Social Change in the History of British Education

This work provides an overall review and analysis of the history of education and of its key research priorities in the British context. It investigates the extent to which education has contributed historically to social change in Britain, how it has itself been moulded by society, and the needs and opportunities that remain for further research in this general area. Contributors review the strengths and limitations of the historical literature on social change in British education over the past forty years, ascertain what this literature tells us about the relationship between education and social change, and map areas and themes for future historical research. They consider both formal and informal education, different levels and stages of the education system, the process and experience of education, and regional and national perspectives. They also engage with broader discussions about theory and methodology. The collection covers a large amount of historical territory, from the sixteenth century to the present, including the emergence of the learned professions, the relationship between society and the economy, the role of formal institutions, the historical experiences of Ireland, Scotland and Wales, the social significance of teaching and learning, and the importance of social class, gender, ethnicity, and disability. It involves personal biography no less than broad national and international movements in its considerations. This book will be a major contribution to research as well as a general resource in the history and historiography of education in Britain.

This book was previously published as a special issue of *History of Education*

Joyce Goodman is Professor of History of Education at the University of Winchester, president of the History of Education Society, and secretary of the International Standing Conference for the History of Education.

Gary McCulloch is Brian Simon Professor of the History of Education at the Institute of Education, University of London, and is past president of the History of Education Society.

William Richardson is Professor of Education at the School of Education and Lifelong Learning at the University of Exeter.

Social Change in the History of British Education

Edited by Joyce Goodman, Gary McCulloch and William Richardson

Routledge
Taylor & Francis Group

LONDON AND NEW YORK

First published 2008 by Routledge
2 Park Square, Milton Park, Abingdon, Oxon, OX14 4RN

Simultaneously published in the USA and Canada
by Routledge
270 Madison Avenue, New York, NY 10016

Routledge is an imprint of the Taylor & Francis Group, an informa business

Transferred to Digital Printing 2009

© 2008 Taylor & Francis

Typeset in Plantin by Genesis Typesetting Ltd, Rochester, Kent

British Library Cataloguing in Publication Data
A catalogue record for this book is available from the British Library

ISBN 10: 0-415-45339-9 (hbk)
ISBN 10: 0-415-49556-3 (pbk)

ISBN 13: 978-0-415-45339-4 (hbk)
ISBN 13: 978-0-415-49556-1 (pbk)

CONTENTS

Introduction: Social Change in the History of Education

Gary McCulloch, Joyce Goodman and William Richardson

'Fortunately in England at any rate, education produces no effect whatsoever. If it did, it would prove a serious danger to the upper classes, and probably lead to acts of violence in Grosvenor Square'. Lady Bracknell's famous assertion, in Oscar Wilde's play *The Importance of Being Earnest* (1895), has long been challenged for its view of the ineffectiveness of education. Historians of education have been to the fore in exploring the relationships that have developed over time between education and the wider society. For over four decades, the most frequently stated objective of research in the history of education in Britain and around the world has been to examine these relationships, and there is now a very large and diverse literature on this topic.[1] This literature requires systematic and critical investigation for how much it explains about the extent to which education has contributed historically to social change, how it, in turn, has been moulded by society, and the needs and opportunities that remain for further research in this area. Such an overall review and analysis of the history of education and of its key research priorities has not been attempted before in the British context. It has now been possible to make a start through a series of six seminars funded by the Economic and Social Research Council on 'Social change in the history of education'.[2]

In the United States, there have been a number of initiatives put in place to review the field and to investigate areas ripe for future development. The most significant of these developed in the 1950s under the auspices of the Ford Foundation.[3] A key outcome of that initiative was the highly influential study produced by Bernard Bailyn in 1960, *Education in the Forming of American Society: Needs and Opportunities for*

---

[1] See e.g. McCulloch, Gary, and William Richardson. *Historical Research in Educational Settings*. Buckingham: Open University Press, 2000.

[2] The ESRC seminar series 'Social change in the history of education' (award RES-451-26-0169) ran from 2004 to 2006, based at the Institute of Education London, the University of Exeter and the University of Winchester. See also McCulloch, Gary, Joyce Goodman, and William Richardson. "Social Change in the History of Education: An ESRC Seminar Series." *History of Education Researcher* 75 (2005): 1–13, for further details.

[3] See Storr, R.J. "The Role of Education in American History: a Memorandum for the Committee Advising the Fund for the advancement of education in Regard to this Subject." *Harvard Educational Review* 46, no. 3 (1976): 331–54.

Study. In this work, Bailyn postulated a straightforward and potent approach to understanding the historical relationships between education and society. He argued that this set of relationships was not simply one-way, reflecting the influence of society on educational configurations, values and processes, but was interactive in its character: 'education not only reflects and adjusts to society; once formed, it turns back upon it and acts upon it'.[4] According to Bailyn, education had 'proved in itself to be an agency of rapid social change, a powerful internal accelerator', which, in its sensitive responses to the immediate pressures of society, had 'released rather than impeded the restless energies and ambitions of groups and individuals'.[5] Moreover, Bailyn continued, education had also 'distinctively shaped the American personality', and thus 'contributed much to the forming of national character'.[6]

A more recent attempt in the United States to mount an overall review of the field took place in March 2000, with a conference funded by the Spencer Foundation to examine new directions in American educational history. This conference revealed an acute awareness of the diversity of research in the history of education, although specific contextual issues in terms of the relationship between education and a wide range of social concerns appeared to be uppermost. A number of contributions emphasized limitations and gaps in previous research, and the need for further consideration of the educational histories of African-American and other ethnic groups, the relationship between history and educational policy, the history of higher education, and the history of women's educational experiences.[7]

Significant initiatives to review the historical relationship between education and the broader society have also been established from time to time in other parts of the world. One such was a collaborative venture that stemmed from an international seminar held in 1979 at the Ruhr-University Bochum, under the auspices of a wider research project on knowledge and society in the nineteenth century. Two additional conferences were held at Leicester in England and again at Bochum that led eventually to the publication of a major edited collection on European secondary and higher education in the late nineteenth and early twentieth centuries.[8] This study was concerned to develop a systematic interpretation of structural change over this period that would take account of underlying similarities or patterns across nations, rather than concentrating on descriptions of specific institutions and particular national accounts. It was found that despite significant differences between the educational structures of England, France and Germany, in each case the processes involved led to hierarchical systems of education that reproduced and reinforced the class and

---

[4] Bailyn, Bernard. *Education in the Forming of American Society: Needs and Opportunities for Study.* Williamsburg: University of North Carolina Press, 1960: 48.

[5] Ibid.

[6] Ibid.

[7] Donato, Ruben, and Marvin Lazerson. "New Directions in American Educational History: Problems and Prospects." *Educational Researcher* 29, no. 8 (2000): 4–15.

[8] Muller, Detlef K., Fritz Ringer, and Brian Simon (eds). *The Rise of the Modern Educational System: Structural Change and Social Reproduction 1870–1920.* Cambridge: Cambridge University Press, 1987.

status structures of society. Clear patterns of interaction were identified between the educational system and the occupational structure, and between established educational traditions and novel social pressures. The leaders of this project came to the conclusion that the educational changes of the period were not only relatively autonomous of, but also partly responsible for, elements in the larger process of social change. Moreover, they added, the outcomes for education and society were often inconsistent with the intentions of many of the agents who helped to bring them about.[9] This set of insights was something of a landmark for the field internationally and highly suggestive as a contribution towards an understanding of the historical relationships between education and society in modern Europe.

Many other instances of work of this type could no doubt be added in different parts of the world. A more modest initiative in New Zealand, sponsored by the New Zealand Association for Research in Education, rallied support for the ideas of Bernard Bailyn applied to the very different context of the Antipodes, with the aim of building and strengthening bridges between education and all other areas of life: leisure, the family, industry, the economy, welfare, health, sport, religion and politics.[10] A special issue of the journal *Paedagogica Historica*, published in 1998, concerned itself with historical and comparative perspectives on schooling in changing societies, including an emphasis on the use of education by governments as the vehicle for the reform of society.[11] In Britain, by contrast, this kind of activity has been conspicuous by its absence. Collaborative, formalized evaluation of the development of the field, as distinct from the historiographical contributions of individual researchers, has not previously been attempted on a national scale in this country. It is vital, as well as somewhat overdue, for those actively involved in the field to appraise its past development in a systematic and focused manner. Yet this is also a highly challenging and even intimidating task in view of the huge output of research in this field within this country over the past 40 years, to say nothing of the diversity of the areas studied during that time.

Sociological treatments of this theme in Britain have developed under the influence of A. H. Halsey, who has expressed scepticism as to the role of education in promoting social change. Halsey has emphasized rather the importance of education in maintaining continuities from the past: 'Education prepares children for society, transforming biological organisms into social personalities. Its capacity is essentially not to create but to recreate society, not to form structures of social life but to maintain the people and the skills that inform these structures. Education as a means of social change is secondary.'[12] Empirical work has been largely preoccupied with the conservative

---

[9] Ibid., xii.

[10] McCulloch, Gary. *Education in the Forming of New Zealand Society: Needs and Opportunities for Study*. Wellington: NZARE, 1986: 28.

[11] *Paedagogica Historica* supplementary series vol. IV (1998). "Schooling in Changing Societies: Historical and Comparative Perspectives." Edited by Czeslaw Majorek, Erwin V. Johanningmaier and Frank Simon. Gent: C.S.H.P., 1998.

[12] Halsey, A. H. *Change in British Society*. Oxford: Oxford University Press, 1978: 133–34.

social effects of education and the processes of 'social reproduction' by which patterns of inequality are reproduced across the generations. According to Richard Breen, such research has demonstrated that social class differentials in educational attainment have remained largely unchanged during much of the last century, although he also notes that sociologists have been more successful in establishing this empirical regularity than explaining it.[13] John Gray too reports that despite a series of efforts to tackle social disadvantage through education, social class remains 'a good (although by no means perfect) predictor of secondary school life-chances'.[14]

Issues of continuity have also figured prominently in the more explicitly historical investigations of the relationships between education and social change in the British context. A starting point in this respect was Fred Clarke's short work *Education and Social Change: An English Interpretation*, published in 1940. This book set out to examine how the English educational tradition, so secure in its general features for many years, should adapt to the challenge of world war and to the changing circumstances of the future. This led him to develop what he described as 'an interpretation, conscious and deliberate, in terms of social economic history, and then, in the light of that interpretation, to estimate the capacity of the English educational tradition to adapt itself without undue friction or shattering to the demands of a changed order'.[15] Clarke was especially concerned to encourage new work that would explore the connections between education and other social institutions and the social structure as a whole.

Brian Simon, the leading historian of education in Britain in the second half of the twentieth century, was strongly influenced by these ideas as well as by a Marxist perspective on social class conflicts.[16] According to Simon, historical studies should be concerned with education as a 'social function', which was of primary importance in every society. He argued in the 1960s that 'It should be one of the main tasks of historical study to trace the development of education in this sense, to try to assess the function it has fulfilled at different stages of social development and so to reach a deeper understanding of the function it fulfils today'.[17] Nearly 30 years later, Simon could still insist that 'A crucial issue to which historical study can and should make a direct contribution, is that of the relation between educational and social change'.[18]

---

[13] Breen, Richard. "Why did Class Inequalities in Educational Attainment Remain Unchanged over Much of the Twentieth Century?" In *Understanding Social Change*, edited by Anthony Heath, John Ermisch and Duncan Gallie. Oxford: Oxford University Press/British Academy, 2005: 68.

[14] Gray, John. "Is Failure Inevitable? The Recent Fate of Secondary School Reforms Intended to Alleviate Social Disadvantage." In *Understanding Social Change*, edited by Heath et al.: 89.

[15] Clarke, Fred. *Education and Social Change: An English Interpretation*. London: Sheldon Books, 1940: 1.

[16] See e.g. McCulloch, Gary. *Education, History and Social Change: the Legacy of Brian Simon* (professorial lecture, Institute of Education, University of London, 2004); and *History of Education* 33, no. 5 (2004). Special issue on Brian Simon, edited by Peter Cunningham and Jane Martin.

[17] Simon, Brian. "The History of Education." In *The Study of Education*, edited by J.W. Tibble. London: Routledge & Kegan Paul, 1966: 91.

[18] Simon, Brian. "The History of Education: Its Importance for Understanding." In idem, *The State and Educational Change: Essays in the History of Education and Pedagogy*. London: Lawrence & Wishart, 1994: 9.

He argued that education had effected social change on a massive scale, despite the efforts of the authorities to maintain control over the mass of the population through the development of schooling. According to Simon, the working class had contested the conservative nature of the educational structures imposed upon them, often with unexpected outcomes. As Simon concluded, modern education systems are 'an area where the interests and objectives of different classes, strata and even groups meet and very often clash'. In this situation, he proposed, 'as the historical record surely makes clear, there is scope for a variety of solutions; which of these will be successful depending on the balance of forces at any particular time'.[19] Many other histories have also been produced over the past 30 years that focus on particular aspects of these relationships, ranging from Geoffrey Sherington's work on education, social change and the First World War to Jonathan Rose's study of the intellectual life of the British working classes.[20]

The present collection includes some of the major contributions to the ESRC seminar series on social change in the history of education. In particular we invited contributors to review the strengths and limitations of the historical literature on social change in British education over the last 40 years, to ascertain what this literature tells us about the relationship between education and social change, and to map areas and themes for future historical research. They consider both formal and informal education, different levels and stages of the education system, the process and experience of education, and regional and national perspectives. They also engage with broader discussions around theory and methodology. The collection covers a large amount of historical territory, from the sixteenth century to the present. Rosemary O'Day considers the emergence of learned professions in England from the sixteenth to the eighteenth centuries. Michael Sanderson examines the dynamics of the relationship between society and economy, and Harold Silver the role of higher technological education in social change. Deirdre Raftery, Jane McDermid and Gareth Elwyn Jones provide comparisons and contrasts between the historical experiences of Ireland, Scotland and Wales. Philip Gardner addresses the social significance of teaching, while Jonathan Rose in particular assesses that of learning through reading. The importance of social class is highlighted by Tom Woodin, gender by Joyce Goodman and Jane Martin, ethnicity by Ian Grosvenor and disability by Felicity Armstrong, involving personal biography no less than broad national and international movements in these considerations. William Richardson contributes a general discussion of British historiography in its international context.

We hope that this collection will be particularly valuable as a basis for developing and prioritizing further substantive research. For example, a further, accompanying collection also deriving from the ESRC series is being planned that will deal in more

---

[19] Simon, Brian. "Can Education Change Society?". In idem, *Does Education Matter?* London: Lawrence & Wishart, 1985: 20.

[20] Sherington, Geoffrey. *English Education, Social Change and War 1911–20.* Manchester: Manchester University Press, 1981; and Rose, Jonathan. *The Intellectual Life of the British Working Classes.* New Haven, CT: Yale University Press, 2001.

detail and depth with colonialism, empire and refugees in terms of social change in the history of education. The present work should moreover afford a means of assessing the potential that now exists for fresh theoretical and methodological approaches to understanding social change in the history of education, as well as addressing fresh agendas. It should also provide a bridge to policy-makers and practitioners considering issues of education and social change. These are key fields for further research and study over the next decade.

Research focusing on the historical relationships between education and social change spans a range of analytical frames. These include variants of Marxism, Bourdieusian 'thinking tools', neo-Weberian approaches and human capital theory; perspectives from feminist, postcolonial, comparative and transnational frameworks; social, economic and cultural history; and historical sociology. As the contributions to this collection demonstrate, approaches differ in the ways in which they deal with the interaction between educational provision, practice and institutions, and aspects of social change. They differ too in the extent to which they blur genres and disciplines in order to recover, reconstruct and interpret the complex historical relationships of education and society, and the influences of each on the other.[21] Together, these authors demonstrate tellingly the many ways in which education has been a major factor in British social change over the past four centuries, a factor which notwithstanding Lady Bracknell has among much else indeed been a serious danger to the upper classes and led to acts of violence in Grosvenor Square.

---

[21] McCulloch and Richardson, *Historical Research in Educational Settings*, chapter 2; Goodman, Joyce and Jane Martin, "*History of Education*: Defining a Field", *History of Education* 33, no. 1 (2004): 1–16.

Social Change in the History of Education: Perspectives on the Emergence of Learned Professions in England, c.1500–1800[*]

Rosemary O'Day

Few historians would disagree that England underwent an educational revolution in the sixteenth and seventeenth centuries and especially during the years 1560–1642. Historians have debated the precise nature and implications of that revolution but agree about its broad characteristics. Even more intriguing is the issue of the social ramifications of this revolution—the subject of the present paper. The paper rehearses the case made in the literature for the development of learned professions as one of the most profound social changes that ensued. It also indicates the manner in which contemporary social concerns have influenced the writing of this history.

In the 1960s, at the same time that the British university system was undergoing tremendous expansion in response to demands for a true meritocracy and that the

[*]Such a broad-sweeping paper inevitably owes a great debt to the work of other scholars. Because historians of the professions draw on so many branches of history, it has been possible to acknowledge by name only a few of the most important works in the field to give a flavour of the debates. I particularly thank Kenneth Charlton and Patrick Collinson for their encouragement past and present.

issue of professionalization was exercising many social scientists, historians of education became interested in the growth of schooling and of college education in the early
modern period and the growth of professions which apparently accompanied it.
Historians drew a backcloth of the general 'explosion' in educational thought and
facilities. A group of historians focused on the universities and their colleges—notably
Lawrence Stone, David Cressy, Elizabeth Russell, Victor Morgan, Hugh Kearney,
Nicholas Tyack and James McConica—and made possible detailed discussion of the
manner in which social as well as geographical mobility was facilitated by education.
There already existed histories of individual professions but Kenneth Charlton spear-
headed work on the early professions with his discussion.[1] Modern historians entered
the discussion, heavily influenced by the work of contemporary sociologists, arguing
that true professions were a feature of the industrial world and that the early modern
professions were not professions at all.[2] The debate frequently descended into one
about semantics. Geoffrey Holmes sought to settle the issue with a detailed exploration of the 'transitional' period.[3] The questions historians now ask about the professions are no longer constrained by Charlton's professionalization 'continuum' but
this dominated much of the work done in the 1960s, '70s and early '80s and formed
an essential basis for later work.

In the two centuries (*c*.1500–1700) there emerged what could be loosely described
as a movement for the formal schooling of males, whether or not they were destined
for a career in the church. As the Simons documented, large numbers of schools
were established—some of them designed to provide able youths of varying social
classes with a classical education, others designed to offer youths what came to be
called a 'commercial' education or an education 'in modern subjects', and still others
offering little more than instruction in basic literacy and numeracy. By the seventeenth century schooling was certainly geographically accessible to most of the population, although it was economically inaccessible and/or less coveted by some
sections of the populations than others. (Notably, young women were, with rare
exceptions, excluded from formal education in the town grammar schools. Before

---

[1] Charlton, Kenneth. "The Professions in Sixteenth-Century England." *University of Birmingham Historical Journal* 12 (1969–70): 20–41.

[2] See Perkin, Harold. *The Rise of Professional Society, England Since 1880*. London: Routledge, 1989.

[3] Holmes, Geoffrey. *Augustan England: Professions, State and Society, 1680–1730*. London: Allen and Unwin, 1982.

the Restoration formal provision for women tended to be at a very basic level and accessible to few.)[4]

Simultaneously, the ancient universities of Oxford and Cambridge also expanded in size (with 'a rise in entry numbers at each university from 150 a year in 1500 to 400–500 by 1600') and apparently changed in their composition. Lawrence Stone posited an educational revolution. There was an enormous influx of undergraduates at both from the 1560s onwards, and moreover of well-born lay students. Once again, women were excluded from participating in university education. At the same time the location and nature of university teaching changed. Undergraduates increasingly received their education within the colleges and received close moral and educational supervision from college tutors. The curriculum was influenced both by the demands of parents for a socially useful (and protected) course and by the impact on the universities and colleges of first of all humanist and later Ramist ideas.[5]

An educational revolution of this kind must have had many causes and many consequences. Establishing them and unravelling them is far beyond the scope of this work. In this paper the emphasis is upon the rise of the professions. The emergence of 'learned professions' in England in the period 1500–1800 must surely present one of the most startling examples of the demonstrable connections between education and social change available to historians and others. (By the early eighteenth century London had 20–25,000 middle-class households and of these between a quarter and a third belonged to learned professionals—5000 lawyers, 1000 clergy, 3000 teachers

---

[4] Good overviews are provided in Charlton, Kenneth. *Education in Renaissance England*. London: Routledge and Kegan Paul, 1965, and Simon, Joan. *Education and Society in Tudor England*. Cambridge, Cambridge University Press, 1967. This expansion built upon traditions already emerging in the middle ages. For detail, see O'Day, Rosemary. *Education and Society, 1500–1800. The Social Foundations of Education in Early Modern Britain*. London: Longman, 1982: 40–42; Orme, Nicholas. *English Schools in the Middle Ages*. London: Methuen, 1973; and *Education in the West of England*. Exeter: University of Exeter, 1976; and Moran, Jo Ann. *The Growth of English Schooling, 1348–1548: Learning, Literacy and Laicization in pre-Reformation York Diocese*. Princeton, NJ, Princeton University Press, 1985. See also O'Day. Rosemary. "Church records and the history of education in early modern England. 1558–1642: A problem in methodology." *History of Education* 2, no. 2 (1973): 115–32. Detailed studies of the expansion in schooling may be found in Fletcher, A. J. "The Expansion of education in Berkshire and Oxfordshire 1500–1670." *British Journal of Educational Studies* 15, no. 1 (1967): 51–59; Simon, Brian. "Leicestershire schools: 1625–1640." *British Journal of Educational Studies* 3, no. 1 (1954–1955): 42–58; Simon, Joan. "Town estates and schools in the sixteenth and early seventeenth centuries." In *Education in Leicestershire: A Regional Study. 1540–1940*, edited by Brian Simon. Leicester: Leicester University Press, 1968; Smith, Alan. "Endowed schools in the diocese of Lichfield and Coventry in the seventeenth century." *History of Education* 4, no. 2 (1975): 5–20 and "Private schools and schoolmasters in the diocese of Lichfield and Coventry in the Seventeenth Century." *History of Education* 5, no. 2 (1976): 117–26; Clark, Peter. *English Provincial Society from the Reformation to the Revolution*. Hassocks, Sussex: Harvester Press, 1977.

[5] See Stone, Lawrence. "The Educational revolution in England. 1560–1640." *Past and Present* 28 (1964): 41–80 and Stone, Lawrence, ed. *The University in Society*. Vol. 1. Princeton, 1974. Russell, Elizabeth. "The Influx of commoners into the University of Oxford before 1581: an optical illusion." *English Historical Review* 92, no. 365 (1977): 721–45 contended that the dramatic nature of this rise in *well-born* lay undergraduates may have been more apparent than real.

and 100 physicians.) These connections can sometimes seem to point to one of 'cause and effect' although to 'prove' such was the case will always be difficult and such claims will always remain contentious.[6]

This paper rests on certain assumptions: that education is not simply concerned with policy, institutions, curriculum and method but also with ethos and the shared educational experience of the educated; that some of the most profound social effects of education may be unintentional or even hostile to the aims of the educators; that the claims made by professionals to an elite status conferred by education were not inevitably acknowledged by the aristocracy who were educated alongside them; that the effects of education on society may not be immediate but rather gradual. The law of unintended consequences frequently came into play. It shows how histories of the professions have moved on from charting how professionals were recruited and trained to showing some of the ramifications of their education in terms of social change and to asking new questions about relationships between state and professions and their institutions as well as between professionals and laity.

The Emergence of Learned Professions

By the late seventeenth century, 'professions' formed a distinct, statistically significant and apparently unremarkable grouping of lawyers, state servants, clergy and 'persons in science and the liberal arts' in Gregory King's table of those increasing the wealth of the nation. Yet 150 years earlier professions, and especially lay professions, scarcely figured. Not only were these professionals numerous, they were self-consciously 'professional' and full of social aspirations. The central argument of this paper is that it was an educational revolution that was at the root of this profound social change. Although professions existed in the Middle Ages—there were clergy who staffed parish ministries, state service, law courts, schools and some parts of the medical service—and there were connections and continuities, professions in the early modern period underwent a sea change. Some of the professions (notably the law in all its aspects and the state service) pulled away from the church and the clergy. These professions became more clearly delineated and their membership much more numerous. Even the parochial clergy began to have more in common with the contemporary lay professions than it did with its medieval antecedents. The difference between the early modern professions and their medieval counterparts lay in the fact that these were learned professions rooted in ideas of a Godly calling (despite the fact that many practitioners were laity) and of academic expertise. (Medieval clergy, for instance, had followed disparate vocations, not simply that of pastoral ministry. Except where medieval lawyers and medics were *also* clerics, they did not profess a religious vocation.) Moreover, the 'professionals' had shared in the educational experience of a large proportion of the aristocracy. Even when close studies of the schools and universities suggests effective social segregation within those institutions, 'professionals' laid claim

---

[6] Earle, Peter. *The Making of the English Middle Class: Business, Society and Family Life in London 1660–1730*. London: Methuen, 1989: 80.

to an identical experience and frequently aped their social superiors. What is more these men employed education as a tool to organize and regulate their professions and to exert control in the marketplace.[7]

It has been extremely important, therefore, for historians to concentrate not only on individual professions (lawyers, clergy, medics) and on what might be termed sub-professions aspiring to higher status (university dons, school teachers, scriveners, attorneys) but also on professions as a group and their relations with the rest of society. Kenneth Charlton pointed the way in this latter regard. Corfield, Hill, Holmes, Prest and O'Day followed up with studies that indicated the immense importance of professions to English social mechanics.[8]

Not only the internal history of the professions mattered but also their relations with government and with other professions and with non-professionals.[9] Nevertheless histories of the individual professions and their institutions have been essential building blocks in this construction of a full social history, as the footnotes to this paper demonstrate. Where, for example, would we be without Wilfrid Prest's *The Inns of Court* (1972) or *The Rise of the Barristers* (1986) or Brian Levack's *The Civil Lawyers* (Oxford, 1973) or W. J. Jones's *The Elizabethan Court of Chancery* (Oxford, 1967) or Louis Knafla's *Law and Politics* (Cambridge, 1977) or David Lemmings, *Gentlemen and Barristers: The Inns of Court and the English Bar, 1680–1730* (Oxford, 1990)?

The development of the professions did not take place in a vacuum. They were not static entities but variables changing in response to more basic social forces. They were rooted in society and responded to both internal and external social pressures. For example, the growth of the legal profession was as much a response to demand in an increasingly litigious society as it was to supply in the form of educated youths. Professions grew because they offered valuable services. They were allowed to regulate themselves to the extent that the state thought safe: for instance the state exerted more control over the clergy and the lawyers than it did over medics because it perceived its stake in the bodily health of the people as less important than its control over the law and religion. The history of any one of the professions was also closely connected to the history of the institutions it worked within (the law courts, the Church of England, the offices of state) but in a paper of this length it is impossible to do more than assert that this was the case. (It is, of course, important from our perspective that attempts by these institutions to create in-house training systems

---

[7] "Aristocracy" is employed in this paper as shorthand for "nobility and upper gentry". See O'Day, *Education and Society*, 90–97 for a summary of work on social segregation.

[8] Corfield, Penelope. *Power and the Professions in Britain, 1700–1850*. London: Routledge, 1995; Hill, Christopher, ed. *Change and Continuity in Seventeenth-century England*. New Haven and London: Yale University Press, 1974; Holmes, Geoffrey. *Augustan England: Professions, State and Society. 1680–1730*. London: Allen & Unwin, 1982; Prest, Wilfrid, ed. *Lawyers in Early Modern Europe and America*. London: Croom Helm, 1981 and *The Professions in Early Modern England*. London: Croom Helm, 1987; O'Day. Rosemary. *The Professions in Early Modern England, 1450–1800: Servants of the Commonweal*. Harlow: Longman, 2000.

[9] A truth amply demonstrated by Penelope Corfield in her *Power and the Professions in Britain, 1700–1850*. London: Routledge, 1995.

were never entirely successful at this time. Even the Inns of Court worked in tandem with the grammar schools and universities in producing young lawyers.) More demonstrable is the way in which the learned professions grew out of a philosophy of life that emerged during the tumults of Renaissance and Reformations and held the educated sectors of society in its thrall. This philosophy of social humanism saw service in Church and State as the raison d'être of the elite and meant that the response of the thousands of young well-educated men who entered these professions was to see their work in terms of vocation, service and commitment rather than of simply earning a living. It was this philosophy which enabled professionals to lay out a professional ethic and to claim authority as well as expertise. It also was the source of a bond between clergymen, lawyers, doctors, teachers and that part of lay society which had been reared and formally educated in the same tradition and the identical institutions—grammar schools, universities and colleges. Education and the professional groups involved in providing it were seen as vital. The exclusion of women from that very educational system determined the exclusion of the female sex from the learned professions. The contribution made to the development of 'elite' learned professions in England by the very peculiarities of the English education system seems both undeniable and fascinating.[10]

That the emergence of lay learned professions did indeed represent a profound social phenomenon seems incontestable. Professionals laid claim to exclusive rights to practise, based on academic and practical learning, experience and expertise. Their development had the effect of closing off opportunities for social and economic advancement to those without access to education. This effect was never total. They had varying degrees of success in enforcing these claims and some historians have seen the Civil Wars (and even the establishment of the American Colonies) as at least partially fuelled by an anti-professional backlash. For while professions had an internal life, they were also involved in discourse within elite society as a whole about their areas of expertise, which were of vital importance to everyone. What, for instance, was appropriate religious belief and who should define it? Why should preaching be limited to men who had been trained in the universities and ordained by bishops? Was Galen's approach to medicine the only acceptable one? Why should women (long guardians of families' and communities' health) defer to university-educated medics whose therapies had doubtful efficacy? What was the nature of the common law? Was it superior to other forms of law then practised in England? The common educational background drew 'laymen' into 'professional' debates—just as today men and women with no 'professional' involvement in medicine may still engage in philosophical debates over the wisdom or efficacy of various policies or of conventional or alternative therapies. This is not purely because they are 'end users' but also

---

[10] For a more detailed consideration see O'Day, *The professions*.

because they share to some extent the same knowledge base as the professionals themselves.[11]

It is possible to argue that it was *only* their common educational background that unified the learned professions during the period 1500–1750. The various branches of the clergy, law and medical professions had precious little in common when it came to their internal or external organization. The organization of the profession of the clergy was closely tied to the institution of the Church and to its teaching. The upper branch of the common law legal profession was largely organized by the Crown, the Privy Council, the judiciary and the barristers through the Inns of Court. The lower branch of that profession, however, was only partly controlled by the same bodies, through the court system and the Inns of Chancery. The upper and lower branches of the civil law legal profession were organized through the universities, the Church and the courts in which they served. Within the medical profession there were attempts at control from several bodies—the Royal College of Physicians, the Company of Barber-Surgeons, the Society of Apothecaries, the medical faculties of the universities, the bishops of the Church—but organization remained weak.

In the final segment of this paper a brief summary is provided of developments within one of the learned professions—the clergy—which serves to suggest that while the educational revolution may have had an enormous role in social change with respect to the development of professions, the ramifications of that change were both many and various. The summary focuses on one or more distinctive features.

The Ethos of the Ruling Elites and of the Professions

Our knowledge of the ethos of the English 'ruling class' stems not from histories of education per se but from a variety of wider studies. In the Middle Ages the upper classes in England were landowners. They did not work with their hands or with their minds. They were in control: others did the hard manual and the hard intellectual work for them. Land conferred status and power. There were other ways of achieving these coveted commodities, most notably via education, the Church and the King's service. Men who acquired status by this route always stressed the non-manual nature of their skill and their non-dependence upon 'work' for their income. To be 'idle' was a virtue; to be 'industrious' was unthinkable. Those who were lawyers, higher clergy

---

[11] There have been major contributions to the history of these professions, too numerous to list here. For individual professions or segments of profession see especially Prest, Wilfrid. *The Inns of Court*. London: Longman, 1972 and *The Rise of the Barristers*. Oxford: Clarendon Press, 1986; Levack, Brian P. *The Civil Lawyers in England. 1603–1641*. Oxford: Clarendon Press, 1973; O'Day, Rosemary. *The English Clergy, 1560–1640*. Leicester: Leicester University Press, 1979; Pruett, John. *The Parish Clergy under the Later Stuarts*. Urbana: University of Illinois Press, 1978; Cook, H. J. *The Decline of the Old Medical Regime in Stuart London*. Ithaca, NY; London: Cornell University Press, 1986; Greaves, R. L. *The Puritan Revolution and Educational Thought*. New Brunswick: Rutgers University Press, 1967 provides an excellent introduction to the controversies surrounding education and profession in the mid seventeenth century. See also O'Day, *The Professions*, 147–49 for a discussion of ethics in the legal profession.

or physicians in the Middle Ages, therefore, laid little emphasis upon what they *did* for a living. Historians have described them as belonging to status professions. They possessed the skill to offer advice in given area of life, not to do anything. This emphasis on the consultative nature of the professional's role has survived into the twenty-first century as has, of course, the idea that 'profession' is status conferring.

But this land-based society was being modified during the later Middle Ages and the early modern period. Men with land still possessed status and power and deplored manual labour. Yet as groups of lawyers, doctors and clergy grew in number and claimed greater influence, subtle changes were afoot. As Quentin Skinner has made clear, the early humanists launched attacks on the Aristotelian ideal of the contemplative life and promoted a Ciceronian morality that saw men actively pursuing the good life in search of salvation. Their concept of the way to honesty, rooted as it was in a vision of action leading to self-knowledge, had much in common with the world of learning. The gentleman could pursue this course with the help of education and reason. Learning was useful to the gentleman and must be deployed in the interests of the commonweal and for the public discussion of relevant issues.[12]

In early sixteenth-century England the idea that the landed aristocrat (including nobility and gentry) would lead an active life of service in the state and that it would be based on a deliberate education (or intellectual preparation) was foreign:

> It becomes the sons of gentlemen to blow the horn nicely, to hunt skilfully, and elegantly to carry and train a hawk ... the study of letters was for rustics....[13]

Yet such views *were* already under attack. When Archbishop Thomas Cranmer argued with the commissioners regarding the refounding of Canterbury Cathedral School in 1541, the commissioners wished to restrict entry to the sons of the aristocracy because 'gentlemen's children are meet to have the knowledge of government and rule in the commonwealth'.

This new attitude to the relationship between learning and the gentleman's social duties had practical manifestations. The aristocracy began, in larger numbers, to send their sons to school—Winchester, Eton, Shrewsbury—or to provide them with a classical education at home. They sent their sons to the universities. By the 1560s there were large numbers of gentle-born students in the colleges of the ancient universities of Oxford and Cambridge. It seems that the majority of these students had no need to earn a living. They were, instead, being educated to practise the art of being a gentleman, with all that that implied in terms of governmental responsibilities at local and national levels. Arthur Ferguson called it 'active citizenship' and 'applied learning'. Being a gentleman had become a calling: as Sir Thomas Elyot bore testimony when he wrote in *The Boke named the governour* a chapter entitled 'The education or

---

[12] Skinner, Quentin. *The Foundations of Modern Political Thought*, 2 vols. Cambridge: Cambridge University Press, 1978.

[13] Hexter, J. H. "The Education of the aristocracy in the Renaissance" in his *Reappraisals in history*. London: Longmans, 1961.

form of bringing up the child of a gentleman, which is to have authority in a public weal'.[14]

The English gentleman of the sixteenth century aspired not to become a well-rounded individual but rather a man active in civil life; there was no emphasis on learning for learning's sake. This helps explain why so many sons of the aristocracy flooded into the universities and the Inns of Court, especially in the years between 1590 and 1639. From here they were prepared to take on the work of leadership and administration in the parishes and counties of England and Wales.

The similarities between the aristocracy's conception of its role in society and the conception of the role of the learned professions are striking. The gentleman's calling was altruistic—for the good of society (in contemporary parlance 'the common weal') as well as in his and his family's self-interest. There is little emphasis on economic need as the motivator. There is enormous emphasis upon the need for education (provided by teachers, schools, colleges and books). The skills practised are non-manual and involve the giving of advice, based on intellectual expertise as well as experience and the execution of magisterial duties. This concept of the gentleman's calling came to be shared by the learned professions.[15]

More important for the future of the learned professions (and for our understanding of the connection between education and their growth) was the extent to which the social ambience and the curriculum followed in the grammar schools and at the universities and Inns of Court was shared by intending clergy, teachers, medics and lawyers who came from rather more humble backgrounds. Professionals in the early modern period came to share the same preliminary preparation for life as many young nobles and gentlemen, albeit sometimes in different foundations. Schools and colleges grew in number to satisfy the demand from all these groups. The curriculum they offered was modified to suit the new Renaissance philosophy of education: that study of the classics could be used to restore virtue to civic and religious life and could be duly Christianized. Schools such as St Paul's, London, were founded to realize this goal and many grammar schools were founded thereafter on broadly similar lines.

The substance of the school curriculum was the study of Latin and, sometimes, Greek authors. The assumption was that a boy would be able to read and write in English before he entered the grammar school or grammar forms. The classical curriculum was accompanied by daily religious exercises, catechizing and attendance at church. Thus the boys of Ashbourne Grammar School sat each Sunday in a special gallery within the church and were taught the creed, the Ten Commandments and the catechism.

Just to give some idea of the social range of pupils who shared the benefits of a grammar school education it is worth looking briefly at the ultimate career destinations of boys from one of the largest endowed schools. At Shrewsbury School in the 1560s the

---

[14] Hugh Kearney's *Scholars and gentlemen: Universities and Society*. London: Faber, 1970 remains the most accessible discussion. See Ferguson, A. B. *The Articulate Citizen and the English Renaissance*. Durham, NC: Duke University Press, 1965: passim. Elyot, Thomas. *The Boke named the governour. 1531*, edited by Crofts. H.H.S, 1883.

[15] See O'Day, *Education and Society*, 77–164 and *The Professions*, 25–43.

following were contemporaries: Andrew Downes (later professor of Greek at Cambridge); Meredith Hanmer (later Archdeacon of Ross, historian); Robert Wright (later MP), William Middleton (Protestant controversialist); Philip Sidney (soldier, diplomat and poet); Fulke Greville (Lord Brooke, later Chancellor of the Exchequer). The 1570s saw the school welcoming an even more varied cohort, which included: Randolph Crew (later Speaker of the House of Commons and Chief Justice of the King's Bench); Abraham Fraunce (poet and translator); Richard Harris (theologian), Rowland Heylin (Sheriff of London) and William Leighton (poet and composer). Men like these pursued the same Christian humanist curriculum and imbibed a common value system. To a degree this was also true of boys who received education from a home tutor. Some schools, like Shrewsbury, taught boys drawn from many different social strata but others were exclusive in their clientele, as gentle and noble students drove out the boys specified by the founder as the chief objects of their concern.[16]

The influence of Renaissance philosophy on the schools was paralleled by its influence on the universities. Initially the English humanists did not see the universities as appropriate for the function of training statesmen or gentlemen: they promoted instead the idea of an academy for the elite, either by adapting the Inns of Court or by setting up a separate 'House of Students' or an academy. The most detailed such proposal collapsed with the fall of Thomas Cromwell from power. It seems that the annexation of the universities and their colleges as a training ground for gentlemen occurred by default as far as the humanists were concerned. By the reign of Elizabeth I it was common not only for boys intending a career in the Church or the law but also for gentle youths to attend university, at least for a short while. All had been educated to believe that a course at university would be useful to them, enabling them to fulfil their social obligations and follow their vocation.[17]

By the early sixteenth century the role of the colleges in the teaching and supervision of undergraduates in the arts faculties of the universities was established and the matriculation regulations forced into residence in these societies students who had formerly lived in private lodgings in the towns of Oxford and Cambridge and escaped control. The facilities were there, for the first time, for the large-scale accommodation in colleges of lay youth.[18]

Some have argued that, when at university, gentlemen and prospective lawyers followed a different course of study from that pursued by students intending to take a degree and enter holy orders. The evidence suggests that although there may have been varying emphases in the teaching accorded so-called 'lay' and 'clerical' students, there was no formal difference in the courses they took. And although there was certainly social separation at the universities and in the colleges (as, for example, in fashionable colleges between fellow-commoners and other undergraduates, or

---

[16] Oldham, J. B. *A Short History of Shrewsbury School*. Oxford: Basil Blackwell, 1952: 286–87; O'Day. *Education and Society*, 25–42, 77–105 and 196–216.

[17] Fisher, R. M. "Thomas Cromwell: humanism and educational reform, 1530–1540." *Bulletin of the Institute of Historical Research* 50 (1977): 151–63.

[18] Russell, "The Influx of commoners".

between one fashionable college and another less fashionable one) there were sufficient points of contact socially as well as academically to produce a common college
and university culture.[19]

Thus a new concept of profession, which embraced the idea of learning and practice (especially in the sense of a service) came out of the social humanism of the
Renaissance aristocracy and the grammar schools and colleges in which they were
educated. It was embraced by members of all three *learned* professions (law, church
and medicine) alongside the elite with whom they were educated. By the middle of
Elizabeth's reign the following dialogue was possible:

> *Question*: But tell mee, are not the lawes a study very fit for a gentleman?
> *Answer*: Yes, surely, both the lawes civill & common are studies most excellent, & to speake
> breefely, all learnings, that tend to action in the state either civill, or martiall.[20]

Case Study of one of the Learned Professions: The Clergy

A brief case study of the clergy in Elizabethan and early Stuart England shows how
this became a graduate profession as a result of the educational revolution and indicates the several unintended effects of this development—many of which were
regarded as unwelcome by the Church hierarchy or by puritan ministers, who sought
to seize control of the situation and shape the graduate ordinands. They wanted a
well-educated clergy but not at any price. Once graduate entry to the profession
became established, it was self-generating and nigh-on unstoppable, but did not as it
turned out guarantee the quality or vocational suitability of recruits. Education alone
could not achieve this: it required a thoroughgoing reform of the patronage and
placement system that was not forthcoming. Moreover, as was the case with the law
(and medicine) the new shared culture of the clergy and elite served to separate them
ever more from the people and led to an antagonism on the part of sections of the
laity that may well have been more profound than that felt towards the Catholic
priesthood.

There had been a clergy in England throughout the Middle Ages and in many ways
they already possessed, in combination, the features of a recognizable professional
structure: hierarchical organisation; emphasis upon service; internal control of recruitment, training and placement; internal enforcement of standards and discipline; stress
upon the importance of expertise, both academic and practical; a developed career
structure and a tremendous *esprit de corps*. Historians remain indebted, for example,
to the work of Hamilton Thompson in the 1930s and of Peter Heath in the 1960s and

---

[19] Curtis, Mark. *Oxford and Cambridge in Transition*. Oxford: Clarendon Press, 1959: 85–92;
O'Day, *Education and Society*, 88–131 and especially 112–18, 24; Looney, Jefferson. "Undergraduate education at early Stuart Cambridge." *History of Education* 10, no. 1 (1981): 9–19. See also Mc-
Conica, James, ed. *The History of the University of Oxford*: Vol. 3: *The Collegiate University*. Oxford:
Clarendon Press, 1986, especially 1–68, 157–99.
[20] Anon. *Cyvile and uncyvile life*. 1586 edn: 21. See Skinner, *Foundations of Modern Political
thought*, Vol. 1: 213–41.

after.[21] Yet this profession underwent profound changes in the period of England's long reformation. The main features of this development have been studied by many historians. Their work indicates the profound influence upon studies of the professions of Lewis Namier's prosopographical methods and, increasingly, the grafting on to this of techniques made possible by the introduction of the computer and statistical study. But it has also always been accompanied by an interest in the religious, political, cultural and institutional context in which professionals' lives were lived.[22] The cultural pervasiveness of clerical thought was early highlighted by the Georges and continued to preoccupy other historians of the clergy and the laity.[23] The emergence of the profession was not the focus of the majority of such studies. O'Day, however, attempted to show the impact of religious and educational change upon the clergy themselves and their response in terms of professionalization. O'Day's view is that before the Reformation the clergy formed one of the three vertical estates of the realm, defined by status. Not all of the 35,000 or so clergy, by any means, were involved in pastoral ministry: many staffed the schools, universities and law courts and the administration or belonged to contemplative religious orders.[24] After the Reformation, she argues, they formed a profession—a hierarchically organized but occupationally defined group, which was much reduced in size and which claimed status in society on the basis of expert services that it offered the commonweal. There were, however, differing views within the Church about the nature of the profession and especially its claims to specialist expertise. Its very existence even was hotly contested by radical reformers such as John Hooper, who believed that the minister

---

[21] Thompson, A. Hamilton. *The English Clergy and their Organization in the Later Middle Ages (1933)*. Oxford: Clarendon Press, 1947. Oxford University Press reprint 1966; Heath, Peter. *English Parish Clergy on the Eve of the Reformation*. London: Routledge & Kegan Paul, 1969.

[22] For the varied approaches of historians see for example, Barratt, D.M. "Conditions of the Parish Clergy from the Reformation to 1660." D.Phil. thesis, Oxford University, 1950; Foster, Andrew "The Function of a Bishop: The Career of Richard Neile, 1562–1640." In *Continuity and Change: Personnel and Administration of the Church in England. 1500–1642*, edited by R. O'Day and F. Heal. Leicester: Leicester University Press, 1976; Hirschenberg, Daniel. "A Social History of the Anglican Episcopate. 1660–1760." Ph.D. diss., University of Michigan, 1976; Zell, Michael. "Economic problems of the parochial clergy." In *Princes and Paupers in the English Church. 1500–1800*, edited by R. O'Day and F. Heal. Leicester: Leicester University Press, 1981; Tyler, Richard. "Children of Disobedience." Ph.D. diss., University of California at Berkeley, 1976; Cross, Claire. "Priests into Ministers: The Establishment of Protestant Practice in the City of York. 1530 to 1630." In *Reformation Principle and Practice*, edited by P. N. Brooks. 1980.

[23] George, Charles H., and Katherine George. *The Protestant Mind of the English Reformation, 1570–1640*. Princeton, NJ: Princeton University Press, 1962; Greaves, *Puritan Revolution and Educational Thought*; Morgan, John. *Godly Learning: Puritan Attitudes Towards Reason, Learning and Education, 1560–1640*. Cambridge: Cambridge University Press, 1986; Collinson, Patrick. *The Religion of Protestants*. Oxford: Clarendon Press, 1982.

[24] See Zell, "Economic problems", 21–22 and Knowles, D., and R. N. Hadcock. *Medieval Religious Houses*. London: Longman Group, 1971: 364 for estimates of the various 'segments' of the medieval clergy.

had no special access to God and that his only role was to evangelize and bring people to God.[25]

The early Elizabethan episcopate was faced with an acute shortage of clergy and, especially, of well-educated clergy to serve the parishes of England and Wales. The unsettled state of the realm and the impoverishment of livings combined to make entering holy orders an unattractive proposition. Yet the episcopate thought a graduate clergy the ideal. Stop-gap measures were introduced but bishops proved reluctant to admit men without adequate scriptural learning. Outside London and the university ordination centres of Ely and Oxford, the educational standards of recruits improved only gradually. Only one out of 282 Chester ordinands between 1560 and 1570 was a graduate. By the 1590s the situation had improved but was still far from wholly graduate. As these ordinands were fed almost exclusively into livings within that diocese, it followed that Chester ministers remained poorly qualified well into the seventeenth century. In 1584 only 14% of clergy in the huge Coventry and Lichfield diocese were graduates; by 1603 the percentage was still only 24%. Matters were made more difficult by the patronage system. Placement of ministers was largely in the hands of laymen, who often selected ministers not on the basis of their education and vocational suitability but rather of their connection and submissiveness.[26] The efforts of the bishops were best helped when patrons, such as the Crown and the Lord Chancellor, themselves conscientiously examined applicants for livings but even here ecclesiastical patronage was too often seen as a way of rewarding particular groups of petitioners, such as nobility and statesmen, rather than of placing educated worthy men in parishes.

At every turn the efforts of the hierarchy to control recruitment into the profession and the placement of these men were stymied by the structure and law of patronage. (Virgin's work on the late Georgian Clergy demonstrates that this problem had not been solved by 1840.[27]) In order to defeat this system, the choice of clients before patrons would have to be limited to educated, worthy individuals. This dream was apparently realized by the early seventeenth century when the expansion of university numbers that had begun in the 1560s was well established. Between the beginning of 1600 and the end of 1606, 82 out of 109 candidates for deacon's orders in the London diocese were graduate and 12 were students. By the 1620s recruitment throughout the London diocese was wholly graduate. Even more remarkable was the position in more 'backward' areas: of the 87 ordained deacons in Gloucester between June 1609 and May 1621, 52 were graduates; 43 of the 60 ordained priests were graduate. Four-fifths of the candidates at Lichfield between 1614 and 1632 were coming out of the universities. And all this leaves out of account the staggering impression of total university recruitment, which is obtained by reading the ordination lists of the

---

[25] See O'Day, *Professions*. 55–57, for discussion of differing views within the Church of England regarding the claims of the reformed priesthood.

[26] For Episcopal attempts to circumvent the patronage system see O'Day, *English Clergy*, 49–74.

[27] Virgin, P. N. "Church and Society in late Georgian England. 1800–1840." Ph.D. thesis, University of Cambridge, 1979: passim.

centres at Oxford, Peterborough, Ely and Lincoln, traditionally fed by their local universities.[28]

This situation was not brought about entirely by the efforts of the hierarchy to encourage potential ordinands to attend university.[29] Boys and their parents learned by example: they noticed that graduates not only gained places in the Church but also preferment. This, combined with the enlarged provision of educational facilities within the provinces, made progression to the university appear an attractive route for the intending cleric. The universities and colleges themselves maintained efficient and extensive communications with schools in the provinces, making certain that able boys were advised about the desirability of further education. Parents, godparents, career writers such as Tom Powell, teachers and local clergy added their voices to the clamour.[30]

O'Day argues that once it was accepted that preferment was within the grasp only of the well educated, the re-routing of ordinands via the universities was self-generating. Richard Baxter was almost deterred from entering the ministry because his 'want of academical honours and degrees was like to make me contemptible with the most, and consequently hinder the success of my endeavours'. Adam Martindale expressed similar fears. In fact, there is little evidence that on the lower echelons of the clerical ladder educational qualifications cut more ice with patrons than did connection, but ordinands believed that a degree provided the key to preferment. By the late 1620s and the 1630s, a bachelor's degree was held by so many recruits that it could not itself provide a positive advantage or act as an effective discriminator. Higher and higher qualifications were demanded if the cleric coveted a wealthy position in the Church. The Master of Arts became the most popular degree with clergymen. For example, of 1380 presentees to benefices by the Lord Keeper between 1627 and 1640, 825 were MAs, 301 held higher degrees, 97 were just BAs and only 157 had no degree at all. The ambitious were encouraged to study theology in what today we would call a postgraduate course.[31]

The Church hierarchy still faced problems in attracting able men. Partly this was because livings remained impoverished. The costs of clerical training were rarely repaid. So wrote Robert Harris:

> After you have spent your time, and your patrimony (two or three hundred pounds it may be) for learnings sake to fit you for the ministry, a small meanes shall be thought to much for you.

---

[28] See O'Day, *English Clergy*, 49–65 for detail.

[29] For example, by subsidizing the costs of the education of grammar school boys at particular colleges.

[30] See O'Day, *Education and Society*, 77–105; O'Day, Rosemary. "Room at the Top." *History Today* 34 (1984): 31–38; Morgan, Victor. "Cambridge university and the 'Country'." In *The University and Society*, Vol. I, edited by L. Stone; Tyler, "Children of disobedience", passim.

[31] Baxter, Richard. *Reliquiae Baxterianae*, edited by M.Sylvester. London, 1696: 12; Parkinson, Richard. ed. *Life of Adam Martindale*. Manchester: Chetham Society, 1845: 49; O'Day, *Education and Society*, 174; O'Day, *English Clergy*, 14. 21–23. 135–39; Green, Ian. "Career prospects and clerical conformity." *Past and Present* 90 (1977): 71–115; O'Day, "The Ecclesiastical Patronage of the Lord Keeper. 1558–1642". *Transactions of the Royal Historical Society* 5th Series, 23 (1973): 105.

Some well-qualified men had to kick their heels in a poorly paid teaching position, linger longer than they might have wished in the universities, or take up a parish lecture-ship before finding a 'tenured' position as a minister. Also the fact that the distribution of livings was still not controlled centrally and the longevity of many clergy meant that it was not always the able who found positions quickly and the less able who had to wait. For example, Weston-on-Trent, Staffordshire, was served in 1620 by 'Mr French [who reads without authority] … [and there are] noe monethly sermons, noe catechis-inge & his swine rooting in the churchyard'. (The situation does seem to have eased by the 1630s.) Moreover, the more scrupulous bishops began to question the vocational value of the BA degree—the men who presented themselves for ordination seemed woefully ignorant when it came to knowledge of the Scriptures. The practice of sending intending ministers to live with revered churchmen and serve a kind of 'apprenticeship' was recommended. John Cosin, Denis Granville, Richard Kidder and Thomas Morton were leading churchmen who educated and trained others in their households.[32]

Parish clergy also took it upon themselves to educate and train young ministers. Bernard Gilpin and Richard Greenham are well-known examples from the sixteenth century but there were many others during the sixteenth and seventeenth centuries. John Cotton, at Boston between 1612 and 1633, educated young men from Cambridge on the direct recommendation of John Preston, Master of Emmanuel College. Other parochial seminaries were run by Thomas Gataker at Rotherhithe, Thomas Taylor at Reading, John Ball at Whitmore, Staffordshire, Francis Higginson at Leicester and Alexander Richardson at Barking. Plans of study began to be produced for use in vocational training, notably by John Rainolds, Laurence Chaderton and Richard Bernard. In this way senior ministers who held no place in the Church's hier-archy became nonetheless influential. It has been claimed recently that 'by the second decade of the seventeenth century, a period of vocational training under the direction of a godly minister was almost requisite'.[33]

These young men were often, for a short time at least, indentured servants. Late in the seventeenth century Denis Granville (or Grenville), Archdeacon and Dean of Durham, employed his own nephew Roger Prideaux as his personal assistant with a view to testing his suitability for holy orders. Prideaux was expected to be a paragon of virtue. In this he failed, having 'too much fondnesse of his owne judgement' arguing for and against matters that 'ought not to be disputed with mee'. He also played cards, drank too much, criticized his master before others and took offence when he was corrected. Nonetheless, Granville liked his nephew and thought he would make a good clergyman but was unprepared as yet to provide him with a reference for ordination:

---

[32] Harris, Robert. *The way to true happinesse.* London, 1632: 246; Green, "Career prospects", passim; O'Day, *English Clergy,* 75–125, 152–54.

[33] Marcombe, David. "Bernard Gilpin: Anatomy of an Elizabethan legend." *Northern History* 16 (1980): 20–39; Shipps, Kenneth W. "Lay patronage of East Anglian puritan clerics in pre-revolutionary England." Ph.D. thesis, Yale University, 1971: 351–56. Webster, Tom. *Godly Clergy in Early Stuart England: The Caroline Puritan Movement, c.1620–1643.* Cambridge: Cambridge University Press, 1997: 25.

> His studies have been hitherto ... chiefly to secure a foundation of humane learning, without any particular respect to this or that calling. It would be convenient that he did for some yeares (or for one yeare at least) addict himselfe to divinity and devotion and such studies as may make him a good preist and churchman, and converse a little with men abroad in the world, who doe not smell of a colledge; which last will not only bee a certaine ornament to him, but qualify him the better to discharge his function....[34]

By the 1630s, then, the clergy was a graduate profession but it was one which did not, strictly speaking, control the means of education and training. Although the colleges of the universities continued to be staffed by clerics and although certain colleges took their role as seminaries seriously, the universities did little to adapt their formal curriculum to the needs of a Church that set great store by preaching and pastoral care. It was an entirely academic regimen that produced classical scholars and theologians, not pastors. It was only outside the universities, through ad hoc schemes of in-service training, that the bishops could tackle directly the problems of providing more vocational expertise. Unfortunately such schemes became ever thinner on the ground after Elizabeth's reign—it was as if the hierarchy took refuge behind the outward success of the drive to produce a graduate profession.

The lack of vocational training inevitably had an impact on the relationship between clergy and congregations. It led some lay men and women to question the value of the cleric's expertise. Partly this was because some of the clergy seemed determined to hide the 'mystery' of the Scriptures from the people behind obscure language and incomprehensible scholarly techniques in order to justify their own monopoly of religious teaching in the state. Thomas Gataker remembered a conversation he once had had with the Oxford don Daniel Featley in the presence of a woman:

> When he and my selfe were in her presence talking together, of the occurrents of the time, and some points of schoole-learning, somewhat out of her element, and above her spheare, she strooke in with us, and requested us to discourse rather of somewhat, that she might also receive some benefit by, that we might be useful as well to her as to us.

Professional works such as William Perkins's *Arte of Prophecying*, 1592, were commonly issued first in Latin and access was therefore denied to all but gentry (with grammar school and/or university education) and recruits to the ministry. A claim to theoretical expertise formed one of the foundations of the clergy's monopoly.[35]

John Morgan's important *Godly Learning* has shown us that the precise position of the clergy themselves on the role of humane learning varied enormously. Many were concerned about the ministerial use of reason to demonstrate religious truth. John Donne wrote:

> The Scriptures will be out of thy reach, and out of thy use, if thou cast and scatter them upon reason, upon philosophy, upon morality, to try how the Scriptures will fit them, and believe them but so far as they agree with thy reason; but draw the Scripture to thine own heart, and to thine own actions, and thou shall find it made for that.

---

[34] Ornsby, G., ed. *The Remains of Denis Granville, D.D., Dean and Archdeacon of Durham*. Surtees Society 47 (1865): paper LXXXVII.

[35] Gataker, Thomas. *St Steven's last will and testament*. London, 1638: 15.

Humane learning, thought John Penry, was only necessary for a minister in order that he should make matters of salvation plain to the laity: rhetoric and logic, Latin and Greek and Hebrew were handmaids to knowledge of the Word of God. They were, however, essential. An educated minister was 'a thing necessarily required at our hands by God almighty...'. Laurence Chaderton believed that 'knowledge of Greke and Lattin histories, and chronologies, [is appropriate] for the better understanding of the histories in the scriptures and the reconciling of many places, which otherwise might seem doubtfull'. Yet the minister, with this education behind him, must put over the Gospel to the people in plain, readily comprehensible language and above 40 printed manuals were available to show him how. More ornate sermon forms—such as those adopted by John Donne—seem to have been characteristic of the so-called Anglican tradition.[36]

There were, of course, many other reasons for distance between clergy and their congregations: their position of authority, their imposition of discipline, their collection of tithes, and sometimes their very public failure to live up to the ideals of the godly life they preached. Nevertheless, education separated the Caroline clergy from most of the laity and served to unite them with well-educated gentry and other professionals. That the Elizabethan and Stuart clergy developed a sense of corporate identity is incontrovertible. It was as true of the post- as of the pre-Restoration clergy, of the Puritan as the non-Puritan. In part this was because of the emergence of clerical dynasties. In part it was because of shared professional life and interests, as they met at exercises, conferences, prophesyings, fast days, combination lectures, visitations, clergy councils, and courts. To a very real extent, however, common educational background drew clergy ever closer once they left the ivory towers of Oxbridge. Henry Clarke, vicar of Willoughby, Warwickshire, became fast friends with George Beale, vicar of the adjacent parish of Grandborough. They had attended Oxford together and had both graduated in 1612. Beale took up his Warwickshire living soon after taking his MA in 1615. Clarke remained for a while at Magdalen but in 1621 was presented by his college to Willoughby, near his boyhood home. Here he resumed his long friendship with Beale and, when he made his will, he left George all his 'Lattin bookes standing in the sayd press [cupboard] in my studdye' and forgave him a debt of £30.[37] Tom Webster's stimulating *Godly Clergy in Early Stuart England* paints with admirable detail the picture of clerical sociability sketched earlier by O'Day although any suggestion that this sociability was confined to the puritan wing of the church remains unproven.[38]

The clerical profession, of course, consisted of more than the lower clergy—the parish clergy who, while the most numerous of the segments, were not the most influential or powerful. Histories of the English professions have rarely concentrated on

---

[36] See O'Day, *Professions*. 75; See Morgan, *Godly learning*, especially 112–20.

[37] Tom Webster's *Godly Clergy* contains much of interest on clerical sociability. O'Day's *The Professions*, 92–107, summarizes the life style and duties of the clergy using clerical diaries and papers.

[38] Webster, Tom. *Godly Clergy in Early Stuart England: The Caroline Puritan Movement, c.1620–1643*. Cambridge: Cambridge University Press, 1997.

segmentation although indirectly we can learn much about the structure of the profession and relationships between its distinct segments from both ecclesio-political studies and histories of church institutions. Broadly speaking the clerical profession could be divided into the bench of bishops; other upper clergy, including archdeacons, Deans and prebendaries of Cathedrals; and lower clergy (a term that embraced not only beneficed (and secure) parish clergy but also assistant curates and lecturers who aspired to but did not yet hold benefices. But there were also other groups of clergy whom it is difficult to place: the many university dons in holy orders; the school masters in orders; the church (civil) lawyers who practised law but were also often in orders. Work has been done on the promotion criteria governing appointment to the episcopate which shows that educational and vocational suitability were far from the only determinants. Ian Green pinpointed one important influence upon entry to the elite.[39] John Pruett highlighted the internal prospects of the clerical elite within the cathedral close.[40] For the historian of the professions one of the questions will always be: did more unite these disparate groups than divided them? One approach may help us here: studying the career prospects and paths of clerical recruits. O'Day, for example, showed that there was no single career ladder in the English church, reaching from assistant curate to bishop, which was accessible to all recruits to the profession. Unsurprisingly preferment did not come through pastoral experience. It came more readily via service in the bishops' households; through university and college degrees (a higher degree and a college fellowship provided an established route to a prebendal stall); and through a network of connection that defeats statistical analysis. This suggests that there was a divide between lower clergy who could aspire to become members of a clerical elite and those who could not. This was not a case of 'alienated intellectuals' but of impatient and disappointed clergy of some education who could not realistically find a wealthy benefice or even a secure post. This may have been disastrous for the economic prospects of some clergy but for the Church hierarchy it offered some hope for proper leadership of the profession as a whole because well-qualified men could be placed in strategic positions.

Conclusion

> You know well that we are they to whose charge that rich treasure, both of church and commonwealth is committed to trust ... and the hope of a more happy age hereafter to come. We are they who help either to make or mar all; for that all the flower of our nation, and those who become the leaders of all the rest, are committed to our education and instruction; that if we bring them up aright, there is great hope, that they shall prove godly lights, and marks to all the rest of the land ... and clean contrarily, most woeful examples ... if they be spoiled through us, for the lack of better care.... We are therefore the men upon whom the flourishing of this our Canaan doth very much depend.[41]

---

[39] Green, "Career Prospects", passim.
[40] Pruett, John. "Career Patterns among the Clergy of Lincoln Cathedral. 1660–1750." *Church History* 44, no. 2 (1975): 204–16.
[41] Brinsley, John. *A Consolation for our grammar schooles.* London, 1622: 45.

John Brinsley noted the enormous responsibility shouldered by grammar school masters as they prepared their charges to become leaders of the commonwealth. These leaders included noble and gentle men as well as young professionals. The common background of reformed Christianity and social humanism initially bound together not only members of the learned professions but also the social elite who followed the same curriculum, often in identical institutions. Education underpinned the course of development of learned professions in sixteenth- and seventeenth-century England.

Professionals regarded one another highly, albeit each profession demanded differing attributes from its members. 'The divine, the lawyer, the physicion must all have these three things: reason, experience and authority, but eache in a severall degree; the divine must begin with the autoritie of Scripture, the lawyer must rely upon reason, and the physicion trust to experience' opined John Manningham, himself a common lawyer. The members of one profession could make common cause with those of another and willingly debated the internal affairs of other professions. This unity (the product of a common culture) became more pronounced when the learned professions came under attack during the civil wars, commonwealth and republic, from those excluded from or disillusioned by that culture.

Indeed, historians have shown that while the period witnessed an educational revolution, which drew into elite culture large numbers of gentlemen, lawyers, clergy and medics, it did not create a one-culture nation. Rather it confirmed and extended an existing separation between the first and second estates (nobility and clergy) on the one hand and the third estate on the other, by creating a new group of professionals who made common cause with educated nobles and gentry. That this sense of division was not based on cynical self-interest but upon deep conviction made it all the stronger.[42] This sowed seeds of dissent within the nation. Professions developed an ethos of service to the commonweal but it was one that rested on an insistence upon the separation between the expert and the client. The anti-monopolistic and anti-professional lobbies of the mid-seventeenth century frequently dissolved into an opposition to academic learning itself.[43]

Current historians, reflecting the development of today's mass educational system, appear to have turned their back on the professions themselves and to be intent on studying the ways in which the laity in the period 1500–1800 continued to practise

---

[42] See Fincham, Kenneth. *Prelate as Pastor: The Episcopate of James I.* Oxford: Clarendon Press, 1990; O'Day, Rosemary. "Hugh Latimer: Prophet of the Kingdom." *Historical Research* 65 (1992): 258–76; Dippel, Stewart A. *The Professionalization of the English Church from 1560 to 1700: Ambassadors for Christ.* Lewiston, NY: Lampeter: E. Mellen Press, c1999.

[43] See O'Day, *Professions*, 14–16; Hill, Christopher. "The radical critics of Oxford and Cambridge in the 1650s." In *Change and Continuity in Seventeenth-century England*, edited by Christopher Hill. 1974; Greaves, R. L. "The Ordination controversy and the spirit of reform in puritan England." *Journal of Ecclesiastical History* 21, no. 3 (1970): 225–41.

theology, law and medicine, despite professional claims to exclusive expertise.[44] This is a fascinating subject but there should be no assumption that we know all that we can or should know about the professions themselves. In our anxiety to write a history of 'the people' we should not turn our backs on one of the most profound social changes brought about by the rise of 'the expert'. The broad outlines have been drawn but there is a crying need for more comparable studies of the learned professions and sub-professions. The story of segmentation must be told.[45] This is one area studied by British and American sociologists that historians of early modern society have neglected. Issues surrounding autonomy and external interference must be addressed. The nature of professional education and training must be charted further. If we are to progress much further we need to have more truly parallel studies that begin with the premises that 'professions' had much in common and that this common ground deserves study. Such studies must also follow the story through from the 1500s to the 1800s: there is far too little detailed work for the post Civil Wars period.

---

[44] The most notable representatives of this trend are Porter, Roy. *Patients and Practitioners: Lay Perceptions of Medicine in Pre-Industrial Society.* Cambridge: Cambridge University Press, 1985; Pelling, Margaret. *The Common Lot. Medical Occupations and the Urban Poor in Early Modern England.* London: Longman, 1998.

[45] Brooks, Christopher. *Pettyfoggers and Vipers of the Commonwealth: The 'Lower Branch' of the Legal Profession in Early Modern England.* Cambridge: Cambridge University Press, 1986. and Miles, M. W. "A Haven for the Privileged." *Social History* 11, no. 2 (1986): 197–210, for example, have helped us towards a fuller understanding of the legal profession as a whole but we need more such detailed studies.

Educational and Economic History: The Good Neighbours

Michael Sanderson

In 1971 the economic historian Peter Mathias addressed the connection of his discipline with its 'neighbours'. He was chiefly concerned with economics, but observed that there were also increasing links with areas such as law, sociology, demography and also education. He saw education as one of the 'newly fashionable themes' arising from the concern about developing areas and noted that 'the knowledge and motivations imported by particular styles of education have become relevant things for economic historians to unearth'.[1] There are many ways in which education relates to economic development. Most clearly a modern economy depends on various levels of science and technology. Before the nineteenth century much technology arose from learning and experimenting 'on the job'. Yet with the institutionalizing of innovation in universities and firms the economy needed trained scientists in chemistry, physics and all forms of engineering. At a lower level, technical schools and colleges produced the mechanics and artisans usually in conjunction with apprenticeship. Yet science was far from the only requirement since other disciplines have shaped a safe

[1] Mathias, Peter. "Living with the Neighbours, the role of Economic History." Oxford: Clarendon press, 1971. Inaugural lecture as Chichele Professor of Economic history, University of Oxford, 24 November 1970: 5, 12.

and efficient society as the framework for economic enterprise. These included financial and business education for management and the City, legal education to produce lawyers operating systems of commercial law and devising the concept of the business corporation, and medicine especially in public health to reduce the initially high mortality of urban living. Beyond such specific skills all manner of secondary and higher educated people run an efficient administrative state, from police to planning, taxation to social work. The economy ultimately depends on them all.

Although literacy was of disputable relevance to industrialization for job performance in many occupations before the early nineteenth century, schooling inculcated other values desirable for industrialization. The discipline of attending school at regular hours, sitting in rows, accepting authority and paying attention prepared the young worker for factory work as opposed to the wider discretions of the domestic system. Concomitant urbanization was made possible by workers with the capacity to read adverts for jobs, safety instructions, shop and street signs while the reading of other advertisements expanded the desire for consumption on which the economy depended. Schooling could also instil moral, often religious, attitudes no less important for industrialization — honesty regarding materials and money, charity to smooth the wealth differentials of industrial society and the virtues of work to encourage enterprise, innovation and widening horizons. Compulsory schooling contributed to the decline of juvenile delinquency in the late nineteenth century. As there are connections between education and the economy so there have been neighbourly connections between economic and educational history, as Peter Mathias pointed out. This essay explores some of these connections and how they have come about. It will be confined largely to England and to the period since the Industrial Revolution.

The Context

Many forms of academic historical study in modern times have arisen from the needs of professional development. The establishment of the Regius Chairs of Modern History at Oxford and Cambridge in 1724 was intended to facilitate the training of diplomats. Law and History were combined at Cambridge from 1848 and at Oxford from 1850. Ecclesiastical, military and art history were integral parts of the training of clergymen, army officers and artists in the nineteenth century. Accordingly 19 teacher training colleges, which had grown rapidly in the 1890s, taught history as a complement to their professional training in the period 1890–1902.[2] There was a heavy emphasis on the thoughts of great educators of the past and the legislative and administrative aspects of educational institutions. These legal, administrative and quasi-philosophical approaches gave an academic respectability to the fledgling subject of education—as Anglo Saxon did to English Literature and mathematics to

---

[2] Gordon, Peter, and Richard Szreter. *History of Education, the Making of a Discipline*. London: Woburn Press, 1989. Richardson, William. "Historians and Educationists, the history of education as a field of study in post war England Part I 1945–72, Part II 1972–96." *History of Education* 28 (1999), nos 1, 1–30 and 2, 109–41.

economics at the same time. So the subject developed usefully, if narrowly, in its particular training context. As such it was aside from the mainstream of political, constitutional and diplomatic historical studies.

At about the same time economic history was emerging for more varied reasons. Early Socialists and 'new' trade unionists needed a working-class labour history to praise and validate preceding forms of social protest and collective labour action— Luddites, Chartists etc.—in the capitalist system. On the other side professors in the civic universities, wishing to show their relevance to their host cities, produced economic historical studies of the Lancashire cotton industry, Yorkshire woollens, the Midland industries. Third, an interest in foreign trade and mercantilism arose from contemporary pre-1914 debates concerning free trade and protectionism. As economics departments began in universities in the 1890s and 1900s, so economic history was usually part of the curriculum. But their focus, so they claimed, was training future businessmen and the history of education was not part of this.

However, the divisions between these two rather distinct fields became less clear from the 1960s for various reasons. In spite of the foundation of the History of Education Society in 1967 and the *History of Education* journal in 1972 the subject threatened to atrophy as teacher training colleges' curricula became overloaded, then merged with university departments in the 1970s and 1980s, often dropping history altogether. Yet at the same time the general study of history continued to thrive in the universities and even grew in the expansion of the 1960s and after. The content of history also broadened from high politics and diplomacy into wider areas of economic and social history with its various elaborations into social class, urban, labour, women's history and so forth. *The Economic History Review* doubled its size and tripled its circulation between 1950 and 1970.[3] The history of education found ready connections with these new interests. It also fitted with the changing student body— a bit more working class, a lot more female—looking for themes with which their life experiences could engage: childhood lifestyles, schooling, the world of work.

Most importantly economists began to take a keen interest in education and its possible contribution to economic growth. Arthur Lewis's *Theory of Economic Growth*, which was published in 1955 and had eight re-issues by 1965, contained a long section on Knowledge which had a wide influence beyond specialist economists.[4] Gary Becker popularized the concept of Human Capital in 1964.[5] The OECD was created in 1960 and formed a Study Group in the Economics of Education. This held an important conference on the subject in 1961 and published a further set of papers on the Residual Factor, including education and technical change, in 1962.[6] Riding this wave of interest the International Economic Association held a conference on the

[3] Cannadine, David. "British History, Past Present and Future." *Past and Present* no. 116 (1987):169–91
[4] Lewis, W. Arthur. *Theory of Economic Growth*. London: George Allen & Unwin, 1955: section 4.
[5] Becker, Gary. *Human Capital*. New York: National Bureau of Economic Research, 1964.
[6] OECD. "Policy Conference on Economic Growth and Investment in Education." In OECD *The Residual Factor in Economic Growth*. Paris: OECD, 1962. Conference held in 1961.

Economics of Education in 1963.[7] The concern to promote the industrialization and economic development of 'Third World' countries placed a new emphasis on the role of education. Growth could no longer be assured by inputs of land, labour and capital, there was a mysterious 'residual' factor—technical change, and the quality and skill of the labourer and entrepreneur created by education. If economists were taking education seriously so the historians of both disciplines drew closer together. In the 1960s notable addresses on the development of the history of education as a subject began repeatedly to use the phrase 'economic and social'. Brian Simon noted in 1966 that, 'the trend in historical studies away from predominantly political and constitutional matters towards economic and social developments ... is a material aid to the history of education'.[8] Few indicators illustrate better the closer engagement of economic and educational history than the *Cambridge Economic History of Britain*. In the 1981 version there were passing references to education; relevant and appropriate, if slight. In the 2003 version each volume has a substantial and important chapter devoted to education.[9]

Contributions and Engagements

Let us focus on some areas where educational history has had an impact on economic history. First, historians have been interested in the relevance of education for the Industrial Revolution. At the level of elementary education and literacy there has been a shift of view. The older view, following the modern finding that education plays a vital part in industrialization, reasonably held that it must have been so in the classic English 1760–1830 period. Lawrence Stone showed a steady rise in literacy from 56 per cent in 1775 to around 65 per cent by 1800 and 66 per cent by 1840.[10] Stone saw this as an 'upsurge of literacy after 1780' underlying a demand for a literate labour force in an industrializing society. This was questioned by Schofield's findings that literacy stagnated after 1750 and those of Sanderson and Laquer that it actually fell in the industrializing districts of Lancashire and Cheshire.[11] Of particular interest was the work of Stephen Nicholas who found from Australian convict

---

[7] Robinson, E. A. G., and J. E. Vaizey. *The Economics of Education.* London: Macmillan, 1966. Proceedings of the International Economic Association Conference 1963.

[8] Simon, Brian. No. 5 in Gordon and Szreter, 1966, op. cit., 66.

[9] Compare Floud, R., and D. McCloskey. *The Economic History of Britain since 1700*, 3 vols. Cambridge: Cambridge University Press, 1981 and Floud, Roderick, and Paul Johnson. *The Cambridge Economic History of Modern Britain*, 3 vols. Cambridge: Cambridge University Press, 2003 and 2004.

[10] Stone, Lawrence. "Literacy and Education in England 1540–1900." *Past and Present* 42 (February 1969): 69–139.

[11] Schofield, R. S. "Dimensions of Illiteracy 1750–1850." *Explorations in Economic History* 10, no. 4 (Summer 1973): 437–54. Sanderson, Michael. "Literacy and Social Mobility in the Industrial Revolution in England." *Past and Present* 56 (August 1972). Laqueur, Thomas W. "Literacy and Social Mobility in the Industrial Revolution in England." *Past and Present* 64 (August 1974): 96–107. The literature has vastly expanded since; see the footnotes in Elaine Brown's article cited later.

data that urban literacy continued to rise to 1808 and rural literacy to 1817 but both fell until the 1840s.[12]

Although his view of the down-turning point is later than that of historians using English data he agrees from occupational evidence that the English Industrial Revolution did not require advancing literacy and did not get it. Those who still regard education as important could fairly point to the sharp rise in literacy between the 1690s and the 1760s as establishing a threshold for industrialization, whatever dip ensued subsequently.

Here was an intriguing disjunction between economic historians of education and the new economists of education. The latter strongly argued the positive contribution of education to industrialization: the former had detected an important case where it was not so. It raised the wider point that history is not always a relevant guide as to what is appropriate or even possible in contemporary situations. This point was interestingly finessed by two distinguished economic historians in the early 1980s. Richard Easterlin showed from long-run statistical data that at least since the 1830s (if not from the 1760s) education has been the decisive element in whether countries have become developed or not.[13] Then Lars Sandberg in an original view on the topic argued that the literacy rates of a country at any particular time did not necessarily relate to its level of economic advance of that time. But curiously literacy levels of earlier times did predict or project forward future levels of economic prosperity.[14] High levels of literacy do eventually pay off as neglect of education will eventually catch up in diminished performance. It is notable that Easterlin and Sandberg were writing in major economic history journals, relating a long view of education to a wide range of economies.

The other area where education is thought to have contributed to the Industrial Revolution is that of scientific education. Here is a long tradition of educational historians writing on dissenting academies, travelling lecturers and scientific clubs in the eighteenth century. T. S. Ashton was already indicating their importance to the Industrial Revolution in 1948.[15] This was embodied in a major statement by Musson and Robinson arguing as to the closer contribution of scientific education and culture to the economy.[16] There is modified dissent. We are reminded that popular science is not necessarily technological innovation[17] and that it could easily degenerate into

---

[12] Nicholas, Stephen. "Literacy and the Industrial Revolution." In *Education and Economic Development since the Industrial Revolution*, edited by Gabriel Tortella. València: Generalitat Valenciana, 1990. Nicholas, Stephen J., and Jacqueline M. Nicholas. "Male Literacy, Deskilling and the Industrial Revolution." *Journal of Interdisciplinary History* XXIII.I (Summer 1992): 1–18.

[13] Easterlin, Richard. "Why isn't the whole World Developed?" *Journal of Economic History* 41, no. 1 (1981): 1–19.

[14] Sandberg, Lars. "Ignorance, Poverty and Economic Backwardness." *Journal of European Economic History* 11, no. 3 (1982): 675–97.

[15] Ashton, T. S. *The Industrial Revolution*. London: Oxford University Press, 1948: 21–21.

[16] Musson, A. E., and E. Robinson. *Science and Technology in the Industrial Revolution*. Manchester: Manchester University Press, 1969.

[17] Hall, A. Rupert. "What did the Industrial Revolution owe to Science." In *Historical Perspectives, Studies in honour of J.H. Plumb*, edited by N. McKendrick. London: Europa, 1974.

polite socializing.[18] But the Musson and Robinson view has been widely absorbed into the economic history of the Industrial Revolution.

A second area where educational and economic history have closely engaged is that of the 'decline of the British economy', 1870–1914. That defects of education were hampering Britain's competitiveness with an emergent Germany after 1870 was widely believed at the time and expressed in Government reports and popular writing. These have been taken up by historians and crystallized into an 'declinist' orthodoxy of culpability by various writers: Derek Aldcroft, Martin Wiener, Correlli Barnett, Gordon Roderick, Michael Stephens and others.[19] Their view was that technical education was inferior to that in Germany and insufficient, and that the public service ethos and classical curriculum of the public schools and ancient universities were inimical to entrepreneurship and the skill formation of the labour force. This view was comforting for various reasons. It was an easier argument to present than more intricate matters such as the balance of home and foreign investment, the merits of tariffs and free trade, the costs and benefits of Empire. It also appealed to businessmen and politicians who could pass the blame for their shortcomings on to the education system. This was still so in the 1980s when Margaret Thatcher and Keith Joseph urged the cabinet to read Wiener's book as a root explanation of Britain's economic difficulties.

This orthodoxy has been shrewdly challenged, notably by Stephen Nicholas[20] and Sir Roderick Floud.[21] They argue that it is irrelevant to compare educational institutions in Britain with those in Germany and France to Britain's disadvantage. The British way of training was not through impressive state-financed buildings but by apprenticeship. Apprenticeship balanced costs and benefits between employers and employed. The apprentice accepted low wages in training and recouped himself later with a wage differential as a skilled craftsman. The employer paid the apprentice probably more than he was worth in his unqualified state but recouped the advantage of a skilled workforce he could rely on as trained on-the-job and not too much in the classroom. This minimized the burden of cost on the consumer or the state through the taxpayer while assuring both of quality skilled labour evident in products from battleships to teacups. British skill formation was not inferior to the Germans, it was just different. It is also pointed out that the neat period 1870-1914 is misleading since there was a very considerable and rapid increase of technical and scientific education

---

[18] Porter, R.S. "Science, Provincial Culture and Public Opinion in Enlightenment England." *British Journal of Eighteenth Century Studies* 3, no.1 (Spring 1980):20–46.

[19] For example, Aldcroft, Derek. "Investment and Utilisation of Manpower: Great Britain and her Rivals 1870–1914." In *Great Britain and her World*, edited by B. M. Ratcliffe. Manchester: Manchester University Press, 1975. Wiener, Martin. *English Culture and the Decline of the Industrial Spirit 1850–1980*. Cambridge: Cambridge University Press, 1981. Barnett, Correlli. *The Collapse of British Power*. London: Eyre Methuen, 1972. Roderick, G. S., and Michael Stephens. *Education and Industry in the Nineteenth Century*. London: Longman, 1972.

[20] Nicholas, Stephen. "Technical Education and the Decline of Britain 1870–1914." In *The Steam Intellect Societies*, edited by Ian Inkster. Nottingham: University of Nottingham, 1985.

[21] Floud, Roderick. "Technical Education and Economic Performance in Britain 1850–1914." *Albion* 14 (1982): 153–71.

from 1890 making the period 1890–1914 quite different from that of 1870–1890 whence much critical comment came. The debate on the public schools has likewise shifted from an outright condemnation of their classics and anti-industrial ethos. It is appreciated that there was a fair expansion of science in the public schools after the Clarendon Commission and in any case very few industrialists were ex-public school men so their virtues and defects were largely irrelevant to British industrial performance. The real value of the public schools was in the more important worlds of commerce and finance in the City. Here their inculcated qualities of gentlemanly trustworthiness and a capacity for wide social networking underlay the strengths of the institutions of the City of London. This has been perhaps the closest area of engagement of educational and economic history and this aspect of the debate has received full coverage in the major textbooks of Francois Crouzet and Sidney Pollard.[22] It would now be unthinkable for an economic historian to survey this period without discussing it.

A third area is the rise of interest in women's education, itself borne along by the general tide of feminist studies. For many decades since the 1890s the historiography was dominated by studies celebrating the path-breaking work of early women's schools and colleges and of individual pioneers. In recent years this aspect of women's educational history and economic and social history have drawn closer over the relevance of education to the changing female labour market.

At the level of the middle class and higher education Janet Howarth and Mark Curthoys have shown just how narrow were the outlets for women graduates before 1914, mostly studying arts subjects and becoming school teachers.[23] Otherwise 'ladies' who had no intention of taking paid employment attended for social and cultural reasons prior to marriage. As such, neither group was attractive to private or state benefactors or of much interest to economic historians. In the interwar years the occupational opportunities of women graduates burgeoned into industrial social work (personnel managers), factory inspectors, engineering, medicine, advertising and marketing, publishing, store management and scientific research.[24] They benefited from the gender imbalance of the interwar years, the need for good taste and lack of need for physical strength in many of the new consumer industries of the 1930s.

However, some of the most interesting work has been in the area of working class girls' education in the first half of the twentieth century. This period was marked by rapid occupational change from old declining Victorian industries, new opportunities for modestly paid girl labour and a confused and incomplete movement towards limited

[22] Crouzet, François. *The Victorian Economy*. London: Methuen, 1982. Pollard, Sidney. *Britain's Prime and Britain's Decline 1870–1914*. London: Edward Arnold, 1989.

[23] Howarth, Janet, and Mark Curthoys. "The Political Economy of Women's Higher Education in late Nineteenth and Early Twentieth Century Britain." *Historical Research* 60, no. 142 (June 1987): 208–31 and "Gender, Curriculum and Career: a Case Study of Women University Students in England before 1914." In *Women, Education and the Professions*, edited by Penny Summerfield. *History of Education Society Occasional Publication*, no. 8 (1987).

[24] Sanderson, Michael. *The Universities and British Industry 1850–1970*. London: Routledge & Kegan Paul, 1972: ch. 11.

secondary education for all. In the nineteenth century working-class girls' elementary education was seen to a great extent as turning them into 'good wives and little mothers' at home or in service through domestic science, or temporary factory hands to whose work their schooling was of little direct relevance.[25] The twentieth century saw a marked change which has best been addressed through local studies. In Lancashire Penny Summerfield has shown the collapse of textiles and domestic service as occupations for working-class girls between 1911 and 1951. They fell from 65 to 19 per cent. These were replaced by commercial and secretarial work and shop assistants (both rising from 6 per cent in 1911 to 62 per cent by 1950). The new grammar schools decanted working-class girls into teaching but the new post-Hadow Central and Senior schools, at levels above the old Victorian elementary school but below that of the Secondary (grammar) school, were producing better educated, upwardly mobile working-class girls. These rose to non-manual jobs where good literacy, self-presentation and dealing with the public ironically could provide better chances of advancement to management than school teaching.[26] Jenny Zmroczek has likewise found it so in Norwich in the period 1900–1939.[27] In the 1900s domestic service was the largest employment for working-class girls followed by the needle trades, boot factories and food packing. By the 1930s there was a large decline in domestic service and the needle trades and a corresponding increase in shop and office work. This closely related to new educational opportunities provided by a Central School and Municipal Secondary School. Nearly half of Central School and two-thirds of Secondary School girls went into office work in the 1930s. This is the real White Blouse Revolution in Gregory Anderson's vivid phrase.[28] This interconnection of educational and occupational change is of great interest to the economic historian. It is a good example of a formerly rather inward-looking branch of educational history becoming highly relevant to wider economic themes of upward mobility and the labour market.

Finally, the urgent issue to have been addressed by recent literature is how far educational policy since the war has contributed to Britain's supposed relative economic decline in the second half of the twentieth century. Here history merges with contemporary comment and protagonists of the pre-1914 period see it as a continuation of the earlier theme. Most notably, Derek Aldcroft, a critic of the education of the entrepreneur before the First World War, returns to the matter.[29] He finds the

---

[25] Dyhouse, Carol. "Good Wives and Little Mothers: Social Anxieties and the Schoolgirl's Curriculum 1890–1920." *Oxford Review of Education* 3, no. 1 (1977): 21–35.

[26] Summerfield, Penny. "Family, School and Work, Girls' Education and Employment in Lancashire1900–1950." in History of Education Society Conference Papers *Education and Employment Initiatives and Experiences 1780 to the Present*, edited by Malcolm Dick, 1988.

[27] Zmroczek, Jenny. "The Education and Employment of Girls in Norwich 1870–1939." Ph.D. diss., University of East Anglia, 2004. "'If girls would take more kindly to domestic work' Norwich 1900–1939." *Women's History* 44 (June 2003): Pagination not available.

[28] Anderson, Gregory. *The White Blouse Revolution*. Manchester: Manchester University Press, 1988.

[29] Aldcroft, Derek. *Education, Training and Economic Performance*. Manchester: Manchester University Press, 1992.

defects of education not in the underinvestment but the low rates of return to the economy resulting from it. This he attributes to a range of factors: the academic bias of the educational system too concerned to sieve out the academically able, an under-valuing of vocational education, the plethora of schemes and initiatives in technical education qualifications with no coherent programme of good quality, an excessive emphasis on arts and social studies in the expansion of higher education, the neglect of managerial education, the excessive discretion of Local Education Authorities and lack of central control to impose a more industry-oriented education. It was a powerful statement very much of its time, its effect enhanced by Aldcroft's reputation among economic historians. Between 1981 and 2002 there have been at least nine books or popular booklets on Britain's economic decline or poor economic performance. They have stressed the 'skills gap', anti-industrial public schools, the decline of apprentice-ship, politicians' and civil servants' greater emphasis on social equality than on the needs of industry and the arts bias of the education of such policy-makers. It is notable in this 'declinist' literature how the focus on education intensified between 1981 and 2001; also how much was published or being written in the Thatcher years.

Three other themes have also attracted attention. Alison Wolf sees parallels between the pre-1914 and pre-2000 moral panics about 'backward' education contributing to a 'declining' economy.[30] She has brilliantly attacked the whole Manpower Services Commission attempt to create a plethora of initiatives, largely devised by businessmen, as a way out of slow growth.[31] In particular she condemns the National Vocational Qualifications, much beloved of the Confederation of British Industry (CBI) but with 364 of the qualifications never taken by anyone and only 2 per cent of the workforce ever taking any of them. In any case the relentless drive to expand the universities swept young people past the NVQs into A levels. Accordingly too many mediocre young people were going into an over-expanded further and higher education sector only to be decanted untrained into low-grade jobs they might have been better starting at 16. Wolf's clear view is that the Government's duty is to provide good primary and secondary education but not to waste money by seeking to micromanage the rest.

Second, Gary McCulloch and associates have focused on the failure to develop school science and technology due to a lack of agreement regarding curricular content.[32] The Nuffield Project from 1962 envisaged it as largely academic science but to the neglect of technology and engineering. By contrast the Schools Council Project 1965–1972 wanted to emphasize craft skills. By the late 1960s–1970s there were too many competing groups with acrimoniously differing views that effectively prevented the reception of technology in the school curriculum. Third, associated with this, some historians have been attracted to the old idea of the Junior Technical School

---

[30] Wolf, Alison. "Politicians and Economic Panic." *History of Education* 27, no. 3 (1998): 219–34.

[31] Wolf, Alison. *Does Education Matter? Myths about Education and Economic Growth*. London: Penguin, 2002.

[32] McCulloch, Gary, Edgar Jenkins, and David Layton. *Technological Revolution, The Politics of School Science and Technology in England and Wales since 1945*. Lewes: Falmer Press, 1985.

of the 1900s (JTS) and later post-Butler Secondary Technical School (STS). These were schools which took children at age 13 to give them a specialized curriculum emphasizing, for example, engineering, building and specific crafts to prepare them for apprenticeships and the world of work. Gary McCulloch has considered whether it is a 'usable past' and regards such specialization as inappropriate for the present day.[33] Alison Wolf is also critical of targeting vocational education at 14-year-olds as a solution to the skills shortage. Michael Sanderson finds more merit in these schools and sees Sir David Eccles's decision not to support them after 1953 as one of the most significant adverse policy changes of the postwar years.[34] They might have acted as feeders for a stronger Technical University sector, supplied the skilled labour whose lack we deplore, and provided mid-teenagers bored by academic study with the greater satisfactions of making and doing. Many of these stop-gap schemes of which Aldcroft and Wolf are sceptical were attempts to fill the void left by the old JTS/STS. Another 'might have been' is the Higher Grade School championed by Meriel Vlaeminke.[35] She deplores their destruction by Sir Robert Morant, believing that if they had been allowed to develop it might have led to a comprehensive school sector earlier than the 1960s. It is notable that McCulloch, Sanderson and Vlaeminke are all historians looking back to the Morant years of the 1900s and still finding issues there of relevance to modern policy thinking—grammar schools; technical schools; proto-comprehensives? The failure of skill formation and hence of productivity since 1945 was still at the heart of Britain's laggardly economic growth and some of the issues went back historically to the 1900s.

These debates were especially strong in the 1980s and 1990s and were encouraged by many studies of the contemporary scene in the 1980s by S. J. Prais, the National Institute of Economic and Social Research and others in which Britain compared especially badly with Germany.[36] They suggested that Britain's backwardness in the technical training of non-academic teenagers was leading to a skills shortage frustrating our productivity and economic growth. British annual percentage GDP growth was certainly lower in than France, Germany and Japan for 1950–1973 and labour productivity of GDP per hour worked was lower in the period 1950–1983 (except for the USA). Yet this has changed in recent years in ways that would surprise the critics of the 1980s. British GPD growth 1990–1998 was faster than that of Japan, Germany and France and has been consistently higher in the UK than in Germany and France since 2000 and higher than Japan in three of the five years 2000–2005.[37] The underswell of economic anxiety that drew attention to education and hence stimulated

[33] McCulloch, Gary. *The Secondary Technical School, a Usable Past?* Lewes: Falmer Press, 1989.

[34] Sanderson, Michael. *The Missing Stratum, Technical School Education in England 1900–1990s.* London: Athlone Press, 1994.

[35] Vlaeminke, Meriel. *The English Higher Grade Schools, a Lost Opportunity.* London: Woburn Press, 2000.

[36] For example, Prais, S. J. *Schooling Standards in Britain and Germany, some summary comparisons bearing on economic efficiency.* London: NIESR, 1982.

[37] Maddison, Angus. *The World Economy, a Millennial Perspective.* OECD, 2001. *OECD Economic Outlook* 5, no. 75 (June 2004).

historians both economic and educational has (for the moment) abated. Was our education really so bad in the 1960s–1980s, did we catch up or is it that education is not quite so important for economic growth as the clichés of the 'knowledge driven' economy suggest?

New Methods and Approaches

The interest in educational history taken by 'neighbours' has brought some fresh methods and approaches to the discipline. Of course the traditional methods remain the description and evaluation of the development of institutions and policy through the research of original archival documents. This links the history of education methodologically with mainstream historical research of all kinds and will certainly continue to give the ballast of credibility and factual certainty as the subject sometimes launches off into more speculative cliometric directions.

Among the most insightful of the more quantitative approaches is that of social mobility. Andrew Miles's outstanding study of social mobility in the nineteenth and early twentieth century finds that improving education did have an effect in increasing mobility.[38] It was in the 1870–1914 period that increasingly literate sons of Class V fathers most sharply moved into higher classes, rarely to Class I but most commonly to the labour aristocracy of Classes III and IV. On the other hand, two-thirds of illiterate sons of Class I fathers and three-quarters of such sons of Class V fathers ended up themselves in Class V. With this Miles sees a psychological change—that mobility up or down came to be seen in terms of personal industry in both education and life and not part of a divine scheme of things. He concluded that 'the battle to seek out any advantage switched from the labour market to education'.[39] Education had created a more open society by 1914 than it had been in 1839.

A. H. Halsey as a sociologist taking a historical perspective had likewise shown for the twentieth century the close association of educational and mobility experience.[40] To take two indications over the sweep of the twentieth century back from 1972, 58 per cent of people moving from working to middle class had taken school examinations and 12.8 per cent had gone to university. Yet only 15.1 per cent of those falling from middle to working class had taken school examinations and a tiny 0.5 per cent had been to university. Education was the path for and to the middle class; lack of it the trap perpetuating immobility at the bottom of society. Some of the most illuminating studies, not just of educational institutions but of their output, have been of inestimable value to economic historians of the labour market. Bishop and Wilkinson on Winchester[41] and the essays of Mark Curthoys and Daniel Greenstein on the

---

[38] Miles, Andrew. *Social Mobility in Nineteenth and Early Twentieth Century England*. Basingstoke: Macmillan, 1999.

[39] Ibid., 144.

[40] Halsey, A. H. *Change in British Society*. Oxford: Oxford University Press, 1986.

[41] Bishop, T. H. J. H., and R. Wilkinson. *Winchester and the Public School Elite*. London: Faber, 1967.

careers of Oxford graduates in the superb modern volumes of the History of Oxford University are exemplars.[42] No serious history of an educational institution would now neglect some attempt to study the career outcomes of their students.

Second, some historians have tried to relate the growth of education to economic growth. As we have seen, Easterlin in 1981 traced statistical data on education and economic growth back to the 1830s and argued that the spread of education was a decisive factor. At about the same time Matthews, Feinstein and Odling Smee sought to advance the methodology by measuring the number of years of formal schooling embodied in the whole labour force in census years 1871–1961.[43] This showed a steady progression and they estimate that the growth in labour quality resulting from improvements in education rose from 0.3 per cent annually in the period 1856–1873 to 0.5 per cent in 1873–1937, rising to 0.6 per cent in 1937–1964. More recently Stephen Broadberry and Mary O'Mahoney have related the growth of education to that of productivity and GDP and find the connection broadly satisfactory apart from the 1960s and 1970s.[44] Likewise Vincent Carpentier has measured the growth of public expenditure since 1833 and related this to growth cycles.[45] His finding was that before 1945 public expenditure on education grew counter-cyclically over times of downturn in the economy, in effect reviving it. After 1945 it has tended to grow with the expansion of the economy. He concludes that only since 1945 has educational expenditure been seen as a driving force in the economic system rather than just a means of correction. This ingenious matching by various scholars of the statistics of education and economic growth over the long term has much to yield in throwing new light on the subject and all tend to confirm education as a significant contribution to growth.

There are difficulties in these studies sometimes more evident to the historian than the economist. For instance it is not possible, though it is tempting, to measure the increase in elementary education between 1818 and 1833 by comparing the Brougham and Kerry returns of those years since the former were about 'the poor' and the latter 'the people' and many respondents to the first survey were quite unsure what they should measure. Also many university statistics are incomplete before 1914, sometimes aggregate returns being made but without it being possible to distinguish students in different disciplines. As such it is problematic to relate numbers of university students not likely to relate to economic growth (medical students, theologians) to those that may (engineers, chemists). Matthews and associates generously admit the impossibility

---

[42] Greenstein, Daniel I. "The Junior Members 1980–1990: a profile." in *The History of the University of Oxford*, VIII: *The Twentieth Century*, edited by Brian Harrison. Oxford: Clarendon Press, 1994. Curthoys, M. C. "The Careers of Oxford Men." In *The History of the University of Oxford*, VI: *Nineteenth Century Oxford Pt I*, by M. G. Brock and M. C. Curthoys. Oxford: Clarendon Press, 1997.

[43] Matthews, R. C. O., C. H. Feinstein, and J. C. Odling Smee. *British Economic Growth 1856–1973*. Oxford: Clarendon Press, 1982: 105–13.

[44] Broadberry, Stephen. "Human Capital and Skills." And O'Mahoney, Mary. "Employment, Education and Human Capital." In *The Cambridge Economic History of Modern Britain*, Vols 3 and 4, edited by Roderick Floud and Paul Johnson. Cambridge: Cambridge University Press, 2003.

[45] Carpentier, Vincent. "Public Expenditure on Education and Economic Growth in the UK 1833–2000." *History of Education* 32, no. 1 (2003): 1–15.

of measuring technical education since much of it was on-the-job training and the system was 'extremely complicated with a wide variety of types and places of training and types of qualification and it is impossible to derive summary measures from published data'.[46] They admit their figures may be 'very rough', possibly subject to errors of 50 per cent or more. It is an odd paradox that econometricians writing educational history and supposedly bringing sharper statistical precision can end up writing history that may be only half true, if that. However, their findings have an acceptability to historians since they do relate to commonsense expectations of what historians know of the track of educational development of the time. Also the important and painstaking work in the 2003 *Cambridge Economic History of Britain* with its clear divisions of primary, secondary and higher education raises questions in the mind of historians aware of just how messy early twentieth-century education was. Were higher grade schools primary or secondary? What of post-elementary senior classes in primary schools in the 1920s? Does a part-time evening class boot maker in Norwich 'Tech' rank as 'higher' along with the Cambridge University engineering student in the 1930s?

There are also difficulties of cause and effect. Showing similarities of economic and educational growth is tempting but can lead to ambiguous conclusions. For instance in 1997 the History of Education Society held a conference on education and economic performance. Harold Perkin showed the clear correspondence between GNP per head, the percentage of the labour force in the service sector and the percentage of an age group in higher education and how these differed widely between high-, middle- and low-income countries. All these indicators increased between 1960 and 1990 while the differentials between them were maintained.[47] One might as well argue that higher levels of higher education yielded higher GNP per head as that only societies with a high GNP could afford generous provision of higher education whether relevant for economic growth or not. Michael Kaser in a famous essay in 1963 likewise showed the close connection between rates of economic growth and university students per 1000 primary school students.[48] It would have been tempting in that year of the Robbins Report to argue simply that more university students would lead to more economic growth and many would have been willing to believe it. Yet Kaser demurred; the causal connections could flow in either direction and it was impossible to tell which. In practice there have been historical anomalies. Egypt's vast expansion of education did not yield economic growth: Switzerland as the richest per capita country in the world has low levels of university provision.[49]

Finally there is a contemporary approach to evaluating education through measuring the rate of return. That is to say, the costs of education including foregone earnings are calculated and then related to the extra earnings that would accrue from a career

---

[46] Matthews, R. C. O. and associates, op. cit., 109.

[47] Perkin, H. J. "Higher Education and Social Progress." *History of Education* 27, no.3 (1998): 207–17.

[48] Kaser, Michael. "Education and Economic Progress: Experience in Industrialised Market Economies", in E. A. G. Robinson, 1996, op. cit.

[49] Wolf, *Does Education Matter? Myths about Education and Economic Growth*, 39, 42.

enhanced with such qualifications—A levels or a degree or whatever else. The extra earnings are represented as a yield on the investment in the initial education over a working lifetime and expressed as an annualized percentage. Gary Becker elaborated these techniques in his 1964 book. Various estimates over the last 40 years tend to be optimistic. Ziderman found the rate of return for graduates was 15 per cent in 1961 before the expansion of the new universities though falling to a still respectable 7 per cent by 1973.[50] A BP/LSE Survey made in the late 1980s found the returns on higher education were 7.08 per cent for males and 5.84 per cent for females.[51] Sir Ron Dearing's Committee in 1997 estimated that the return on doing a degree was of the order of 11–13 per cent.[52] Finally Charles Clarke's major policy statement of 2003 stressed that honours graduates earn on average 64 per cent more than non-graduates. He claimed that the rate of return enjoyed by university graduates in the UK was higher than that in any other OECD country.[53] But intriguingly he does not say what it was, though clearly civil servants will be calculating this regularly. The key issue is whether the continued expansion of graduates is driving down their rate of return below the earlier findings of 7 per cent let alone the more optimistic Dearing calculations. Historical calculations are rare. David Mitch found that the lowest rates of return to literacy for males fell from 9 per cent in 1839–1843 to 3.75 per cent in 1869–1873 and remained constant at below 1 per cent for females for both periods.[54] These returns were good compared with alternative investments and the fall was a convergence to these other alternative rates as a consequence of rising and hence more commonly diffused literacy.

Alison Wolf, however, draws attention to certain conceptual problems regarding the rate of return.[55] There is a difference between the return to the individuals and the social rate of return. For example the best individual rate of return is yielded by studying law yet this is clearly not the best way to boost the economic growth of society at large. Also since the costs of producing (useful) science, engineering or medical graduates is much higher than that for producing (less useful) arts graduates so the benefit to the individual 'useful' graduate is higher through the wages premium than the social rate of return—still vastly worth having—due to the higher costs of producing such graduates.

Forward Paths?

As economic and educational history have drawn closer we may speculate on some further areas of developing research. It is now a matter of urgency to write the first

[50] Ziderman, A. "Does it Pay to Take a Degree?" *Oxford Economic Papers* (1973): 262–74.

[51] Bennett, Robert, and others. *Learning Should Pay*. London: BP/LSE, n.d. 1992.

[52] *National Committee of Inquiry into Higher Education: Higher Education in a Learning Society* (Sir Ron Dearing). London: HMSO, July 1997.

[53] *The Future of Higher Education* (Charles Clarke) CM5735. London: HMSO, January 2003.

[54] Mitch, David. "Under investment in Literacy? The potential contribution of government involvement in elementary education to economic growth in nineteenth century England." *Journal of Economic History* XLIV, no. 2 (June 1984): 557–66.

[55] Wolf, Alison., 2002, op. cit., 22–28.

histories of the new universities of the 1960s. We are in a window of time, fast closing, when early pioneers and practitioners are still alive and capable of being interviewed and their papers sought. But we are sufficiently distant from the early days that confidential papers may be made available and even embarrassing events like student unrest discussed dispassionately and analytically. Some early assessment of their contribution to the labour supply, technological innovation and their relation to their regional economy is now appropriate. The new universities of the 1960s were initially the subject of adulation and then vilification. Now is the time for a more balanced view that the historian of education can provide.[56]

Second, the theme of literacy is far from exhausted. We need further regional studies relating to the Industrial Revolution.[57] Were the West Riding woollen textile districts of Yorkshire similar to Lancashire with the urban–rural divide; was there a decline in literacy under the impact of population increase; what were the literary levels of factory and domestic workers and were they relevant for either? Was it greatly different in Birmingham with its greater reliance on small independent craftsmen and engineering rather than machine-minding mill workers? Furthermore interest is moving to the mid–late nineteenth century where further economic questions arise. With rising literacy from the 1840s and especially after 1870 the literacy of various occupational groups converged. So did occupations that formerly required little literacy now require more of it—and get it? David Mitch suggests that between 1841 and 1891 jobs requiring literacy rose from 27.4 per cent of the male labour force to 37.2 per cent and those to which it was irrelevant fell from 46.9 per cent to 37 per cent.[58] If there was a premium to literacy reflected in wages, as found by Mitch for the middle century, did it diminish and ultimately vanish with virtually total compulsory literacy, and were there occupational variations in this? Mitch has also shown by econometric methods that the rise in public finance for state school education markedly increased working-class access to such schools.[59] Interest is also being taken in gender variations in the literacy convergence. Elaine Brown's recent work on Leicester has shown that female literacy remained consistently below that of men through most of the nineteenth century but converged sharply after 1870.[60] She relates this pre-1870 divergence to an economy heavily dependent on domestic industries and the reliance on female

---

[56] For example, Sanderson, Michael. *The History of the University of East Anglia 1918–2000.* London: Hambledon and London, 2002.

[57] Stephens, W. B., ed. *Studies in the History of Literacy: England and North America.* Leeds: University of Leeds, 1983, extends the study to five new areas showing variously falls, rises and no clear trends in literacy. The problem of the direction of literacy can only be addressed by such regional studies.

[58] Mitch, David. *The Rise of Popular Literacy in Victorian England.* Philadelphia: University of Pennsylvania Press, 1992.

[59] Mitch, David F. "The Impact of Subsidies to Elementary Schooling on Enrolment Rates in Nineteenth Century England." *Economic History Review* 2nd Ser. XXXIX, no. 3 (1986): 371–91.

[60] Brown, Elaine. "Gender, occupation, illiteracy and the urban economic environment: Leicester 1760–1890." *Urban History* 31, no. 2 (2004):191–209 and "Working class education and illiteracy in Leicester." Ph.D. diss., University of Leicester, 2002.

labour in these industries with a 'culture of illiteracy'. The detailed documentation on marriage and literacy from 1837 also yields insights into gender, occupation and social mobility, notably Mitch's finding that literate middle-class women would marry literate working-class men of illiterate fathers who showed themselves to be potentially upwardly mobile. It was a rational response to the 'surplus women' problem, with education and the acquirement of literacy as a proxy for economic prospects. Maggie Hobson's 'Hobson's Choice' of her father's workman Will Mossop as a husband was not only fiction but reflected a reality.[61]

Third, we could be paying more attention to the difficult area of the junction between education and employment. How, historically, did you train to be an actor, stockbroker, lorry driver and how appropriate was educational provision for this? Some occupations achieve an efficient elision of education–training–job. Such would be actors for example (English and drama at school and university, amateur dramatics, drama school, profession); the same would be so for musicians. Yet others like university lecturers have had virtually no training at all and learned by doing. The constant complaints by employers, notably the CBI, about the education of their recruits suggest defects in this junction. In this amorphous borderland between education and doing the job lie various issues—careers advisory services, the perception of occupations by school and university leavers, what influence employers in Sector Skills Councils have in the curricula of subjects supposedly relating to the employment they provide,[62] the role of private training agencies (secretarial colleges, HGV driving schools), the role of family in finding jobs,[63] the efficiency of recruitment and induction systems of firms. This no-man's land through which labour is distributed from education to employment is of as much interest to the economic historian as the formal education system.

Both economic history and the history of education stand fairly close together at the more vocational end of the liberal arts spectrum. Economic history most clearly relates to the study of economics giving it a human dimension and grounding it in the reality of economic change over time. The history of education is one of those areas of social history which are essential mental baggage for thinking about, for example, old age, the changing role of women, sexuality, poverty, social structure and so forth. Many of the issues of education today need the illumination of a historical perspective for a fuller understanding. The desirability (or not) of elite private education, grammar schools or comprehensives as vehicles of social mobility, the role of education in

---

[61] Harold Brighouse's famous play was staged in 1916 but represented prewar years. Maggie spends part of her honeymoon improving her husband's literacy. By the final act he is a confident middle-class businessman.

[62] *Financial Times*, 18 August 2006, Advertisement for the Sector Skills Councils. This also claims that 57 per cent of employers are dissatisfied with the education of recruits. See also *FT*, 14 August 2006, "CBI in science warning over 'dire' school leavers".

[63] Zmroczek, op. cit., in extensive historical interviewing of Norwich women who were girls in the interwar years shows the importance of family connections, notably uncles, in getting jobs. Also she shows the importance of private secretarial colleges for non-university middle-class girls and the ablest of the working class.

economic growth and decline, how far the state should be involved in education at all, the justification of education 'for its own sake' or for employment—are all live issues with roots some going back to the Morant era of the 1900s and many beyond, at least to the Victorians.

Of course there are differences in the approaches of those with a historical bias and those more economically inclined, as we have seen.[64] Historians place an emphasis on archival research, factual, documentary and often unpublished evidence. Researching mountains of documents gives a sense of the complexity, variability and sheer messiness of reality. This can often be glossed over by the economically minded seeking broad trends from aggregated published material which (they hope) can lead to conceptual generalization—if it was so there and then it must be so here and now. Those with an economic approach bring mathematical techniques, in which historians *purs sangs* are usually untrained, and theoretical assumptions. And they are often more willing to take a long-run view based on printed statistics which can yield insights hidden from more cautious historians. They in turn are suspicious of the historians' presentation of endless factual data, sometimes contradictory (as in the literacy debate), which defies the creation of a theoretical model. They can be unappreciative of the historian's awareness of contingencies and the role of individual actors and policies (Sir James Kay Shuttleworth's expansion of the role of the state in public education in the 1830s and 1840s, Sir Robert Morant's determination to eliminate the Higher Grade Schools in the 1900s and Sir David Eccles's halt to the development of the STS in the 1950s). The historian inclines to the empirical, the narrative and the analysis of policy: the economist to the search for the conceptual and resultant theory. The history of education is especially fortunate in having both kinds of worker in the field. The discipline needs both and their neighbourly receptiveness to work 'over the garden fence' ensures the subject's continued vibrancy and progress.

---

[64] Mathias, op. cit., is perceptive on the differences in the historians' and the economists' approaches to economic history, which are fruitful here.

Social Change and Education in Ireland, Scotland and Wales: Historiography on Nineteenth-century Schooling

Deirdre Raftery, Jane McDermid and Gareth Elwyn Jones

Education and Change in the Nineteenth Century[1]

The nineteenth century was a period of unprecedented change in educational provision in Ireland, Scotland and Wales, and this change reflected and responded to rapid social and economic change. In Ireland, the population declined significantly as a consequence of the Great Famine (1845–49) which brought death and emigration. By 1851, the population had fallen to six million, from a pre-famine figure of over eight million. Population decline continued to the end of the century. There was also severe depopulation of rural areas, as people emigrated in search of work, or migrated to towns and cities for poor relief. By contrast, in Scotland and Wales there was significant population growth. Throughout the nineteenth century, Scotland's population increased (though at a lower rate than that of England and Wales). The 1911 census

---

[1] Scholars are referred to in this paper by their full names, excepting in a few instances where scholars write using initials and surname.

revealed around 4.76 million people living in Scotland, almost three times as many as in 1801. However, Scotland—like Ireland—witnessed significant depopulation of rural areas, except for the North-East. In Scotland, emigration was both significant and in excess of immigration (the latter mainly to the Central belt). Between 1830 and 1914, around two million people left Scotland for overseas, which 'probably places Scotland in second place to Ireland in a European league table of proportion of population involved in emigration overseas, and it implies a gross emigration rate of around one and half times that of England and Wales'.[2]

Industrialization transformed both the number and location of the population of Wales. The population of Wales increased from about 600,000 at the turn of the nineteenth century to more than two million at the turn of the twentieth. In the late eighteenth century, 80 per cent of Welsh people lived in rural areas; at the beginning of the twentieth century 80 per cent lived in centres of industry, with one of the 13 counties, Glamorgan, having a population of one and a quarter million. The demographic changes in Ireland, Scotland and Wales had a direct impact on the demand for education. They were part of the economic reality of famine in Ireland, and of industrialization in Wales. These realities conditioned the educational history of the three nations, bringing about dramatic change.

Any discussion of 'change' requires some understanding of the conditions that preceded change. In the case of the provision of schooling in nineteenth-century Ireland, Scotland and Wales, these conditions invite comparison and merit further study. In brief it can be noted, for example, that traditionally the local schoolmaster in Ireland and Scotland was held in esteem and local schools were—for different reasons—of great importance. In Ireland, from penal times, British legislation had curtailed all educational opportunities for the majority of the Irish population: the Catholic labouring and middle ranks. Catholics subverted the penal laws by developing a haphazard system of 'hedge schools' or pay schools. The history of the hedge schools of Ireland has been studied in some depth by Antonia McManus (2002), who developed on a shorter study by P. J. Dowling (1931).[3] In 1824, an official commission calculated that there were about 11,000 schools in Ireland, of which 9000 were 'hedge schools' or pay schools. Four out of every five children participated in this unofficial system. Families living in great poverty managed to pay for lessons with goods such as eggs or turf. The curriculum typically included reading, writing and arithmetic, with the addition of history, geography, Latin and Greek in some schools. The survival of such a system was a reflection of the great status associated with learning. As McManus notes, 'next to the ministry of the priesthood, the teaching

---

[2] Anderson, M., and D. J. Morse. "The People." In *People and Society in Scotland*, Vol. 2: *1830–1914*, edited by W. H. Fraser and R. J. Morris. Edinburgh: John Donald, 1990: Ch. 1. The same authors note that around a third of those who left before the First World War eventually returned (16). See also Knox, William W. *Industrial Nation: Works, Culture and Society in Scotland, 1800-Present*. Edinburgh: Edinburgh University Press, 1999: Chs. 2, 8, 14, 20, 26.

[3] McManus, Antonia. *The Irish Hedge School and its Books, 1695–1831*. Dublin: Four Courts Press, 2002; Dowling, P. J. *The Hedge Schools of Ireland*. Cork: Mercier, 1931.

profession was regarded as a noble and elevated calling ... hedge school masters were given special treatment in society'.[4] Student teachers were known as 'poor scholars', and underwent rigorous training under schoolmasters of repute. People extended great hospitality to poor scholars and schoolmasters, providing accommodation and food. In addition, the status of the teacher ensured that he was 'the master of ceremonies at all wakes and funerals', while a visit from an erudite master or dominie was considered an honour.[5]

In a recent study of Scottish education, Lindsay Paterson (2003) noted the traditional status of the local teacher in Scottish schools.[6] He reflected the historical consensus that the tradition from the Reformation was for local or community schools, with the schoolteacher and the educational authorities playing a central role in determining educational policy and practice. This tradition, or myth, of the democratic intellect was embedded in the Education Act of 1696, and revived by an Act of 1803 which improved the position of the dominie (schoolmaster). From the Reformation, by law there was to be a school and a schoolmaster in every parish, paid for from the local rates. Fees were charged, but the school was to be provided, the master to be paid a minimum wage, and the children of the poor were to be supported by the local community of ratepayers. A great deal of national sentiment was invested in the figure of the 'lad of parts' from remote villages and humble social origins being empowered by parish schooling to climb into the professions. Just as the 'poor scholar' became a schoolmaster in Ireland, the dominie in Scotland was often a former 'lad of parts'.

William Fyfe Hendrie (1997) has published a study of the dominie in Scotland.[7] The dominie had to subscribe to the Established Church, and was expected to have had a university education (if not a complete degree). Thus, the dominie was the embodiment of the educational tradition, serving as the link between parish school and university, which was distinctive to Scotland. The parish school over which he presided was believed to develop a common culture for the whole nation, in contrast to the social (and indeed sexual) segregation of English education.

Studies of particular aspects of education, such as those by McManus and Hendrie mentioned above, demonstrate distinctive features of schooling in Ireland and Scotland. In Wales, such elements of distinctiveness were minimal, at least until the eighteenth century, although Wales merited special attention during the interregnum of 1649–1660. The lack of indigenous educational initiatives reflected the fact that legally England and Wales constituted a single state after the Acts of Union, 1536–1543. Then the organization of a distinctively Welsh system of Circulating schools was initiated by Griffith Jones in the 1730s, constituting a breakthrough in spreading

---

[4] McManus. *The Irish Hedge School*, 87.

[5] Ibid., 94–95.

[6] Paterson, Lindsay. *Scottish Education in the Twentieth Century*. Edinburgh: Edinburgh University Press, 2003.

[7] Hendrie, William Fyfe. *The Dominie: A Profile of the Scottish Headmaster*. Edinburgh: John Donald, 1997.

literacy (defined by the ability to read) to the mass of the population. However, the provision of adequate elementary education remained sporadic in the first half of the nineteenth century. From 1833, the British state became directly involved in financing education, though significant change only came about in the last decades of the nineteenth century, after the passing of the Education Act of 1870.

Educational changes in the later nineteenth century reflected the nature of state control in Wales, which was modified in the last quarter of the nineteenth century due to suffrage reform, reflecting Welsh centrality to the economy through the coal, steel and non-ferrous industries, and the Liberal ascendancy. Cultural nationalism was increasingly reflected in national institutions, nowhere more so than in education. In this context the creation of a national federal university in 1893 was of symbolic as well as practical importance. The 1889 Welsh Intermediate Education Act was very significant, representing the first tentative, unplanned step on the road to devolution. It resulted in a network of nearly a hundred state secondary schools across Wales by 1900, schools which had no English parallel until after 1902, and the creation of the Central Welsh Board in 1896 for inspection and examination purposes.[8] Because this was such a significant recognition of specifically Welsh needs, and because of its institutional significance in education, the Act of 1889 has attracted considerable attention. Its centenary occasioned a major volume of authoritative essays published by the Welsh Office (1990), and it was also examined by Gareth Evans in a special issue of *History of Education* (1990), and by David Allsobrook in the *Welsh Journal of Education* (1989).[9] The educational structure that emerged from the Act of 1889 has been analysed by Gareth Elwyn Jones (1982), and the curriculum which characterized the schools, with its social and occupational implications, by Wynford Davies (1982).[10]

In contrast to the development of a state-supported education system that, in Wales, eventually supported cultural nationalism and responded to Welsh needs, the state-funded system that was developed in Ireland in the nineteenth century was designed to support the British cultural assimilation policy for Ireland. The state became fully involved in the control of education in 1831, when the government of Earl Grey established a system of primary education for the Irish poor. The system was to be known as the National System, although for many this was merely a label, and the system failed to take into account the needs of an evolving nation.[11] The

---

[8] Evans, W. Gareth. *An Elected National Body for Wales: the Centenary of the Central Welsh Board.* Cardiff: WJEC, 1997.

[9] Jones, O. E., ed. *The Welsh Intermediate Act: A Centenary Appraisal.* Published in Welsh and English. Cardiff: Welsh Office, 1990; Evans, W. Gareth. "The Welsh Intermediate and Technical Education Act, 1889: a centenary appreciation." *History of Education* 19, no. 3 (1990): 195–210; Allsobrook, David. "'A Benevolent Prophet of Old': Reflections on the Welsh Intermediate Act of 1889." *Welsh Journal of Education* no. 1 (1989): 1–10.

[10] Jones, Gareth Elwyn. *Controls and Conflicts in Welsh Secondary Education, 1889–1944.* Cardiff: University of Wales Press, 1982; Davies, Wynford. *The Curriculum and Organization of the County Intermediate Schools, 1880–1926.* Cardiff: University of Wales Press, 1982.

[11] See Raftery, Deirdre, and Susan M. Parkes. *Female Education in Ireland, 1700–1900: Minerva or Madonna.* Ontario and Dublin: Irish Academic Press, 2007.

system effectively erased the Irish language, history and culture from the curriculum. Its aim was to provide literary education for the poorer classes. National education in Ireland pre-dated the similar system in England, and has often been viewed as a *corpus vile* for the English system. Modern social historians of Irish educational systems have tended to interpret the provision of education, by the solidly upper-middle-class National Board, as an attempt to control the poor. Scholars such as J. M. Goldstrom (1972) adopted the 'social control' perspective.[12] The only major study of the system is Donald Akenson's *The Irish Education Experiment: The National System of Education in the Nineteenth Century* (1971), although aspects of national schooling have been examined in shorter studies, such as Eustás Ó Héideáin's *National School Inspection in Ireland: The Beginnings* (1967), and Paul Connell's *Parson, Priest and Master, National Education in Co. Meath, 1824–1841* (1995).[13]

Although the national system attracted some criticism from Catholics, it remained the main form of mass education, and the number of national schools rose from 789 in 1832 to 6,520 by 1867. However, pupils made modest progress, in part because of the high levels of absenteeism (approximately 75 per cent of Irish children absented themselves from school, compared with almost 56 per cent in Wales and about 63 per cent in Scotland), and also because of the devastating impact of famine. To secure the efficiency of the national system of education, in 1868 the British treasury supported the establishment of a Royal Commission of Inquiry into Primary Education, under the chairmanship of Lord Powis. Arguably the most significant outcome of the commissioners' reports was the introduction of a system of payment-by-results, whereby payments were made to teachers dependent on their pupils' results in examinations. The introduction of this system in Ireland was doubtless influenced by similar recommendations by the Newcastle Commission (1858) in England and the Argyll Commission (1864) in Scotland. It is not surprising to note that the introduction of payment-by-results brought about a mechanical approach to teaching and learning. It also continued the delivery of a curriculum that promoted English practices, and thereby brought an end to Irish educational traditions including the oral transmission of culture.

It has been argued that, in contrast to Wales and Ireland, the Union of 1707 left Scotland's three national institutions intact: the Church, the legal system and the educational system.[14] Two key themes since the Union were integration and

---

[12] Goldstrom, J. M. *The Social Content of Education, 1808–1870: A Study of the Working Class School Reader in England and Ireland.* Shannon: Irish University Press, 1972.

[13] Coolahan, John. *Irish Education, History and Structure.* Dublin: Institute of Public Administration, 1981; Akenson, Donald. *The Irish Education Experiment: The National System of Education in the Nineteenth Century.* London: Routledge & Kegan Paul, 1971; Ó Héideáin, Eustás. *National School Inspection in Ireland: The Beginnings.* Dublin: Sceptre Publications, 1967, and Connell, Paul. *Parson, Priest and Master, National Education in Co. Meath, 1824–1841.* Dublin: Irish Academic Press, 1995.

[14] See Brown, A., D. McCrone, and L. Paterson. *Politics and Society in Scotland.* Basingstoke: Macmillan Press, 1996; Paterson, Lindsay. *The Autonomy of Modern Scotland.* Edinburgh: Edinburgh University Press, 1994.

autonomy. David McCrone (1994, 1996) and Lindsay Paterson (1996) have argued that Scotland retained a high degree of civil autonomy within the post-1707 British and later UK state.[15] By the nineteenth century, Scots were enthusiastic about membership of the Union, and especially participation in the British Empire. There is, however, a longstanding debate over whether the 1872 Education (Scotland) Act dealt a death blow to the educational tradition by introducing English practices.[16] It has also recently been argued that the school boards set up by that Act continued the tradition of common provision.[17] Historians, educational sociologists and policy-makers have all identified key elements in the Scottish educational tradition, or myth, of the democratic intellect, notably the importance of Presbyterianism and the integral role played by the dominie who served as the link between parish school and university, which, as noted above, was distinctive to Scotland.[18]

Linked to common provision was a belief in Scotland in the need for a uniform curriculum, to foster a common citizenship. At the core of this curriculum was literacy in English, confirming the Lowland basis of the educational tradition. This emphasis on literacy in English had a considerable impact on Gaelic-speaking Scots, since the educational tradition was hostile to Gaelic. In contrast to Wales and Ireland, Gaelic was either not associated with Scottish national feeling, or was regarded as a backward-looking patriotism, particularly due to its association with Catholicism. The Napier Commission of 1883 recommended the use of Gaelic in schools in Gaelic-speaking areas, but the aim was still to spread literacy in English. As Robert Anderson has noted, 'there was more sympathy for Gaelic as an academic study than as a living language'.[19]

In Ireland, during the nineteenth century the Irish language went into decline, and the English language became more widespread. This was partly because English was increasingly recognized as the language of politics and commerce in Ireland, but also because the National System of education that was introduced by the British Government from 1831 made no provision for the teaching of the national language, and did not permit its use in school. Lessons were delivered with constant reference to the textbooks provided by the National Board, which contained extracts from English literature, moral lessons, and some British history and geography. The failure to teach English through Irish severely compromised the education of pupils in Gaeltacht areas where almost all schoolchildren would have been monoglot Irish speakers. In these rural areas, illiteracy remained a serious problem which, coupled

---

[15] See McCrone, David. *Understanding Scotland: The Sociology of a Stateless Nation.* Edinburgh: Edinburgh University Press, 1994.

[16] See *Scottish Educational Studies* 4, no.2 (1972).

[17] Paterson, *Scottish Education in the Twentieth Century,* 37–39.

[18] See for example Raffe, David. "How Distinctive is Scottish Education? Five Perspectives on Distinctiveness." *Scottish Affairs* 49 (2004): 50–72. See also Carter, J., and D. J. Witherington. *Scottish Universities: Distinctiveness and Diversity.* Edinburgh: John Donald, 1992.

[19] Anderson, R. D. *Education and the Scottish People.* Oxford: Clarendon Press, 1995: 217.

with lack of spoken English, had a lasting impact on the economy. The relationship between economic circumstance and language use in Ireland has been examined by Mary Daly.[20] She has noted, for example, that the economy of West Galway was dominated by agriculture and fishing, with a dependence on local resources (such as turf and kelp). There was poor road access, little migratory labour and outsiders were virtually unknown. The transmission of English culture via schooling in the English language, using the English textbooks of the National Board, would have been limited. In areas of Ireland with a tradition of migratory labour, employment by English speakers (in service or industry) and greater educational participation, the relative impact of the content of National Board schoolbooks was probably more significant. In these areas, the English language was viewed as the language of progress, and parents recognized the benefits of bringing their children up speaking English.

In Wales, at the beginning of the nineteenth century, the predominant language of the people was Welsh. However, the language of 'getting on' was English, just as it was in Ireland and Scotland. Only the Sunday schools used Welsh as their normal language of communication, and the role of the Welsh language in school and university education, despite some official encouragement from the 1880s, was very limited. In 1847, a government report, *Report of the Education Commissioners into the State of Education in Wales*, was utterly condemnatory of the Welsh language, as of every other aspect of Welsh life.[21] The report also insulted the morals of the nation and, more accurately, its education provision, and prompted a nationalist backlash. Two recent studies have examined the 1847 Report (Prys Morgan, 1991; Gwyneth Tyson Roberts, 1998).[22]

From the beginning of the nineteenth century tensions in the education system in Wales were inevitable given that the minority Anglican Church provided the majority of elementary schools, particularly in rural areas. Anglican schools, bolstered by the activities of the National Society in the early decades of the century, therefore provided much of the education on offer. The non-denominational British Society had little impact until after 1843 when Welsh Nonconformists were strongly urged to establish schools under its aegis. The historiography associated with both types of schools is largely limited to the general textbooks on Welsh history, although substantial essays on both are to be found in the first attempt at a general history of education in Wales.[23] Because of the denominational distance from the favoured Established Church and its schools, major state intervention in the form of the Education Acts of

[20] Daly, Mary. "Literacy and language change in the late nineteenth and early twentieth centuries." In *The Experience of Reading: Irish Historical Perspectives*, edited by B. Cunningham and M. Kennedy. Dublin: ESHSI, 1999.

[21] *Report of the Commissioners of Inquiry into the State of Education in Wales.* London: 1847.

[22] Morgan, P., ed. *Brad Y Llyfrau Gleision.* Llandysul: Gwasg Gomer, 1991; Roberts, Gwyneth Tyson. *The Language of the Blue Books.* Cardiff: University of Wales Press, 1998.

[23] Williams, J. L., and G. R. Hughes. *History of Education in Wales.* Llandysul: Christopher Davies, 1978.

1870 and 1902 caused considerable perturbation in Welsh religious circles. The 1902 Education Act, particularly, produced something of a constitutional crisis as all but two of the Welsh local authorities refused to administer the Act. This 'Welsh Revolt' has been studied in some detail, but there has been no large-scale study of the inter-relationship between religion and education in Wales.[24]

In the case of Scottish education in the nineteenth century, the influence of the Presbyterian Reformation has been recognized in Paterson's recent study (2003). In addition, research into the schooling of working-class girls in Victorian Scotland has highlighted the significance of the Catholic minority by the later nineteenth century, and attempted to integrate the Catholic educational experience into the national one.[25] Such research suggests that while female religious orders were important for middle-class schooling and teacher-training, and provided care for the very poor and for delinquent children, they did not play as significant a role in the schooling of Catholic working-class girls in Scotland in the later nineteenth century as they did in Ireland. Recent research, however, claims that religious orders, male as well as female, were integral in establishing the Catholic system in Glasgow, Scotland's largest city. They maintained their influence, despite the fact that by the early twentieth century the vast majority of Scotland's Catholic schoolteachers were lay people.[26]

The particular ethos of some Catholic schools, and their contribution to the spread of literacy and instruction in Ireland, has received attention. The nineteenth century witnessed great change in the relative power of the Established Church and the Catholic Church. As Donal McCartney (1987) has noted, 'not only were the churches responsive to the external forces of change, but [they] were powerful and persuasive enough to be themselves a major cause of those changes that were taking place in society'.[27] This was particularly true of the Catholic Church and educational change. The nineteenth-century National System attempted to establish non-denominational education. With the growth of the Catholic Emancipation movement, and the increasing power of the Catholic hierarchy by the middle of the nineteenth century, the education of Catholics at distinctively 'Catholic' schools was made an imperative. The revival of Irish Catholicism was evident in the great expansion that took place in the building of convent schools, boys' colleges, seminaries, orphanages and diocesan colleges between 1845 and 1871. During this period, the number of convents and monasteries or brothers' schools more than doubled. The education provided by the Catholic Church for its members was to have a major influence on the growth of a new Catholic middle class, as educated

---

[24] The fullest treatment of the educational aspects of the post-1902 conflict is in Jones, Gareth Elwyn. *Which Nation's Schools? Direction and Devolution in Welsh Education in the Twentieth Century.* Cardiff: University of Wales Press, 1990, and references therein.

[25] McDermid, Jane. *The Schooling of Working-class Girls in Victorian Scotland: Gender, Education and Identity.* London: Routledge, 2005.

[26] O'Hagan, Francis J. *The Contribution of the Religious Orders to Education in Glasgow during the period 1847–1918.* London: Edwin Mellen, 2006.

[27] McCartney, Donal. *The Dawning of Democracy: Ireland 1800–1870.* Dublin: Helicon, 1987, 26.

children of the farming classes went into business, banking, the civil service, teaching, medicine, the law, and into the Church itself.[28]

The nineteenth century witnessed significant economic and social change in Ireland, Scotland and Wales. Changing demographics, industrialization, emigration, famine, denominational tensions and political pressures variously affected the provision and purpose of schooling in this period. Significant historical research has been produced, documenting and analysing education in the nineteenth century. This paper now offers an overview of scholarship that engages with the various themes identified above, and suggests areas that demand either revision or original research. For convenience and clarity, Ireland, Scotland and Wales are treated in three separate sections. The paper includes, within the footnotes, an extensive, though not exhaustive, bibliography of relevant research.

Published Research and Emerging Areas

Ireland

One of the most distinguished scholars in the field, Donald Akenson, commented in 1971 that 'much educational history in the British Isles was concerned with describing the evolution of educational institutions *in vacuo*' (Donald Akenson, 1971). A review of research in the history of education in Ireland indicates that educational and curricular systems are described as if they existed independent of the society from which they grew. Even in general histories of Irish education, the content is typically ordered in 'thematic' chapters and there is evidence of a reluctance to draw overarching conclusions. The early general studies of Irish educational history fit this style of writing, and include *Education in Ireland* (T. J. McElligott, 1966) and *Irish Education, A History of Educational Institutions* (Norman Atkinson, 1969). The mid-1970s, however, saw the publication of Donald Akenson's *A Mirror to Kathleen's Face: Education in Independent Ireland, 1922–60* (1975), which pushed out the boundaries of traditional narrative accounts of schooling, and explored the complex interrelations between Irish education institutions and society.

There is a paucity of research that deals explicitly with the history of education and economic development. Where research explores economic expansion and technical developments, it is located in short studies that have an eye on social and cultural change, such as John Coolahan's study, 'The ideological framework of the payment by results policy in nineteenth-century education' (*Irish Educational Studies*, 1977), and Muiris O'Riordan's work on 'Technical vocational education, 1922–52: the cultural emphasis' (*Irish Educational Studies*, 1977). Other short studies document change and innovation, but are not located within a major study of education and economic development.[29]

---

[28] See McCartney. *The Dawning of Democracy*, 36–39.

[29] See for example Byrne, Kieran. "Mechanics Institutes in Ireland, 1925–50." *Irish Educational Studies* (1979).

There has, on the other hand, been a sustained interest in social change and particularly in the development of a system of national education in the nineteenth century. In the early 1970s, major studies appeared which explored facets of national schooling. *The Irish Education Experiment: The National System of Education in the Nineteenth Century* (Donald Akenson, 1971), and *The Social Content of Education 1808–70: A Study of Irish School Textbooks* (J. M. Goldstrom, 1972) remain the standard university reading on the delivery of national schooling. Other scholars have published shorter works on national schooling (for example Mary Daly, 'The development of the national school system, 1831–40', *Studies in Irish History*, 1979).

Perhaps unsurprisingly, a number of scholars have worked on the contributions of religious orders to the development of schooling in Ireland. Such studies have typically focused on the work of founders of religious teaching orders, and on the schools under their direction. These works were rarely critical of the systems that they documented. Because of the dominant role of the Catholic teaching orders in the delivery of schooling, there is a particularly pressing need for rigorous research in this area. Similarly, the role of the Church of Ireland and of other groups (including Presbyterians and Quakers) has been under-examined. There are some studies of 'prestigious' Protestant schools, and of education systems under the management of Protestant voluntary groups (such as Kenneth Milne's *The Irish Charter Schools*, 1998), but there remains a need to bring such research together within a study that will provide the analytical tools to understand the tensions and dynamics between the various churches involved in education in Ireland.

The relationship between Church and State has interested some scholars though it is surprising that more work has not been done in this field, given that the control of education in Ireland has been openly contested by Church and State. One study which has provided an analysis of an aspect of Church–State relations is E. Brian Titley's *Church, State and the Control of Schooling in Ireland, 1900–1944* (1983). Titley's work was controversial in that it provided a frank and eloquent critique of the 'hostile response' of the Catholic Church to the British model of national schooling, at a time when the more popular reading of the period was that the national system was part of the British cultural assimilation policy for Ireland. Donald Akenson had, in 1983, expressed a hope that Titley's work would provoke debate—something which he viewed as the 'prerequisite of educational advance in Ireland'. But it is only in the last few years that a new generation of scholars has been asking questions about the 'received' versions of the history of Irish education, and pushing out the boundaries of traditional research.

Our understanding of the nature and content of 'indigenous' schooling has been enriched by new work. For example, the standard reference tool on the illegal 'hedge-school' or pay school system was P. J. Dowling's *The Hedge Schools of Ireland* (1968). This long-neglected area of education has recently been the subject of a thoroughly researched and authoritative new study: *The Irish Hedge School and its books* (Antonia McManus, 2002). McManus's work erases the 'stage-Irish' image of the hedge-school master, and presents us with compelling evidence of what actually took place in these illegal schools.

One area that has had some attention is pauper education, although there remains much work to be done on systems of education for destitute and indigent children. In 1989, Jane Barnes's *Irish Industrial Schools, 1868–1908*, was published. Like McManus's study of the hedge schools, this book emerged from thesis research. It has opened the way for more work into industrial and reformatory schooling, and pointed to a range of important sources in this area. The education provided at the workhouse schools and the gaol schools remains unexamined. Surprisingly, there is no major study of the impact of the Great Famine on Irish education, and no survey of pupil participation in workhouse schools during the famine years. This is an area that demands attention.

There is also a paucity of research focusing specifically on the education of women and girls. Standard studies in the history of education which appeared in the 1960s and 1970s (see above) did not give specific attention to the very different experience of education that most girls had in the nineteenth and twentieth centuries. While there are some Master's and Ph.D. theses on female education (particularly on convent schools), there remains a need for research in this area that allows comparison. New studies such as *Female Education in Ireland, 1700–1900: Minerva or Madonna* by Deirdre Raftery and Susan M. Parkes (2007), have attempted to respond to this need, while other shorter studies provide information on specific areas.[30]

Scotland

Because Scotland had a separate system of education, embedded within an educational tradition dating back to the Presbyterian Reformation, its educational history is usually treated as distinct from that of England and Wales. This is the perspective in works such as *Education and the Scottish People* (R. D. Anderson, 1995); *Two Hundred and Fifty Years of Scottish Education* (Henry Macdonald Knox, 1953); *Scottish Education in the Twentieth Century* (Lindsay Paterson, 2003), and *The History of Scottish Education* (James Scotland, 1969).[31] Histories of English or British education generally do not refer to Scotland, except to point to differences. For example, differences in the administration of education and teacher training are noted by

---

[30] See for example O'Connor, Anne V. "The revolution in girls' secondary education in Ireland, 1860–1910." In *Girls Don't do Honours: Irish Women in Education in the 19th and 20th Centuries*, edited by M. Cullen. Dublin: WEB, 1987; Breathnach, Eibhlín. "Charting new waters: women's experience in higher education, 1879–1908." In M. Cullen, ibid.; Raftery, Deirdre. "Female education in late nineteenth century Ireland." In *A History of Women at Trinity College Dublin*, edited by S. M. Parkes. Dublin: Lilliput Press, 2004; Raftery, Deirdre. "The nineteenth century governess: image and reality." In *Women and Work in Ireland, 1500–1930*, edited by B. Whelan. Dublin: Four Courts Press, 2000.

[31] See Anderson, *Education and the Scottish People*; Knox, Henry Macdonald. *Two Hundred and Fifty Years of Scottish Education*. Edinburgh: Oliver & Boyd, 1953; Paterson, *Scottish Education in the Twentieth Century*; Scotland, James. *The History of Scottish Education*. London: London University Press, 1969.

A. S. Bishop in *The Rise of a Central Authority for English Education* (1971) and by B. Lawrence, *The Administration of Education in Britain* (1972), respectively.[32] Michael Sanderson (1983) has noted Scottish influences on English education.[33] A few studies take a broadly comparative approach, useful in pointing to similarities as well as differences between Scotland and England and Wales, as well as for questioning the supposed superiority of Scottish education.[34]

The work of Lindsay Paterson and David Raffe reveals the importance of sociologists for educational history in Scotland, with contributions to research in the history of gender and education, rural education and adult education.[35] In practice there is little research being done in history departments in Scottish universities, with the noted exception of R. D. Anderson of Edinburgh, though there are valuable studies of local educational history conducted outside the universities.[36] There are also some interesting publications in areas such as institutional histories.[37] It is noteworthy, however, that the educational tradition was male-centred, as is much of the

---

[32] See Bishop, A. S. *The Rise of a Central Authority for English Education.* Cambridge: Cambridge University Press, 1971: 110; see also Lawrence, B. *The Administration of Education in Britain.* London: B. T. Batsford, 1972: 122.

[33] Sanderson, Michael. *Education, Economic Change and Society in England 1780–1870.* Basingstoke: Macmillan, 1983: 26.

[34] Stephens, W. B. *Education in Britain 1750–1914.* Basingstoke: Macmillan, 1998; Smelser, Neil. *Social Paralysis and Social Change: British Working-class Education in the Nineteenth Century.* Berkeley: California University Press, 1991. This study also looks at Ireland. See also Houston, R. A. *Scottish Literacy and Scottish Identity: Illiteracy and Society in Scotland and Northern England 1600–1800.* Cambridge: Cambridge University Press, 1985.

[35] In addition to the work of Paterson and Raffe, see Corr, Helen. "An Exploration into Scottish Education." In *People and Society in Scotland*, Vol. II: *1830–1914*, edited by W. H. Fraser and R. J. Morris. Edinburgh: John Donald, 1990: Ch. 10; Jamieson, L., and C. Toynbee. *Country Bairns: Growing Up, 1900–1930.* Edinburgh: Edinburgh University Press, 1992; Barr, Jean. *Liberating Knowledge: Research, Feminism and Adult Education.* Leicester: National Institute of Continuing Education, 1999.

[36] See for example Bain, Andrew. *Education in Stirlingshire: From the Reformation to the Act of 1872.* London: London University Press, 1965, and *Patterns of Error: The Teacher and External Authority in Central Scotland 1581–1861.* Edinburgh: Moray House, 1989. For Anderson, see also his "Education and Society in Modern Scotland: A Comparative Perspective." *History of Education Quarterly* 25, no.4 (1985): 459–81.

[37] See Harrison, M., and W. Marker. *Teaching the Teachers: the History of Jordanhill College of Education.* Edinburgh: John Donald, 1996; Holmes, H., ed. *Scottish Life and Society: Institutions of Scotland: Education.* East Linton: Tuckwell Press, 2000; Begg, Tom. *The Excellent Women: the Origins and History of Queen Margaret College.* Edinburgh: John Donald, 1994; Thompson, W., and C. McCallum. *Glasgow Caledonian University: Its Origins and Evolution.* East Linton: Tuckwell Press, 1998; Hutchison, Iain C. G. *The University and the State: The Case of Aberdeen 1860–1963.* Aberdeen: Aberdeen University Press, 1993; Moore, Lindy. *Bajanellas and Semilinas: Aberdeen University and the Education of Women, 1860–1920.* Aberdeen: Aberdeen University Press, 1991; Kirk, Gordon. *Moray House and the Road to Merger.* Edinburgh: Dunedin Academic Press, 2002; Anderson, R., M. Lynch, and N. Phillipson. *The University of Edinburgh: An Illustrated History.* Edinburgh: Edinburgh University Press, 2003.

historiography.[38] This is despite the fact that the post-1872 growth in educational provision resulted in the feminization of the teaching profession, in numbers at least. Helen Corr (1997) has commented on the male-centred tradition and the gendered division of labour, which favoured the dominie.[39] This has been attributed by some to the peculiarly patriarchal nature of Scottish society.[40] This suggests a rather static understanding of the term when there needs to be an examination of the historical specificity of patriarchy in Scotland.[41] Another issue that might be pursued here is the Scottish preference for mixed-sex education over single-sex schooling. There is also scope for more research into both the educational role of religious orders, indeed of religion generally, and the history of minorities and education in Scotland.

The influence and attractions of empire from the later nineteenth century particularly affected educated Scotsmen, though as Marjorie Theobald (1993, 1996) has noted, women also had an impact on the shaping of educational systems elsewhere.[42] There is scope for further research into the imperial connection. Robert Bell and Malcolm Tight (1993) have shown the international influence from 1877 of St Andrews University's LLA (Lady Licentiate in Arts), which offered distance learning, while the Scottish tradition of relatively open access may have influenced the university extension movement and the development of adult education in nineteenth-century England.[43] Roy Lowe (2003) has looked into Scottish influence on educational planning in England, but there is also room for research into the influence of external educational ideals and practices in developing Scottish education.[44] This could add new challenges to the claim for the distinctiveness and implied superiority of the Scottish system within the UK.[45]

---

[38] See for example Knox, *Two Hundred and Fifty Years of Scottish Education*; Scotland, *The History of Scottish Education*.

[39] Corr, Helen. "Teachers and Gender: debating the myths of equal opportunities in Scottish education 1800–1914." *Cambridge Journal of Education* 27, no.3 (November 1997): 355–63.

[40] See Paterson, F. M. S., and J. Fewell, eds. *Girls in their Prime: Scottish Education Revisited*. Edinburgh: Scottish Academic Press, 1990; Corr, Helen. "An Exploration into Scottish Education." In *People and Society in Scotland*, edited by W. H. Fraser and R. J. Morris. Edinburgh: John Donald, 1990: Ch. 10; Moore, Lindy. "Education and Learning." In *Gender in Scottish History*, edited by L. Abrams, E. Gordon, D. Simonton and E. J. Yeo. Edinburgh: Edinburgh University Press, 2006: Ch. 5.

[41] Miller, Pavla. *Transformation of Patriarchy in the West, 1500–1900*. Bloomington and Indianapolis: Indiana University Press, 1998.

[42] See for example Theobald, Marjorie. "Boundaries, Bridges and the History of Education: An Australian Response to Maxine Schwartz Seller." *History of Education Quarterly* 33, no. 4 (1993): 497–510; Theobald, Marjorie. *Knowing Women: Origins of Women's Education in Nineteenth-century Australia*. Cambridge: Cambridge University Press, 1996.

[43] See Bell, R., and M. Tight. *Open Universities: A British Tradition*. Milton Keynes: Open University Press, 1993.

[44] Lowe, Roy. "A Scottish diaspora: influences on educational planning in twentieth-century England." *History of Education* 32, no. 3 (2003): 319–30.

[45] See for example Paterson, Lindsay. "How Distinctive is Scottish Higher Education?" *Scottish Affairs* 7 (1994): 86–92.

Wales

The study of education has not figured centrally in Welsh historiography, and the first comprehensive history of education in Wales appeared as recently as 2003.[46] The work that has been produced on the history of Welsh education has not been characterized by any obvious ideological bias. There has been no Marxist historiographical tradition so there has been nothing, even on a minor scale, to compare with Brian Simon's four magisterial studies (1960–1991).[47] Historians of education in Wales have been in the historical mainstream methodologically, and have not engaged with the postmodernist perspective. It is arguable that the ideology that underpinned the early history of education was Whig-based. That is to say, education provision in the modern era was seen as a jewel in the Welsh crown, reflecting both the desire of ordinary Welsh people to secure education for their children often against considerable odds, and the links between educational provision and cultural nationalism. Only from the 1980s did works critical of the mythology of the Welsh Intermediate and grammar schools, such as that of Gareth Elwyn Jones (1982), begin to appear.[48] The biases present in the work of virtually all educational historians in Wales are those of a leaning towards orthodox Labour achievement and a commitment to the idea of Wales as a nation.

Arguably, the biggest gap in educational writing in Wales has been that in investigating the relationship between the economy and educational provision. With one notable exception, historians of Wales have not concerned themselves directly in this area. That exception is Gordon W. Roderick (1981, 1989, 1990, 1993) who has written extensively on industrial, vocational and technical education, concentrating on the nineteenth century.[49] The opportunities to build on Roderick's work are significant. He has commented on the fact that Wales produced relatively few scientists and engineers of note in the nineteenth century, and that students were generally biased towards arts and pure science subjects in the intermediate schools and the university colleges.[50] There were few industrially oriented Works' Schools of note in

---

[46] Jones, G. E., and G. W. Roderick. *A History of Education in Wales*. Cardiff: University of Wales Press, 2003.

[47] Simon, Brian. *Two Nations and the Educational Structure, 1780–1870*; *Education and the Labour Movement, 1870–1920*; *The Politics of Educational Reform, 1920–1940*; *Education and the Social Order*. London: Lawrence & Wishart, 1960–1991.

[48] Jones, *Controls and Conflicts*.

[49] Roderick, Gordon Wynne. "The Institute of South Wales engineers and the south Wales economy in the late 19th century." *Welsh History Review* 14, no. 4 (1989): 595–609; Roderick, Gordon Wynne. "Technical instruction committees in south Wales, United Kingdom, 1889–1903 (pts. 1 & 2)." *The Vocational Aspect of Education* 45 (1 & 2) (1993), 59–70 & 145–62; Roderick, Gordon Wynne. "Education in an industrial society." In *The City of Swansea: Challenges and Change*, edited by R. A. Griffiths. Stroud: Alan Sutton, 1990; Roderick, G. W. and M. D. Stephens. "The influence of Welsh culture on scientific and technical education in Wales in the 19th century." *Transactions of the Honourable Society of Cymmrodorion* (1981): 99–108.

[50] See for example Roderick, G. W., and D. Allsobrook. "Welsh Society and University Funding, 1860–1914." *Welsh History Review* 20, no. 1 (2000): 34–61; Roderick, G. W., and M. D. Stephens. "Science and Technical Studies in Welsh Higher Education in the Nineteenth Century." *Bulletin of the History of Education Society* 43 (1989).

the nineteenth century.[51] There were far fewer Mechanics' Institutes or Science and Art classes relative to population than in England or Scotland.[52] In an area where a quarter of a million men worked in the coal industry, Cardiff was the only university college to provide mining education, and even then the provision was affected by in-fighting between coal owners and college authorities, as Peter Harries (2000) has recorded.[53] Research could also develop the question of how far education was linked with the inability to develop secondary industries in Wales in the late nine-teenth century; indeed J. B. Elliott (2002) has made a start by pointing to the lack of schools of design or provision for tool-making.[54]

Apart from some of Roderick's work (1998) only a few studies shed light on how the intermediate and, later, the grammar schools transformed the prospects of chil-dren from skilled and unskilled working-class backgrounds, and educated them to become professionals whose purchasing power had a considerable impact on the Welsh economy.[55] This transformation gives rise to new questions: for example, most of these 'new professionals' left their immediate localities, but where did they go? And how many science graduates ended up in England, thereby contributing to the vulnerability of the Welsh economy between the wars, and since?

While it would be possible to give an extensive list of lacunae in Welsh educational historiography, there are three areas that, arguably, are research priorities. First, the question of gender and education remains under-examined. Gareth Evans's *Education and Female Emancipation, the Welsh Experience, 1847–1914* (1990) provides a thorough examination of one aspect of women's experience in the nineteenth and early twentieth century but like all pioneering works it needs to be supplemented by further investi-gation, and the research could also be taken further into the twentieth century.[56] While two exceptions to the neglect of female education are the work of Deborah James (2001)

[51] Evans, Leslie Wynne. *Education in Industrial Wales, 1700–1900: A Study of the Works' Schools System.* Cardiff: Avalon Books, 1971.

[52] Roderick, Gordon Wynne. "Educating the worker: the Mechanics Institute movement in South Wales." *Transactions of the Honourable Society of Cymmrodorion* (1991): 161–74.

[53] Harries, Peter. "Colleges for Miners: A History of the Provision of Technical Education to the South Wales Mining Industry, 1882–1939." Unpublished Ph.D., University of Wales, 2000.

[54] Elliott, J. B. "The development of secondary industry in the Amman Valley, 1850–1914: a study of the Welsh industrial tragedy." *Welsh History Review* 21, no. 1 (2002): 48–74; Elliott, J. B. *The Industrial Development of the Ebbw Valleys, 1780–1914.* Cardiff: University of Wales Press, 2005.

[55] Roderick, Gordon Wynne. "Social class, curriculum and the concept of relevance in sec-ondary education: industrial Glamorgan, 1889–1914." *Welsh History Review* 19, no. 2 (1998): 289–318.

[56] Evans, W. Gareth. *Education and Female Emancipation, the Welsh Experience, 1847–1914.* Cardiff: University of Wales Press, 1990. See also the work of Williams, Sian Rhiannon. "Women teachers and gender issues in teaching in Wales, circa. 1870–1950." *Welsh Journal of Education* 13, no. 2 (2005); and James, Deborah. "'Teaching girls': intermediate schools and career opportunities for girls in the East Glamorgan valley of Wales, 1896–1914." *History of Education* 30, no. 6 (2001): 513–26.

and Sian Rhiannon Williams (2005), the scholar of women's educational history typically has to piece together information from general histories of Welsh women's lives.[57]

Second, as noted above, significant publication has emerged from study of those educational institutions that helped to give Wales a national identity in the last quarter of the nineteenth century and into the early twentieth century. In particular, interest has been shown in Welsh intermediate schools, which were the first distinctively Welsh types of schooling to be developed in the nineteenth century. These schools transformed the economic and social prospects of a significant minority of Welsh boys and girls. The political and legislative background to the establishment of these schools has been fully investigated, and there are general accounts of the way in which they were managed, and how their curriculum was developed. There are also histories of the formative years of a few intermediate schools. However, research in this area has typically drawn heavily on the official records of central government, the Board of Education and (from 1907) its Welsh Department. Little work has been done utilizing sources such as school magazines, local newspapers and literary works, and glimpses of the experience of pupils, teachers and parents have little historical currency. Until there is a body of research that embraces such sources, it remains impossible to comment conclusively on the question of the centrality of the schools to the community and to the nation at the turn of the century.

Lastly, the Welsh language and bilingualism, now embraced within a national political framework, are increasingly being seen as central to national identity. There is new interest in the history of the Welsh language in education in the nineteenth century. Indeed only recently have historians such as Robert Smith (1999) been prepared to challenge the assumption that 'English' state education attempted to destroy the Welsh language.[58] There remains a need for detailed work on bilingualism in schools and communities, and on the role of education in helping to preserve or undermine the Welsh language.

Conclusion

This paper has provided a survey of scholarship on nineteenth-century history of education in Ireland, Scotland and Wales. There were rapid changes in the economy and population of Ireland, Scotland and Wales in the nineteenth century. These changes had an impact on the demand for education, though it is suggested that there remains a serious need for research that investigates the relationship between the economy and educational provision. There are other areas that also merit analysis. For example, a study of the influence of English education on schooling in Ireland, Scotland and Wales is certainly overdue. Equally, it would be useful to have a comparative study of schooling

---

[57] For example, Betts, S., ed. *Our Daughters' Land: Past and Present.* Cardiff: University of Wales Press, 1996; and Beddoe, Deirdre. *Out of the Shadows: A History of Women in Twentieth Century Wales.* Cardiff: University of Wales Press, 2000.

[58] Smith, Robert. *Schools, Politics and Society: Elementary Education in Wales 1870–1902.* Cardiff: University of Wales Press, 1999.

in these three nations, which would elaborate on themes identified in this paper, such as education and national identity, and the role of the native language in education.

While considerable scholarship in the history of education appeared in Ireland in the 1970s and early 1980s, there followed a period in which little new work appeared. Only recently has there been a new body of research and this has, happily, addressed some of the lacunae in scholarship in areas such as pauper education and female education. In Wales and Scotland there has been a steady output of new research in the history of education, with some significant publications since the 1980s. It has been noted that histories of Welsh education have been based firmly on the pragmatist practice of history and often lack ideological frameworks, while major Irish studies have tended towards description rather than systematic analysis. It has also been noted that there is room for research into how external influences shaped education in Scotland, and into the imperial connection in the case of both Scotland and Ireland. It is beyond the scope of this paper to address issues such as the role of archives and the rapidly changing use of technology in accessing and working with sources in education history. However, the paper identifies many of the strengths and the gaps in extant research on nineteenth-century education, and provides a concise overview of the major research. It is therefore a tool that historians can utilize as they address new sources and identify new perspectives on education in Ireland, Scotland and Wales.

Additionally, however limited its frame of reference, this attempt to compare some aspects of the history and historiography of nineteenth-century education in three of the nations of the UK should have a wider resonance. Since the 1980s, there has been a significant change in the way in which British history has been approached, with attempts to move away from an Anglocentric framework into one in which the UK is viewed as being made up, until 1922, of four national constituents whose histories interrelate. By comparing historiography on nineteenth-century education in Ireland, Scotland and Wales, this paper can conclude that, where education was concerned, Westminster policies and English practices (not always synonymous) were shaped by different national traditions and perceived needs. Certainly comparisons between Ireland, Scotland and Wales show similarities between and differences from both each other and England. But taking English policies and practices as benchmarks, even ones to refute, confirms English dominance in British educational history. Throughout this paper, the relationship between England and each of the other three nations has been the subject of analysis. What has not been undertaken before is a comparative study of these three nations in which their shared education narrative is foregrounded while the relative position of England becomes a backdrop.

Several challenges emerge. First, there are many areas that are under-researched and that demand attention from scholars. Second, it remains to position England in a comparative study of education in the United Kingdom in the nineteenth century. Third, and perhaps most importantly, there is a need to rethink carefully the question of education and national identity (however defined), and to develop an archipelagic view of educational history that both challenges and informs the Anglocentric framework which has dominated historical discourse on education in Ireland, Scotland and Wales.

The 'Life-long Draught': From Learning to Teaching and Back

Philip Gardner

In 1855, Frances Power Cobbe published her notable Kantian study, *The Theory of Intuitive Morals*.[1] Here she celebrated a practical philosophy founded upon 'the glorious thirst after Knowledge', an unquenchable impulse which 'never finds its life-long draught sweet enough'.[2] With these words, Power Cobbe fashioned an early evocation of an association which, in the familiar form of 'lifelong learning' has today become a commonplace: the expectation that all citizens should be open to the nurturing, sustaining influence of educational experiences operating across the span

---

[1] Williamson, Lori. *Power and Protest: Frances Power Cobbe and Victorian Society*. London: Rivers Oram Press, 2005, 29–32.

[2] Power Cobbe, Francis. *The Theory of Intuitive Morals*. 4th ed. London: Swan Sonnenschein, 1902: 189. Power Cobbe's expression here finds a resonance in Albert Mansbridge's much later allusion to adult education as the source of 'deep draughts of knowledge'; quoted in Fieldhouse, Roger. "The 1908 Report: Antidote to Class Struggle?" In *Oxford and Working-Class Education*, edited by Sylvia Harrop. Nottingham: University of Nottingham, 1987: 30–47, 39.

of their entire lives.[3] For historical analysis of social change in education, the powerful contemporary association of the 'lifelong' with learning has tended to deflect attention from the importance of the concept in addressing the other axis of the pedagogical relationship—teaching. This recognition is the foundation for this exploratory investigation of the relationship between conceptual identification and social change in the modern history of education.

The temporal constitution of modern perceptions of teaching was the subject of a recent study, *The Next Generation of Teachers: Changing Conceptions of a Career in Teaching*, an interim report of an ongoing investigation at the Harvard Graduate School. Here, a pervasive change was noted in the accent accorded to the 'lifelong' among new cohorts of trainees seeking to enter the teaching profession. It was a trend that ran counter to the gathering hegemony of lifelong learning. '(R)ather than regarding teaching as a calling and a lifelong commitment, many new teachers ... approach teaching tentatively or conditionally'; 'the next generation of teachers', the report continued, 'will surely differ from the generation that is about to retire'.[4] The fading of the lifelong teacher is not a trend confined to the USA; it is clearly mirrored in patterns of educational change on the other side of the Atlantic as well.[5]

In reflecting on this change, with the aid of Francis Power Cobbe's metaphor with which we began, we might identify three successive and distinctive historical draughts drawn from the lifelong vessel of education: the first distinguished by an emphasis on learning; the second by the hegemony of teaching; and the most recent by a return to

---

[3] Sixty years after *The Theory of Intuitive Morals* was published, policy recognition of the importance of the 'life-long draught' was elaborated in the Final Report of the Ministry of Reconstruction's Adult Education Committee with the declaration that 'adult education is a permanent national necessity, an inseparable aspect of citizenship, and therefore should be both universal and lifelong'. Ministry of Reconstruction Adult Education Committee. *Final Report*. Cmnd. 321. London: HMSO, 1919: 5. Emphasis on lifelong learning has re-emerged as a major concern for the twenty-first century; see, for example, DfEE. *The Learning Age*. London: HMSO, 1998; Field, John. *Lifelong Learning and the New Educational Order*. Stoke-on-Trent: Trentham Books, 2000; Fieldhouse, Roger. *Adult Education History: Why Rake Up the Past?* University of Leeds: School of Continuing Education, 1997; Fieldhouse, Roger, et al. *A History of Modern British Adult Education*. Leicester: NIACE, 1996; Lengrand, Paul. *An Introduction to Lifelong Education*. London: Croom Helm, 1975; Barr, Jean. "Dumbing down intellectual culture: Frank Furedi, lifelong learning and museums." *Museum and Society* 3, no. 2 (2005): 98–114. Also see Tight, Malcolm. *Key Concepts in Adult Education and Training*. London: RoutledgeFalmer, 2002: 39; Edwards, Richard. *Changing Places? Flexibility, Lifelong Learning and a Learning Society*. London: Routledge, 1997: 107.

[4] Peske, Heather G., et al. "The Next Generation of Teachers: changing conceptions of a career in teaching." *Phi Delta Kappan* 83, no. 4 (2001): 304–11.

[5] OECD "Policy Brief: The Quality of the Teaching Workforce." *OECD Observer*, February 2004: 1–8. Coolahan, John. "Teacher Education and the Teaching Career in an Era of Lifelong Learning." *OECD Education Working Paper No.2* 14 (2002): 14. See also Day, Christopher. *Developing Teachers: The Challenge of Lifelong Learning*. London: RoutledgeFalmer, 1999; Ross, Alistair, and Merryn Hutchings. *Attracting, Developing and Retaining Effective Teachers in the United Kingdom of Great Britain and Northern Ireland: OECD Country Background Report*. London: Institute for Policy Studies in Education, 2003; Chevalier, Arnaud, and Peter Dolton. "Teacher Shortage: another impending crisis?" *CentrePiece* Winter (2004): 14–23.

learning. In this paper, the intention is to look particularly at the transition, at the turn of the nineteenth century, from a popular form of lifelong learning to the primacy of a form of lifelong teaching. In relation to the charting of educational and social change, the prime subtextual questions here might be expressed as: What happened to the original lifelong learners and the legacy they left to teaching? What became of the autodidactic tradition in a period of educational modernization?

Frances Power Cobbe's words were written at a time when the great British tradition of working-class autodidacticism was at its height, at a time when 'the British working class enjoyed a reputation for self-education'.[6] This was an extensive tradition of popular learning, which, in the overwhelming majority of cases—that is to say, save for the handful who achieved public celebrity, political influence or patronage on account of their 'pursuit of knowledge under difficulties'—remains buried in obscurity.[7] The culture of individual or mutual informal learning—self-improvement—was an established cultural current long before the nineteenth century, but the social and demographic changes contingent upon industrialization and urbanization accelerated and heightened its impact. Across the century, as David Vincent shows in his still unsurpassed analysis of working-class autobiographical writing, 'the pursuit of knowledge took on a new dimension'.[8] It was not only the material and visual impact of an unprecedented emergent industrial civilization that fascinated foreign visitors to Britain, but also the remarkable image of the proletarian scholar, tirelessly pursuing knowledge in the face of the most daunting hardships. The autodidact sometimes turned to informal or formal intellectual cooperation by way of mutual improvement or experimental varieties of adult education, sometimes to solitary reading, specimen collecting or scientific enquiry, and sometimes to more or less sustained political activism. But however it found its expression, this 'passion for education' was, as Stuart Macintyre notes, 'rooted in (a) larger tradition of individual workers' search for knowledge', best understood 'as a process of individual self-discovery'.[9] Writing much closer to this tradition, in 1920, the great labour historian, A. E. Dobbs, saw its manifestations, achieved through 'unknown depths of sacrifice', as the embodiment of the principle 'that the art of living was as important to the nation as the "science of production"'.[10] It was in the act of 'individual self-discovery', in the engagement with learning as a lifelong devotion, that the autodidact's intellectual struggle defined itself as an 'art of living'

[6] Rose, Jonathan. *The Intellectual Life of the British Working Classes*. New Haven, CT: Yale University Press, 2001: 187; also Harrison, J. F. C. *Learning and Living 1790–1960: A Study in the History of the English Adult Education Movement*. London: Routledge & Kegan Paul, 1961: 44.

[7] Burnett, John. *Destiny Obscure: Autobiographies of Childhood, Education and Family from the 1820s to the 1920s*. London: Allen Lane, 1982.

[8] Vincent, David. *Bread, Knowledge and Freedom: A Study of Nineteenth-Century Working Class Autobiography*. London: Europa Publications, 1981, 133.

[9] Macintyre, Stuart. *A Proletarian Science: Marxism in Britain 1917–1933*. Cambridge: Cambridge University Press, 1980, 72, 70.

[10] Dobbs, A.E. "Historical Survey." In *Cambridge Essays on Adult Education*, edited by R. St John Parry. Cambridge: Cambridge University Press, 1920: 35–63, 48, 55.

rather than being defined, as in the case of formalized elementary schooling, as a sequential preparation merely for a life of work.

A key characteristic of the learning pursued by working-class autodidacts was its unfettered intellectual range. The autodidacts were certainly full of ambition, but for most the object of this ambition was the acquisition of knowledge itself and not the instrumental purposes to which it might be put. Social mobility or the refinement of work skills was not the object of learning.[11] In this respect, the educational orientation of the autodidacts entailed a very particular ontological dimension as well as a specifically epistemological one. The pursuit of 'really useful knowledge' carried its own justification as a way of being in the world. Independent working-class learning was always understood by the pursuers of knowledge themselves to be an inherently emancipatory exercise, and therefore a deeply moral one. Frequently this perception might be inflected by an explicitly critical or political note—a public passion, as in the case of the Chartists or the Owenites, or the proletarian Marxists of the early twentieth century.[12] Sometimes, it might be more inwardly oriented, directed to the private goal of personal transformation through immersion in canonical or improving literature, ancient and modern.[13] As Dobbs put it, throughout the nineteenth century there were many 'busy men (who) would devote their scanty leisure to studies of no pecuniary value, actuated in some cases by social or political interests, in others by a love of knowledge for its own sake'.[14] For the former group, the idea of lifelong education carried a dual meaning in that it promised not only to transform the life of the learner but also the life of society itself, thereby touching the educational lives of all. For the latter, for those who did not see a future heaven on earth for all as a necessary consequence of their own intellectual struggles, the 'lifelong' character of their learning was its principal definition and sole justification. 'Learning' and 'living', as the very title of John Harrison's pioneering work in this field tells us, were here each wrapped in the other; to live was to learn, and to learn was truly to live.[15] But the promiscuous and undisciplined patterns of nineteenth-century autodidactic learning were not at all well suited to the accelerating systematization of national education from 1870 onwards. The traditional pattern of lifelong learning, as it had been experienced and practised by self-learners in the exemplary mould of William Lovett or Thomas Cooper, could not emerge unchanged from the encounter with educational modernization. Though writing from quite different intellectual perspectives, both Stuart Macintyre and Jonathan Rose have each noted across the twentieth century a 'long-term decline in the autodidact tradition',[16] with '(a)utodidacts ... becoming

---

[11] Vincent, *Bread, Knowledge and Freedom*, 148.

[12] Macintyre, *A Proletarian Science*, 70.

[13] Vincent, *Bread, Knowledge and Freedom*, 140.

[14] Dobbs, "Historical Survey", 56.

[15] Harrison, *Learning and Living*. See also Chase, Malcolm, and Ian Dyck. *Living and Learning: essays in honour of J.F.C. Harrison*. Aldershot: Scolar, 1996.

[16] Macintyre, *A Proletarian Science*, 238.

an endangered species'.[17] So what happened to the tradition? One possibility is that the concept of lifelong learning as known to the autodidacts was not entirely over-taken or lost in this way, but was transformed into an equally powerful lifelong commitment—teaching.

The systematization of compulsory elementary schooling from the 1870s and 1880s marked a significant moment in the development of national education and also in the character of working-class educational experience, and therefore of tradi-tional lifelong learning. Patterns of juvenile educational activity that had previously been episodic, uneven, unpredictable, and to some degree under parental or local cultural control were steered into standardized and regulated forms.[18] More than this, a developing conceptual identification between education, schooling and childhood began to define the parameters of learning around narrower and more concentrated spaces and to legitimize them in ways that offered a challenge to the old, expansive tradition of lifelong learning. The conceptualization, as well as the experience of compulsory and, increasingly, post-compulsory schooling impacted directly on cultural expectations of the place of learning after schooling, across the rest of life. At this important point, driven by incremental legislative activity, the two educational currents upon which the working class could draw with a greater or lesser degree of independence came briefly into close proximity. On the one hand stood the long residual tradition of fully independent lifelong learning—'really useful knowl-edge'[19]—in all its manifold forms; on the other, the new and assertive agency of the school boards and their associated publicly funded schools with which wide sections of the working class came to feel a genuine affinity as 'our schools'.[20] This meant that the expression of an independent working-class educational voice might no longer have to be confined solely to the old defensive tradition of self-learning in which phys-ical and institutional separation from established educational agencies might be seen as the only guarantee of intellectual independence. But if the two currents could both be seen, more or less explicitly, to represent a working-class educational interest, profound pedagogical differences remained between them. These centred, most obvi-ously, on the insistence by formal schooling regimes upon severe conventions of limi-tation in relation to age-defined scholarship, curriculum, assessment, learning space and learning mode.

In pedagogical terms it is not difficult to conceive the sum of these limitations on learning as the antithesis of the nineteenth-century tradition of self-learning, as some

---

[17] Rose, *The Intellectual Life*, 296.

[18] Vincent, *Bread, Knowledge and Freedom*, 96–103; Davin, Anna. *Growing Up Poor: Home, School and Street in London 1870–1914*. London: Rivers Oram Press, 1996: Part II; Gardner, Phil. *The Lost Elementary Schools of Victorian England: The People's Education*. London: Croom Helm, 1984: ch. 3.

[19] Johnson, Richard. "Really Useful Knowledge: Radical Education and Working Class Culture." In *Working Class Culture: Studies in History and Theory*, edited by J. Clarke et al. London: Hutchinson, 1979: 75–102; Johnson, Richard. "Educational Policy and Social Control in Early Victorian England." *Past and Present* 49 (1970): 96–119.

[20] Gardner, Philip. "Our schools or theirs? The case of Eliza Duckworth and John Stevenson." *History of Education*, 20, no. 3 (1991): 163–86.

kind of latter-day success for the earlier efforts of the Society for the Diffusion of Useful Knowledge to routinize and discipline independent working-class learning. This is the ground taken by those theoretical positions which equate early twentieth-century elementary schooling with class-cultural domination.[21] Such an analysis would point particularly to the desiccated pedagogical regime of the Revised Code years, contrasting it with the refusal of the old autodidactic tradition to be incorporated within the new, with its rejection of instrumental linkages between learning and work, or between knowledge and formal qualifications.[22] But such a comparison simply begs the key question of what happened to the autodidactic tradition of life-long learning when its twisting path ran into the broad new highway of compulsory schooling that was finally completed in 1880, ultimately 'making education less of an adventure and more a matter of examinations'.[23] The relative lack of schooling endured by self-educators who grew up in the first half of the nineteenth century had often been an important part of their drive to become scholars in the first place, to experience that which they had been denied in the way of schooling. Charles Shaw, the 'Old Potter' from Tunstall, born in 1832, remembered as an eight-year-old mould-runner with 'a strong passion for reading' contrasting his own lot with that of a more favoured boy he one day observed 'reading at his own free will'. The experience, which 'touched me to the quick':

> ... forced upon my mind a sense of painful contrast between his position and mine. I felt a sudden, strange sense of wretchedness. There was a blighting consciousness that my lot was harsher than his and that of others.... I went back to my mould-running and hot stove with my first anguish in my heart. I can remember, though never describe, the acuteness of this first sorrow.[24]

But the very lack of formal schooling could also be a liberation of a negative kind. It meant that the impulse to learn was not prematurely constricted, constrained or distorted, and that creative horizons remained open. It meant that lifelong learning retained an intellectually independent dimension—'quite distinct from that of the national intelligensia'[25]—of a sort that the various strands of the early twentieth-century adult education movement, whether liberal or radical, could not always accommodate.[26] What Vincent calls the 'exuberant catholicism' and 'undisciplined eclecticism' of the autodidacts did not incline very easily either towards the formal school curriculum or to the vocational, rational recreational, or explicitly political goals of institutionally organized adult education.[27] The milestones inhering in lifelong

[21] Humphries, Steve. *Hooligans or Rebels?: An Oral History of Working-Class Childhood and Youth 1889–1939*. Oxford: Basil Blackwell, 1981; Fieldhouse, *Adult Education History,* 36.

[22] Vincent, *Bread, Knowledge and Freedom,* 140–43.

[23] Rose, *The Intellectual Life,* 67.

[24] Shaw, Charles. *When I Was A Child.* Seaford: Caliban Books, 1977: 20–21.

[25] Macintyre, *A Proletarian Science,* 238.

[26] Steele, Tom and Richard Taylor. "Marxism and Adult Education in Britain." *Policy Futures in Education* 2: 3 and 4 (2004): 578–592, 582.

[27] Vincent, *Bread, Knowledge and Freedom,* 120; also Rose, *The Intellectual Life,* 90.

self-education were of a different order from those of a later period when the markers of educational advance were more likely to be formal credentials. The symbols of intellectual growth were more private and intimate: 'Every student workman knows the stages and the progress from no books to books, from books in the kitchen to books in a separate room. These stages are the milestones of his life.'[28]

To the extent that the tradition of self-learning could not flourish easily in the circumscribed and increasingly pervasive intellectual climate of the classroom, it is not surprising, particularly with increasing differentiation through competitive scholarships, that autodidacticism found it difficult to survive in its old form. Moreover, the orientation of potential recruits to adult education was heavily influenced by childhood experiences of schooling. The impulse to lifelong learning could be difficult to reignite where school pupils had come to perceive learning as dull, routine or instrumental, or indeed where they had come to see its sole legitimate association as being with childhood. The elementary school does not therefore present itself as the most immediately promising site in which to search for the continuance of the autodidactic tradition—that is, as long as we focus upon pupils, rather than their teachers.

In tracing the 'lifelong' tradition, history has concentrated the bulk of its analytical attention not upon the school but upon the many strands of the adult education movement, through Working Men's Colleges, University Extension, the Workers' Educational Association and the Labour Colleges, as the true successor to self-learning.[29] But well before the establishment of most of the modern apparatus of adult education, it was the elementary teaching profession that might be seen as the major channel into which flowed the inheritance of the autodidactic tradition, along with some of its key assumptions about life and learning. It is in this confluence that an inchoate but deeply principled culture of proletarian learning came alongside an emergent and still substantially working-class professional culture of teaching. In this meeting, the primary claim upon the unifying principle of lifelong commitment to education can be seen to slip from the realm of learning to that of teaching.

In April 1904, *The Schoolmaster*, the journal of the National Union of Teachers, published a short essay by George Baddeley under the title 'When I Was a Pupil Teacher'.[30] It was the first in a series of 15 weekly contributions from lifelong elementary school teachers, each in turn reflecting on their memories of pupil-teaching in the early decades of the scheme, famously introduced by James Kay Shuttleworth in

---

[28] Jack Lawson, writing in 1949, cited in Rose, *The Intellectual Life*, 88–9. Also see Vincent, *Bread, Knowledge and Freedom*, 120–22.

[29] Harrison, *Learning and Living*, xiv, 43. Also Rose, *The Intellectual Life*; Macintyre, *A Proletarian Science*; Lawrence Goldman. "Intellectuals and the English working class 1870–1945: the case of adult education." *History of Education* 29 (2000): 281–300.

[30] Baddeley, George. "When I Was a Pupil Teacher." *The Schoolmaster*, 23 April 1904: 954. The series clearly originated as an organized expression of the Executive Committee of the National Union of Teachers, with nine of the contributors coming from the ranks of the Executive itself; see *The Schoolmaster*, 2 January 1904, 20. Across the series, male authors outnumbered females by 13 to two.

1846.[31] The series was clearly planned as an affectionate valedictory for a system of school-based apprenticeship training, following the issuing of Morant's 'revolution-ary' new training regulations in July 1903.[32] The tone of the pieces ranges from the light-hearted and anecdotal to the ponderous and philosophical, but at the heart of each is a shared celebration of lives dedicated to teaching from the start. Each also marks a bitter-sweet recognition that a lifelong professional responsibility is passing to a new teaching generation as part of a larger national narrative of educational advance. Here is the self-conscious voice of the nation's first generation of teachers for an age of mass schooling; animated by 'enthusiasm for our profession ... we were, with all our drawbacks, the pioneers of what we all hope will one day be a complete system of national education'.[33] But if this sense of shared professional loyalty and commitment affords some forward glances to the future, its abiding concentration is on the backward gaze, across the landmarks of a life given to teaching.

> I entered the noble army of schoolmasters on the night of 9th September, 1855, the night on which the country celebrated the capture of Sebastopol.... I served my apprenticeship in the Redruth National School under an untrained master, Mr. Wm. Tonkin, a gentle-man who ... spared no time or pains in giving his pupil teachers the best education that the circumstances of the time permitted.[34]

> I became a pupil teacher in the Gloucester British School in April 1857.... Mr. Norton, the master, had the reputation, which was well deserved, of being a good and successful teacher, but also of being a very severe one.... His was not a joyless life. He had as a life-long and inseparable friend, Mr. Moore, of the British School at Cheltenham. But his chief joy and pride was in his own school, his only one, and when he retired after long service in it, he still remained in close connection with it....[35]

In the eleventh week of the series, the format was set aside in favour of an unplanned addition to the original schedule, taking advantage of a local educational story that happily coincided with the spirit of 'When I Was a Pupil Teacher'. As *The Schoolmaster* reported, 'We gave last week some account of the presentations to Mr. Scotson of Manchester, on the occasion of his retirement after no fewer than fifty-six years' work in the elementary schools of Manchester'.[36] Echoing the sentiments of the contribu-tors to the series proper, Scotson, '"the prince of schoolmasters" ... carrying bravely the weight of 69 years' declared '(o)ne of my most pleasing reflections' to be that thanks to the nation's teachers, 'a boy bred in the gutter has before him a prospect of

[31] Selleck, R. J. W. *James Kay Shuttleworth: Journey of an Outsider*. London: Woburn Press, 1994: 224–45; Tropp, Asher. *The School Teachers: The Growth of the Teaching Profession in England and Wales from 1800 to the Present Day*. London: Heinemann, 1957: 18–22.

[32] Dent, H. C. *The Training of Teachers in England and Wales 1800–1975*. London: Hodder & Stoughton, 1977: 50. For a broader context, Schwarz, Leonard. "Professions, Elites, and Universities in England, 1870–1970." *The Historical Journal* 47, no. 4 (2004): 941–62, 947.

[33] Cleghorn, Miss. "When I Was A Pupil Teacher." *The Schoolmaster*, 30 April 1904: 989.

[34] Treglohan, Thomas P. "When I Was A Pupil Teacher." *The Schoolmaster*, 6 August 1904: 230.

[35] McWilliam, R. "When I Was A Pupil Teacher." 24 September 1904: 546–47.

[36] "Half a Century at Work." *The Schoolmaster*, 23 July 1904: 166.

Figure 1.   J. Scotson.

securing the highest scholastic attainments, and of becoming valuable to the city and to the nation'. Scotson's story of lifelong teaching, as with the series itself, comprised something more than a written text. The many common threads of individual recollection that connected all the accounts were further unified through the use of some thoughtful visual imagery (Figure 1).

The pictorial representation that accompanies Scotson's recollections (see Figure 1) shows a much simplified version of the more complex and carefully designed composite image which decorates each of the texts in the main sequence. Here we see, to take two of the contributions to the series as examples (Figures 2 and 3), how inscribed memories of teaching could also be represented symbolically as part of a common educational unity, of a kind and intensity not dissimilar to that which united the experience of the autodidacts. In this respect, lifelong teaching could be seen to match Vincent's description of the autodidact's experience as constituting 'nothing less than … a transformation in consciousness and in relationship with the external world'.[37] The images we see here are a visual attempt to capture and sustain just such a transformative moment.

In the representative cases of Selvage ('we old ones who love our work for its own sake'[38]) and Rankilor ('forty-six years' continuous and not altogether unsuccessful work in the same Birmingham school'[39]), we see the images of two professional lives

---

[37] Vincent, *Bread, Knowledge and Freedom*, 135.
[38] Selvage, Miss A. G. "When I Was a Pupil Teacher." *The Schoolmaster*, 2 July 1904: 34.
[39] Rankilor, G. J. "When I Was A Pupil Teacher." *The Schoolmaster*, 1 October 1904: 640.

Figure 2. Miss A.G. Selvage.

through time encapsulated within shared symbolic identifications of education as a
way of life.

   Each of the lifelong teachers in the series is represented by two portrait images, set
against a stylized background and cropped to fit oval frames reminiscent of the
conjoined halves of a sentimental locket. The images capture each individual at
the start ('Then') and at the end ('Now') of their long period of professional service,

Figure 3. Mr. G.J. Rankilor.

inviting the viewer to reflect on the extent as well as the constancy of the commitment that has been rendered to education by each one. The individual portraits are, week by week, the only elements of the composite image to change. No attempt is made to personalize, localize or otherwise specify the particular character of this or that life in teaching, a task which is reserved for the text itself. Instead, the role of the composite image is to present a collective expression of teaching, represented by a range of invariant devices signifying both an individual commitment to education by each, and the honouring of a professional tradition transcending any single contribution. In this way, the teacher readers of *The Schoolmaster* are invited to place themselves in the tradition, to visualize their own portraits within the common frame, and to declare themselves as lifelong teachers too. The symbolic objects that decorate the pairs of portraits are direct and uncomplicated, and in this lies the source of much of their power. Like the autodidact, they speak of an orientation to education which is straightforward, authentic and without artifice.

Spilling from the open locket, as it were, an assemblage of line-drawn images cluster around the portraits, distilling the characteristics of the elementary teacher's identity. To the left, attaching itself to the youthful portrait, are the markers of sustained personal study and academic labour—the desktop, the learned tomes, the open notebook and the writing pen, all bathed in the bright, directed light of the study lamp. To the right, the senior picture is attended by the single object which most fittingly captures both the faithful and unbroken day-after-day duty of care discharged by the teacher, and the serious, disciplined and responsible manner in which it was recorded—the school log book. This dimension of the teacher's lifelong identity might have been represented by equally mundane images of school bells, desks, playgrounds or, indeed, children themselves. These, however, are absent, and the choice of a book—the only object which is common to all three illustrative dimensions of the image and which stands directly for knowledge and truth—is significant. Moreover, the log book, with its routine associations, is not left unadorned. It serves as a perch for Minerva's Owl, the premier symbol of wisdom, assuring us that despite all that might be repetitive or intellectually unchallenging about teaching, the teacher himself or herself never ceases to be a scholar as well. At the same time, the positioning of the bird alongside the twilight image of the teacher reminds us that in pursuit of true wisdom and understanding, Minerva's Owl spreads its wings only at dusk—an insight which the series itself puts into practice.

Like the image of the book—perhaps the most striking and ubiquitous point of material contact between the cultures of lifelong learning and lifelong teaching[40]—the celebration of wisdom is manifest at every symbolic stage of the image. Most notably,

---

[40] If the image of the book was a dominant one for the lifelong teacher, for the autodidact it was without parallel. 'By "knowledge"', as David Vincent tells us, the autodidacts 'meant book knowledge'. Reflecting on the 'life-long struggle to acquire books', Benjamin Brierley, a Lancashire weaver, remembered that the members of his local mutual improvement society sought to make their precious books lifelong too; it 'became a labour of love to cover the bindings, which we did with stout nankeen, so as to make them last forever'. Vincent, *Bread, Knowledge and Freedom*, 109, 113, 112.

of course, it is to be found at its heart, holding together the two ages of a single exist-ence. Here we find the representation of Minerva herself, the goddess of wisdom setting her touch upon the young and the old sides of life alike, and standing four-square upon the foundation of another learned volume. Above Minerva, and again linking the two images of a single existence, stands a garlanded bush of laurel, signi-fying both lifelong dedication and the just rewards of honour and triumph due to a life given to education.

Like the visual symbols, the only words—'Then and Now'—which attach to the illustration stress continuity in identity across time. Rather than the more abstract terms 'past' and 'present' in which the characteristic quality of absence in the former is to be contrasted with the quality of presence in the latter, 'then' and 'now' are inti-mately connected in the course of a life continuously reflecting, in memory, on that which holds it together across time. In this respect, the composite image may be seen as an active place of memory where that which Paul Ricoeur has distinguished as the *idem* (identity as sameness across time) and the *ipse* (identity as selfhood perceived through the experience of change across time) are bound together in the single construct of narrative identity.[41]

How does the idea of the 'lifelong', and particularly lifelong commitment to education, as deployed in the words and images of 'When I Was a Teacher' connect with the older notion of the lifelong learner? In terms of the representations of the lifelong teacher that we have considered, there are clear parallels with the ways in which history has sought symbolically to represent the image of the autodidact. An evocative example, created by Clifford Harper, is to be found in the cover illustra-tion of Brian Simon's edited volume devoted to working-class adult education in the twentieth century, *The Search for Enlightenment*.[42] Here we see clearly accentuated (Figure 4), if in a very different artistic style, the same elements of self-study—the learned volumes, the notebook, the writing pen, the same intimations of dark, late-night study, and the same triumphant, illuminating beam of light representing, as well as facilitating, the quest for knowledge. It is an image that would have been seen as both quite familiar and eminently praiseworthy by George Baddeley and his co-memorialists.

Teachers were adept and practised self-learners, whether as pupil teachers, college students, or more generally across the course of their teaching careers. But as the disparate educational reforms of Robert Lowe and Robert Morant would recognize, if in quite different ways, the restricted regime and expectations of the elementary school meant that there was always a tension between the level of personal education of teachers and the pedagogical demands of an academically limited curriculum. This meant that there was a persistent sense in which teachers, mirroring the experience of the working-class autodidact, could find their daily work to be an obstacle to the furtherance of their own personal studies. The resolution of this tension was ultimately

---

[41] Ricoeur, Paul. *Oneself as Another*. Chicago: University of Chicago Press, 1992: 2–3.

[42] Simon, B., ed. *The Search for Enlightenment: The Working Class and Adult Education in the Twentieth Century*. Leicester: NIACE, 1990.

Figure 4. The Search For Enlightenment.

the triumph of lifelong teaching over lifelong learning, of professional dedication to the service of education over the personal desire for education.[43] There is of course a substantial irony here in tracing an educational connection between a fading autodidactic tradition and an emergent pedagogic one. The material limitations and administrative strictures of the late nineteenth-century elementary school were in many ways the institutional antithesis of the unfenced learning of the self-educators, with elementary teachers constrained 'to impose themselves on the pursuit of knowledge' in the classroom, 'rarely (able to) exercise much influence over the higher levels of learning'.[44] But the nature of the elementary school learning experience for pupils—whether, like Humphries, we see it as bleak and oppressive or, like Rose, as more likely to be happy and fulfilling—is not the central issue here.[45] Rather, we are concerned with the educational impact of the elementary school ethos upon teachers, and upon its capacity to sustain a lifelong commitment to education, as expressed in the figure of the lifelong teacher.[46] This was an identity which, alongside its professional aspect, could never wholly overlook the ideal of lifelong scholarship—'the higher levels of learning'—as one of its own defining conditions. Despite the rigours and limitations of the pedagogical arenas in which they operated, individual elementary teachers clung

[43] Gardner, Philip. "Teacher Training and Changing Professional Identity in Early Twentieth Century England." *Journal of Education for Teaching* 21, no. 2 (1995): 191–217.

[44] Vincent, *Bread, Knowledge and Freedom*, 157.

[45] Humphries, *Hooligans or Rebels?*, ch. 2; Rose, *The Intellectual Life*, ch. 5.

[46] See Marsden, W. E. *An Anglo-Welsh Reaching Dynasty: the Adams Family from the 1840s to the 1930s*. London: Woburn Press, 1997.

on to the old self-improving tradition as best they might. There is a particular importance here in relation to the participation of women in the culture of learning. The autodidactic tradition had been a highly gendered one in which female voices were very few, partially because of the pervasive time constraints operating on women's labour, and partially because of the exclusive attitudes of male self-learners themselves.[47] If the residue of the old, untrammelled self-learning always held some place within the new tradition of lifelong teaching, it would prove to be particularly important for the large numbers of women who came into elementary teaching in the closing decades of the nineteenth century. The demands of lifelong teaching may have impinged upon the desires and opportunities of all teachers also to be lifelong learners. But, for women, access to a degree of self-learning on such terms was a notable advance on what had been on offer to them during the hegemony of the old autodidactic culture.[48]

If the autodidactic tradition had eschewed any orientation of learning towards the instrumental end of certification or vocational qualification, this injunction was obviously problematical in the special circumstance where the object of certification opened a lifelong involvement with education—if not purely with lifelong study— itself. And, of course, it was in school teaching that just such an avenue to certification was established on a small scale from the mid-nineteenth century, with the demands of effective teacher training thereafter leading the way for more general educational reform—a trend that was to hold good until well into the twentieth century.

It was not, however, until the national reform of elementary education, with the immensely enhanced demand for trained teachers and its ancillary effects—most notably the inception of the National Union of Elementary Teachers—that the culture of lifelong teaching began to take deep root.[49] Here, the establishment of universal childhood compulsion played an important role in introducing a new dimension to the role played by educational differentiation in defining the idea of the 'lifelong'. Traditionally, the autodidact had commonly enjoyed local status and renown as a 'great scholar', one whose wisdom or skills might be admired as being of a superior sort. This was a designation that early trained elementary teachers might also attract. Richard John, a lifelong teacher, remembered the veneration for his own schoolmaster in South Wales in the 1860s. 'The penmanship of the master, Mr. Thomas Davies, was the talk of the district. *"Can't he write!" "Ain't he a scholar!"'*.[50] In the closing decades of the nineteenth century, with every child at school, the old understandings of scholarship were forced to change. All were now 'scholars', if sometimes only of a notional kind. The

---

[47] Vincent, *Bread, Knowledge and Freedom*, 44.

[48] Copelman, Dina M. *London's Women Teachers: Gender, Class and Feminism 1870–1930*. London: Routledge, 1996: 28, 77. The idea of lifelong teaching comprehends both a material career and an associated professional and personal identity. In this respect, women who were obliged to relinquish their posts as a consequence of the operation of marriage bars might, although having lost their material place in the profession, retain and continue to enact elements of the identity of the lifelong teacher.

[49] Dent, *The Training of Teachers*, 26; Copelman, *London's Women Teachers*, 68–9.

[50] John, Richard M. "When I Was a Pupil Teacher". *The Schoolmaster*, 11 June 1904: 1259.

child who might go on to pursue independent learning in adult life shared his or her first years of scholarship alongside those—the majority—who would not. In this changed educational context, a new point of differentiation was called for to demonstrate the mastery of elevated forms of knowledge. And in the figure of the local teacher rather than the local scholar, the idea of scholarship within a working-class community could be redefined.

At the same time, as far as school pupils were concerned, and whatever their particular experience of the classroom might be, the one constant image they had before them every day of their learning lives was that of their teacher. For many, the classroom could be a dull or a frightening place from which they sought escape.[51] For others, despite the routine forms that learning might take, school carried at least the promise of learning, and in that way it caught the attention of those with the same thirst for knowledge as the old self-learners. And this smaller group caught the reciprocal attention of the teacher as well, for a very specific reason. It was amongst the best, the brightest and the most engaged of their pupils that teachers looked for their pupil-teacher apprentices. For such individuals, the offer of a pupil teachership was a marking out, a confirmation to them of their intellectual distinctiveness. Similarly, for those among the early autodidacts who had access to schooling— generally no more than 'a poor little bit of an education'[52]—this early awareness of differentiation was an important stage in their own intellectual growth and resolution. They recognized themselves as special scholars, 'singled out from their contemporaries and informed that they stood at the head of a hierarchy of personal merit'.[53] John Harris, the Cornish tin miner and poet whose education was confined to a dame school, remembered in his 1882 autobiography that, much in the same way as prospective pupil teachers would find themselves singled out, 'I was soon considered the best scholar in her establishment'.[54] And the 1807 memoirs of James Hogg, the shepherd-poet, recalled that on leaving school at the age of six, he had 'had the honour of standing at the head of a juvenile class'.[55] In such intimations of scholarly ability we can see the pre-figuring of the long hours of solitary study that later generations of pupil teachers would have to combine, like the autodidacts, with the pressures of their other work. We also see the unwelcome but unavoidable corollary of the certification of learning, in the substitution of unrestricted reading by the pressures of cramming. As one of the contributors to 'When I Was a Pupil Teacher' recollects:

> But I think I hear someone say, "When did you get your own lessons?" From a quarter to eight until nine, from twelve until twelve-thirty or sometimes nearly one every morning. Back at school at one-thirty, and often lessons again between four and five. After that home lessons quite sufficient to fill up the rest of the evening.... It was necessarily a system of

---

[51] Burnett, *Destiny Obscure*, 152.
[52] Shaw, *When I Was A Child*, 11.
[53] Vincent, *Bread, Knowledge and Freedom*, 104.
[54] Ibid.
[55] Ibid.

cram from the text-books. Try me in Cornwell's Geography. To this day I can repeat whole pages of it.[56]

Yet pupil teachers could also feel they were advancing, in a spirit of true knowledge, towards the ultimate if transitory goal of the training college—in the words of George Baddeley, 'the Mecca of my pilgrimage'.[57] Here, in the true tradition of the autodidact, Baddeley's studies 'day by day extended my knowledge horizon'.[58] The discipline of independent study of the intensity demanded by college and by pupil-teachership were founded, for him, on those qualities of 'grit, self-reliance, and earnestness of purpose'[59] which chimed closely with the characteristic 'sobriety, self-discipline and commitment to rational inquiry' of the autodidacts.[60] Both the lifelong learner and the lifelong teacher shared a reputation for seriousness and for standing apart from the mainstream (widely admired qualities in the case of the former category, widely lampooned in the latter[61]), and both celebrated the triumph of knowledge in the face of adversity. James Scotman, at the end of his lifelong teaching career, could in this way reflect upon a conception of personal study reaching back to the old days of the pursuit of knowledge under difficulties: 'Boys should be thrown more on their own resources, and be taught to take a delight in surmounting a difficulty'.[62]

In overcoming difficulties in this fashion, the lifelong teachers were fortunate in a way that the autodidacts were not. From the first moment of their self-study, from their appointment as pupil teachers, they had regular and sustained access to a mentor, a guide, and occasionally a friend in the form of their head teacher and, sometimes, other pupil-teachers.[63] Here they might enjoy the kind of support and encouragement in the development of a lifelong identity which sometimes proved elusive for the autodidacts who, whilst full of enthusiasm and dedication, so often lacked such guidance. For the autodidact:

> A constantly recurring event ... is a meeting with another working man who has embarked on a similar course of self-improvement. In every case the formation of a relationship with him is ascribed a central role in the course of the ... pursuit of knowledge.[64]

---

[56] Cleghorn, "When I Was a Pupil Teacher", 989.

[57] Baddeley, "When I Was a Pupil Teacher", 954.

[58] Baddeley, "When I Was a Pupil Teacher", 953.

[59] Ibid.

[60] Vincent, *Bread, Knowledge and Freedom*, 133.

[61] See for example the 1899 observations of a correspondent of the *Fortnightly Review* on "The Teacher Problem". Elementary teachers were here described as 'unintellectual, knowing hardly anything well, parochial in sympathies, vulgar in the accent and style of his talking, with a low standard of manners'; cited in Copelman, *London's Women Teachers*, 45. As Marsden indicates, such 'limited and somewhat sinister concept(s) of course derived from (a) ... set of social principles designed to humble elementary schoolteachers and mock their aspirations'. Marsden, *An Anglo-Welsh teaching dynasty*, 264.

[62] "Half a Century of Work." *The Schoolmaster*, 23 July 1904: 166.

[63] Jennings, Ruth. *Lofty Aims and Lowly Duties: Three Victorian Schoolmasters*. Sheffield: Sheffield Academic Press, 1994, ch. 3.

[64] Vincent, *Bread, Knowledge and Freedom*, 126.

There is a further important link connecting the autodidacts and the lifelong teachers of the late nineteenth and early twentieth centuries. Many autodidacts, drawing on their copious stores of knowledge and their high local standing as great scholars, also had some experience of teaching. Many were occasional Sunday school teachers or periodically set up small private elementary schools in order to fill a slow patch in trade or as a stop-gap in a time of poor health or other dislocation. [65] But the fundamental goal of educational life remained emphatically that of learning, not teaching. None saw teaching as a lifelong commitment or as a skilled enterprise requiring intricate preparation. It was, rather, merely a casual and ephemeral by-product of the far greater business of lifelong learning, simply a passing on of the more rudimentary fragments of personal knowledge. In this, the autodidacts were wholly in tune with a dominant popular assumption of the early nineteenth century, namely that teaching was a straightforward task that could be undertaken by any with the requisite academic knowledge.[66] It was not high-status work, requiring professional demarcation from the other trades and crafts of the working man. Christopher Thomson, a one-time shipwright and itinerant performer, wrote in just these terms of his Yorkshire school venture in the 1820s:

> There can be no surprise excited at my 'keeping a school' ... anybody could make a schoolmaster. People must live; and as well to keep a school as do anything else; every sixpence will buy a loaf; and to be a schoolmaster is one of the few comfortable trades which require no previous training.[67]

The incremental professionalization of teaching in the second half of the nineteenth century challenged this assumption by reversing the polarity of teaching and learning. It took the autodidact's most fundamental educational principle—that of the 'lifelong'—and founded a quite new conception of teaching upon it. In popular perception, the emergence of the lifelong teacher stimulated a mix of admiration for lifelong dedication alongside ambivalence about teachers as 'a race apart' leading 'a narrow life'.[68] To this extent, teachers could be regarded with the same kind of bemused popular respect—if usually less generously expressed—as had been the autodidacts.

As for the teachers themselves, whilst they would characteristically remain in their private lives the most enthusiastic of scholars, it was in terms of teaching rather than their own scholarship that, for most of the twentieth century, they came to define their lifelong relationship with education. In so doing, they had refashioned the legacy of the old autodidactic tradition and given to the twentieth century the era of the lifelong teacher.[69] But at the close of that century, a new and very different idea of learning returned to reclaim the ownership rights to the educational 'lifelong'. As it did so,

---

[65] Vincent, *Bread, Knowledge and Freedom*, 101, 149–50.

[66] Gardner, *The Lost Elementary Schools*, 1984, ch. 4.

[67] Quoted in Vincent, *Bread, Knowledge and Freedom*, 150.

[68] Cunningham, Peter and Philip Gardner. *Becoming Teachers: Texts and Testimonies 1907–1950*. London: Woburn Press, 2004, ch. 6.

[69] Gardner, Philip. "Classroom Teachers and Educational Change 1876–1996." *Journal of Education for Teaching* 24, no. 1 (1998): 33–49.

teaching began to surrender its century-long hold on the concept, perhaps making way for a new twenty-first century reworking of that older, porous model of teaching which had dominated the early nineteenth century, with boundaries between teaching and other occupations weak, and occupational movements in and out of teaching common. The approbation of strong categorical distinctions between lifelong teachers and other occupational and social groups, a characteristic that had animated the contributors to 'When I Was a Pupil Teacher', is on the wane in the twenty-first century, taking with it, perhaps for good, the era of the lifelong teacher. In reflecting on this, we might wonder about the attention history has thus far paid to the importance, across time, of 'the life-long draught'. We might ask if it has done enough to develop a category not only of great symbolic significance for education, but also of real conceptual utility for exploring key aspects of the relation between education and social change.

Working-class Education and Social Change in Nineteenth- and Twentieth-century Britain

Tom Woodin

Working-class educational history provides a valuable perspective from which to understand social change in education. The education of the working class has been a continuing and thorny issue that has resonated widely with implications for the organization and values of society in general. Subordinate groups have not only contested dominant discourses within and beyond education but also established their own initiatives. Understanding even the small group or protest draws one into an analysis of the broader canvas within which it operates. In particular adult education and literacy are rich and diverse areas where working-class people have been active.

Although historians of education often trace their work to current debates and policies, early twenty-first-century Britain would not at first sight seem to be a propitious standpoint from which to understand working-class education. Indeed, our current situation provides a very different lens than previously for understanding working class movements. According to one view, processes of 'globalization' have strained adult education through a neo-liberal sieve from which human capital versions of 'lifelong learning' have been retained while liberal education has been discarded. Indicative of the altered situation, two UNESCO reports are often compared: *Learning to Be* (1972) with its nod towards liberal and lifelong education has been dislodged by *Learning: the Treasure Within* (1996) and its embrace of lifelong learning.[1] In this new context a particular notion of learning has become dominant: individuals are expected to take responsibility for updating their skills in order to keep abreast of rapid economic and technological changes. Arguably, this tidal change has left the notion of 'working-class education' stranded, seemingly cut off from mainstream developments. In addition, since the 1980s social class in general has been eclipsed from public life in Britain; in its place we have more fragmented categories such as the socially excluded or, more specifically, those in receipt of free school meals. It has even been claimed the concept of class is 'dead'.[2] Yet examples of social class continue to intrude upon this apparently settled scene—in 2006 even the Conservative Party's Social Justice Unit noted the significant role of social class in education. In short, the working class has become an 'absent presence', rarely spoken of yet pervasive.

A more positive reading of this process would be that marginal forms of educational activity have finally been recognized by policy-makers and entered the mainstream. For instance, adult education is no longer a discrete minority-based practice; rather it is something that everyone potentially does. Indeed, the influence of this thinking in England can be identified in a raft of policies and initiatives such as extended schools, widening participation and family learning to name a few. In 1998 David Blunkett, as secretary of state for education, made much of the educational traditions of working-class self-help in framing *The Learning Age* although this may have been more a result of Blunkett's increasingly distant history in socialist politics and less a reflection of recent Labour Governments in general.[3] This recognition of working-class educational initiatives may in fact be a very selective use of the past to justify contemporary policy.

In order to unravel the connections and discontinuities between the history of working-class education and current developments it is necessary to view the past through a number of variegated lenses. We need to recognize that 'working class' can be a multiple and diffuse category as well as a tightly defined one and that it has been implicated in many contests over education. Paradoxically our current educational world is also beginning to bear more resemblance to an earlier period prior to the advent of the welfare state, a time when class pervaded British society. For instance, supposedly 'new' phenomena such as middle-class fear of failing[4] or the growing privatization of education are two trends where there are similarities to the late

---

[1] Faure, Edgar, et al. *Learning to Be: the World of Education Today and Tomorrow*. Paris: UNESCO, 1972. Delors, Jacques, *Learning: the Treasure Within*. Paris: UNESCO, 1996. See also, "Editorial: From the 'Great Tradition' to 'Celebrity Big Brother': Whatever Became of Adult Education?" *International Journal of Lifelong Education* 24, no. 6 (2005): 455–57.

[2] Pakulski, J., and M. Waters. *The Death of Class*. London: Sage, 1996.

[3] See also Yeo, Stephen. *Organic Learning: Mutual Enterprise and the Learning and Skills Agenda*. Leicester: NIACE, 2000.

[4] McCulloch, Gary. "Education and the Middle Classes: the Case of the English Grammar Schools, 1868–1944." *History of Education* 35, no. 6 (2006): 689–704.

nineteenth and early twentieth centuries.[5] It is also possible that the history of working-class education may come into clearer perspective once again.

The speed of these changes has been remarkable. Social class has passed from being a central category of historical analysis into a state of virtual oblivion decades. Paradoxically, these changes have proceeded during a time of increasing economic inequality throughout the world. For generations of historians, especially in the postwar period, class had been a ubiquitous explanation of social change and was a crucial lens for sifting and analysing evidence. By contrast, we would find class to be almost equally remote from more recent historiography—the class emperor may have had no clothes after all—although this would be less true in history of education.[6] By charting the ways in which working-class education has been conceived historically it may prove possible to work through this conundrum and to see how it may yet enrich our understanding of the past. This provides an opportunity to re-think the nature and contradictions of working-class education, about which much has been written. One place to start this process is the rich and wide-ranging historical work on adult education in which many generations of working-class people were imbricated.

Adult Education

Understanding the nature and significance of this participation has been a major preoccupation of educational historians. However, many histories of adult education have also occluded our vision of the social, political and economic movements which worked for the emancipation of the working class in the nineteenth century. As early histories began to recognize these movements they also systematically downgraded them. Indeed, the growth of adult education into a self-conscious 'movement' during the early twentieth century provided a context from which to mould an understanding of historical change. For instance, the '1919 Report' of the Ministry of Reconstruction Adult Education Committee would be marked by a sense of progressivism and a searching for roots of the present. It usefully surveyed the historical development of adult schools, mechanics institutes, Chartism and cooperation, people's colleges and university extension but, in its eagerness to consider policy implications in terms of a wider educational *system*, these earlier movements were treated as fragmented precursors to the present:

> In the absence of the earlier stages of training, experiments in adult education too often have resembled an attempt to roof a house before the walls were completed ... efforts to build up adult education, which were previously in the nature of forlorn, if heroic,

---

[5] For two different takes on private education see Gardner, Phil. *The Lost Elementary Schools of Victorian England*. London: Croom Helm, 1984 and West, E. G. *Education and the State*. 3rd ed. Indianapolis: Liberty Fund. 1994.

[6] For a critique of class in general see Joyce, Patrick. *Visions of the People*. Cambridge: Cambridge University Press, 1990.

enterprises ... are at length finding their proper place as one element in a training which extends through childhood and adolescence to manhood and womanhood'.[7]

This whiggish interpretation of social change saw earlier 'experiments' as well intentioned but doomed to failure given the lack of preparatory education as well as 'demoralizing industrial conditions'. The committee viewed itself as a fulcrum that would tip the balance away from the patchy initiatives of the past towards a system in which adult education was available to all who needed it. Social change, by implication, had been a one-way process of gradual widening towards more comprehensive provision. Although this approach would seem to have much in common with the views of the Fabians Sidney and Beatrice Webb, who aimed to replace the voluntarism of many working-class associations with the efficiency of state machinery,[8] the committee did in fact support the WEA, a voluntary association. By outlining a system of financial support it also helped to delineate a varied pattern of adult education which was not adopted into policy but did serve as a prompt to further activity and understanding. While this vision recognized the importance of working-class agency it also curtailed and boxed it in as one element of a wider educational structure.

Moreover, aspects of this approach would continue for many years. Even though A. E. Dobbs's 1919 account was much more creative in so far as it analysed education in relation to wider social change, he nevertheless concluded that the WEA had 'drawn together a variety of movements...'.[9] In addition, Robert Peers would later contrast the 'adult education movement' of the twentieth century with the 'isolated experiments' of the nineteenth.[10] Thomas Kelly would also write a history of adult education as an 'autonomous' account, which made few connections to wider social changes. He claimed that a system of adult education had grown incrementally by the 1970s:

> ... this fourfold partnership of the central government, the local education authorities, the universities, and the voluntary organisations, lumbering and creaking as it has sometimes been, has produced a system of adult education that is varied, comprehensive, and infinitely responsive to individual needs.[11]

Thus a well-oiled and efficient system was presented as the outcome of the spontaneous and organic activity of various bodies. In fact, organizational forms represented

---

[7] Ministry of Reconstruction Adult Education Committee. *Final Report*. London: HMSO, 1919, 10.

[8] Yeo, Stephen. "Notes on Three Socialisms." In *Socialism and the Intelligentsia*, edited by Carl Levy. London: Routledge, 1987. Potter, Beatrice. *The Co-operative Movement in Great Britain*. London: Swan Sonnenschein, 1891.

[9] Dobbs, A. E. *Education and Social Movements, 1700–1850*. New York: Augustus Kelly, 1919: 250–51. See also Silver, Harold. "Education and the Labour Movement: a Critical Review of the Literature." *History of Education* 2, no. 2 (1973): 173–202.

[10] Peers, Robert. *Adult Education*. London: Routledge & Kegan Paul, 1972, orig. 1958.

[11] Kelly, Thomas. *A History of Adult Education in Great Britain from the Middle Ages to the Twentieth Century*. 2nd ed. Liverpool: Liverpool University Press, 1970, orig 1962: 395.

by paid professionals delivering a service to the general public had overlaid the activist working-class progenitors of adult education. Thus acceptance into a wider system of adult education came at the price of its continuing institutional marginality.

These perspectives emphasized the notion of liberal education as inextricably linked to adult education. Indeed, 'liberal education' became the key descriptive label for adult education during much of the twentieth century, epitomized by university extra-mural work as well as the WEA, which ran three-year courses modelled on the university degree even though groups were democratically run and generally rejected certification.[12] In the long term critics would note that such liberal studies opened the door to middle-class domination and the WEA would experience continuing insecurities over whether it was in fact a working-class organization.

In reality the idea of liberal adult education was a contested practice and other historians would retain an explicit focus on class. Certainly class conflict within and over forms of adult education is a recurring theme well analysed by both J. F. C. Harrison and Brian Simon.[13] For instance, there were considerable rifts with what became known as 'independent working-class education', which crystallized following the 1909 Ruskin College strike sparked by students who favoured the teaching of Marxist economics. This impulse would spurn the Plebs League, Central Labour College (CLC) and National Council of Labour Colleges (NCLC), organizations that were seen to favour education directly related to class struggle and social action. Activists made much of their independence from state funding and contrasted their work with that of the WEA, which was represented as both dependent and bourgeois.[14] These activities would flourish in the interwar years although after 1945 they lost their radical edge and eventually became incorporated into the increasingly conservative trade union movement. Again this tendency to portray a fall from grace, from an early radicalism to a gradual incorporation into established and conservative forms, has been a constant theme of writing about the working class and radical education. An alternative view would emphasize the strengths of incorporation and the potential to influence mainstream forms from within.[15]

---

[12] For the WEA see: Stocks, Mary. *The Workers' Educational Association: the First Fifty Years.* London: Allen & Unwin, 1953: Fieldhouse, Roger. *The Workers' Educational Association: Aims and Achievements, 1903–1977.* Syracuse, NY: Syracuse University, 1977; and Roberts, Stephen K. *A Ministry of Enthusiasm.* London: Pluto, 2003.

[13] Harrison, J. F. C. *Learning and Living.* London: Routledge, 1961. Simon, Brian. *Studies in the History of Education.* London: Lawrence & Wishart, 1960. *Education and the Labour Movement.* London: Lawrence & Wishart, 1965.

[14] For instance, Simon, Brian, editor. *The Search for Enlightenment.* Leicester: NIACE, 1990; Craik, W. W. *Central Labour College.* London: Lawrence & Wishart, 1964; and and Millar, J. P. M. *The Labour College Movement,* London: NCLC Publishing [1980]. See also Macintyre, Stuart. *A Proletarian Science.* Cambridge: Cambridge University Press, 1980.

[15] Compare McIlroy, John. "The demise of the National Council of Labour Colleges." In *The Search for Enlightenment,* edited by Brian Simon. London: Lawrence & Wishart, 1990 with Holford, John. *Union Education in Britain: A TUC Activity.* Nottingham: Department of Adult Continuing Education, 1994.

These conflicts were also indicative of historical work that mined this oppositional seam of working-class history. Having themselves been saturated in political and educational debates, historians would uncover and develop arguments around class in relation to social change. For example, E. P. Thompson, an adult education tutor, would go on to influence a generation of researchers intent on 'rescuing' alternative working-class traditions that were portrayed as indelibly engrained in British society.[16] Educational initiatives were part of wider movements capable of transformation in their own time; they were not portrayed as well-intentioned forerunners of a contemporary educational framework. This strand of historical writing would also emphasize a conception of past and present in which previous historical moments could be juxtaposed to the present in creative ways that also implied alternative futures were possible.

Despite the richness and quality of this work, the key distinction between radical and liberal education has a tendency to blur in today's climate where both of these approaches can be portrayed as anachronistic. Recent work has also argued that the division between the WEA and 'independent' forms of working-class adult education may have been overplayed; antagonisms regarding curriculum and subservience to the state also deflected issues of competing for similar students.[17] It has proved difficult to draw any direct correlation between education in the WEA and political alignment.[18] Similarly, it may also be true that those involved in independent working-class education received a more 'rounded' liberal education beyond the confines of the class struggle. For instance, novelists such as Lewis Jones and Harold Heslop were nurtured as students in the CLC and intellectuals such as A. J. P. Taylor and Harold Laski were both tutors at the NCLC.[19] Famously, G. D. H. Cole attempted to bridge both liberal and independent working-class education and R. H. Tawney, an icon of 'liberal education', was a complex character who was aware that social and political movements were primary factors in explaining educational change.[20] Thus there is a need to be aware of the fluidity between 'ways of struggle' and 'ways of life',[21] which, from a contemporary perspective, appear to overlap. Whilst one

---

[16] Thompson, E. P. *The Making of the English Working Class*. Harmondsworth: Penguin, 1968, orig. 1963.

[17] Brown, Geoff. "Independence and Incorporation: the Labour College Movement and the Workers' Educational Association before the Second World War." In *Adult Education for a Change*, edited by Jane L. Thompson. London: Hutchinson, 1980: 109–25.

[18] Rose, Jonathon. *The Intellectual Life of the British Working Classes*. New Haven, CT: Yale University Press, 2001.

[19] McIlroy, John. "Independent Working Class Education and Trade Union Education and Training". In *A History of Modern British Adult Education*, edited by Roger Fieldhouse. Leicester: NIACE, 1996: 264.

[20] Tawney, R. H. "Adult Education in the History of the Nation". Paper presented at the Fifth Annual Conference of the History of the British Institute of Adult Education, 1926, quoted in Keith Jackson. Preface to Thompson, *Adult Education...*, 14.

[21] See E. P. Thompson's review of Raymond Williams's early work, "The Long Revolution, Parts 1 & 2." *New Left Review*, 9–10 (1961): 24–33, and 34–39.

strategy may have made sense at one moment, it may have spilled over into another in a different context.

Furthermore, Cole and Tawney also reveal the complexity of middle-class responses to adult education. While working-class education has been represented as a quest for independence, experiences were often enriched by the encounter of middle- and working-class people across the class divide in which mutual learning took place. Middle-class supporters could show great sensitivity and understanding which, in turn, fostered greater independence.[22]

By analysing the work of particular working-class movements, familiar dichotomies have a tendency to break down, such as those between liberal and radical education, vocational and non-vocational, public and voluntary provision. As Roger Fieldhouse has noted, these dichotomies 'might more usefully have been treated as different but not opposite positions along the continuum of adult education'.[23] For instance, the educational work of the co-operative movement engaged with the state but was also at times fiercely independent.[24] The co-op linked practical training to general forms of education in ways that could challenge the division between vocational and non-vocational education. Indeed, co-operatives and other self-help organizations such as friendly societies were themselves built upon entrepreneurial understanding and skills.[25] The co-op was also a forum in which the activism and learning of women can be analysed, especially in the work of the Women's Co-operative Guild, although this has not always been framed in educational terms.[26] Despite the fact that the movement was at the forefront of many educational developments, it is surprising to find that there are no in-depth studies of co-operative education in the way there are for trade unions, the Labour Party and early socialists.[27]

Although the co-op was predominantly a working-class movement it also generated ambiguous class messages in comparison with other class-based movements. Indeed,

---

[22] Rowbotham, Sheila "Travellers in a strange country." In *Threads Through Time*, edited by S. Rowbotham. London: Penguin, 1999, 260–301. Goldman, Lawrence. *Dons and Workers*. Oxford: Clarendon, 1995 and "Intellectuals and the English working class, 1870–1945." *History of Education* 29, no. 4 (2000): 281–300.

[23] Fieldhouse, *History...*, 399.

[24] Some educational aspects of the movement can be found in Gurney, Peter. *Co-operative Culture and the Politics of Consumption in England 1870–1930*. Manchester: Manchester University Press, 1996, chs 2 and 3. Attfield, J. *With Light of Knowledge: a Hundred Years of Education in RACS, 1877–1977*. London: RACS/Journeyman, 1981. MacPherson, Ian, and Stephen Yeo. *Pioneers of Co-operation*. Manchester: Co-operative College, 2005.

[25] Woodin, Tom, "Exploring Themes in the History of Co-operative Education." Paper presented to Institute of Historical Research, London, March 2005.

[26] For instance, Scott, Gillian, *Feminism and the Politics of Working Women*. London: Taylor & Francis, 1998.

[27] Griggs, Clive. *The Trades Union Congress and the Struggle for Education 1868–1925*. Barcombe: Falmer, 1983. *The TUC and Educational Reform 1926–1970*. London: Woburn Press, 2002. Dennis Lawton. *Education and Labour Party Ideologies 1900–2001 and Beyond*. London: RoutledgeFalmer, 2004. Manton, Kevin. *Socialism and Education in Britain 1883–1902*. London: Woburn, 1999.

as the concept of class was stretched to encompass such an increasing variety of experiences, the ubiquitous nature of the concept would come under scrutiny. For instance, from the 1970s an increasing range of voices became uneasy that historical understandings of class had been too unitary and homogenous and implied overly-deterministic models of social change. Richard Johnson returned to similar material worked on by E. P. Thompson and found evidence of the 'really useful knowledge' that early nineteenth-century movements connected to their social emancipation in order to parody the notion of 'useful knowledge' favoured by elites. However, contrary to Thompson's argument, this was not seen as evidence for the formation of the working class, a claim which testified to a broader concern that social class should not simply be applied to an increasing diversity of historical situations.[28]

Furthermore, feminist historians problematized the fixed categories of the working class, which universalized the experiences of white male workers. The work of the Co-operative Women's Guild is also evidence of the fact that women's participation in adult education has been highly significant although rarely recognized and much harder to find.[29] Jane Martin has shown how the significant role of women like Mary Bridges Adams in educational debates has been written out of the historical record.[30] In addition, in the nineteenth century the growing formalization of education often led to the increasing marginalization of women in working-class communities where their influence is harder to detect[31] and less easily squared with versions of class based on a male breadwinner. It has also been argued that 'heroic' and 'romantic' accounts of the male working class are less applicable to women.[32] Despite significant studies that have focused on the development of the private and public and on contested forms of femininity,[33] working-class women's education remains an area with huge historical potential. Similarly the histories of immigrant and minority ethnic communities are waiting to be written in relation to a number of educational and cultural movements and campaigns in Britain as well as in its

---

[28] Johnson, Richard. "Really Useful Knowledge." In *Working Class Culture*, edited by J. Clarke et al. London: Hutchinson, 1979.

[29] For a recent example see Munby, Zoe. *Raising Our Voices: One Hundred Years of Women in the WEA*. Barton on Humber: WEA, 2003.

[30] Martin, Jane. "Contesting Knowledge: Mary Bridges Adams and the Workers' Education Movement, 1900–1918". In *Gender, Colonialism and Education*, edited by J. Goodman and J. Martin. London, Woburn Press, 2002: 124–47.

[31] Thompson, Dorothy. "Women and Nineteenth Century Radical Politics: A Lost Dimension." In *Outsiders. Class, Gender and Nation*. London: Verso, 1993. Also Vincent, *Literacy*...

[32] For instance, Scott, Joan Wallach. *Gender and the Politics of History*. New York: Columbia University Press, 1999. Swindells, Julia, and Lisa Jardine. *What's Left?* London: Routledge, 1989. Steedman, Carolyn. "The Price of Experience: Women and the Making of the English Working Class". *Radical History Review* 59 (1994): 108–19.

[33] For instance, Dyhouse, Carol. *Girls Growing up in Late Victorian and Edwardian England*. London: Routledge, 1981. Taylor, Barbara. *Eve and the New Jerusalem*. London: Virago, 1983. Purvis, June. *Hard Lessons*. Cambridge: Polity, 1989. *A History of Women's Education in England*. Milton Keynes: Open University Press, 1991. Martin, J., and J. Goodman. *Women and Education 1800–1980*. London: Palgrave, 2004.

former colonies.[34] In comparison with the weight of historical work, race and gender remain under-utilized concepts and it seems likely that accounts of working-class education in the future will be more marked by notions of masculinity and whiteness. For instance, gendered and racialized debates on whether working-class and colonial subjects were capable of being educated and 'civilized', so as to earn the right to participate politically, were at the heart of Victorian society and empire. Similar educational issues also informed debates on slavery and empire.[35]

Changing Perspectives

These challenges to class in historical study have been coterminous with the transformations alluded to at the beginning of this paper. 'Traditional' labour movements have declined and transformed themselves in the face of increasingly complex, fragmented and contradictory identities.[36] As a result the frameworks to study working-class education have altered considerably. In 1961 J. F. C. Harrison could draw a distinction between purposive adult education and the more diffuse education of adults in general.[37] However, in the current context where obituaries for the movement have proliferated in recent years, this division has begun to break down. Indeed, in the absence of a contemporary movement to provide meaning and direction to historical study, it has become more difficult to exclude the general arena of adult learning. While researching educational institutions has distinct advantages in terms of definition and clarity such studies can only be enriched by placing them alongside the diverse range of learning processes that may be taking place at any one time. This claim was staked out by Lawrence Cremin and remains an approach that may also help to resuscitate working-class education in new ways.

This trend has become increasingly significant in recent years and a broad interest in literacy has surfaced, a focus that considerably widens the study of working-class learning and education.[38] David Vincent's key introductory work to the historical

---

[34] For instance, Walmsley, Anne. *The Caribbean Artists Movement*. London: New Beacon Books, 1992. From a policy perspective, see Grosvenor, Ian. *Assimilating Identities. Racism and Educational Policy in Post 1945 Britain*. London: Lawrence & Wishart, 1997.

[35] For instance, Hall, Catherine. *White, Male and Middle Class*. Cambridge: Polity, 1992. Hall, C., K. McClelland, and J. Rendall. *Defining the Victorian Nation: Class, Race, Gender and the British Reform Act of 1867*. Cambridge: Cambridge University Press, 2000. On slavery in the Caribbean see Blouet, Olwyn Mary. "Slavery and Freedom in the British West Indies, 1823–33: The Role of Education." *History of Education Quarterly* 30, no. 4 (Winter 1990): 625–43.

[36] For different approaches see Rowbotham, S., L. Segal, and H. Wainwright. *Beyond the Fragments*. London: Merlin, 1980. Jacques, M., and Mulhern, F. *The Forward March of Labour Halted?* London: Verso, 1981.

[37] Harrison, *Learning…*, xiv.

[38] In part influenced by contemporary movements in adult literacy which pointed to the absence of such practices in the past. See Hamilton, Mary. "Literacy and Basic Education." In Fieldhouse, *History*. Hamilton, M., and Y. Hillier. *Changing Faces of Adult Literacy, Language and Numeracy: A Critical History*. Stoke-on-Trent: Trentham, 2006. Woodin, Tom. "'A Beginner Reader is not a Beginner Thinker'. Student Publishing Since the 1970s". *Pedagogica Historica* (forthcoming).

study of literacy, *Literacy and Popular Culture 1750–1914*, focused attention on the myriad uses and purposes to which reading and writing has been put: 'the often discrete categories of education, family, work, popular beliefs, the imagination and politics must be studied together...'.[39] Vincent also employs quantitative data to provide a longer term account of change giving due prominence to wider social forces in stimulating and directing literacy practices. For instance, he examined the role of the state in channelling the development of literacy through a universal postal system. His account attempts to capture the overall transformation from orality to literacy as well as some of the subjective nuances of such transitions.

The meanings and contradictions apparent within these wider accounts of change have also offered new perspectives on working-class education. Indeed, writing about adult education has suffered from too great a focus on national debates and structures rather than the experience of learning in a wider cultural context. One means of addressing this issue has been through an analysis of the written works of working-class people themselves. Although limited in number these significant autobiographies allow us to follow the trajectories of individual lives as they make sense of the world, albeit from a perspective later in life.[40] In addition, historians of reading have developed studies that construct accounts of the cultural experience of learning. Jonathon Rose's *Intellectual Life of the British Working Classes*, which aimed to provide 'a more representative portrait of the working class as a whole', examined how working-class people avidly read 'classic' literature not as a symbol of class oppression but for their own personal reasons. Rose's focus on the individual is driven by his desire to 'step outside' the collective modes traditionally occupied by labour historians. He warns of the 'ideology' implicit in 'Marxism, feminism, Christianity, Islam, liberalism, the traditional British class structure, or any other intellectual system...' and emphasizes the need to return to the reception and lived meanings of such collective forms.[41]

These accounts of literacy can be further enriched by a greater awareness of subjectivity and the cultural creation of working people. For example, the literature on working-class writing is still quite separate from that on education, reading and

---

[39] Vincent, David. *Literacy and Popular Culture: England 1750–1914*. Cambridge: Cambridge University Press, 1989, preface and 15.

[40] Burnett, John. *Useful Toil*. London: Allen Lane, 1974. Burnett, John, D. Vincent, and D. Mayall. *The Autobiography of the Working Classes*. 3 vols, 1790–1900, 1900–1945, Supplement 1790–1945. Brighton: Harvester, 1984, 1987, 1989. Vincent, David. *Bread, Knowledge and Freedom*. London: Europa, 1981; *Literacy and Popular Culture. England 1750–1914*. Cambridge: Cambridge University Press, 1989. Howard, Ursula. "Self-education and Writing in Nineteenth Century English Communities." In *Writing in the Community*, edited by D. Barton and R. Ivanic. London: Sage Publications, 1991, 78–108.

[41] Rose, *Intellectual Life*, 8. Rose built on earlier studies, notably Altick, Richard D. *The English Common Reader*. Chicago: University of Chicago Press, 1957. See also Webb, R. K. *The British Working Class Reader 1790–1848*. London: George Allen & Unwin, 1955. David Vincent asserts that this approach may involve a methodological arbitrariness; see Vincent, David. "The Progress of Literacy." *Victorian Studies* (Spring 2003), 405–31. For claims that Rose underestimated working-class sympathy for modernism see Christopher Hilliard. "Modernism and the Common Writer." *The Historical Journal* 48, no. 3 (2005): 769–97.

autobiography.[42] Writers are not just readers who tell us about their society, learning and cultural consumption; they also speak for themselves and are engaged in cultural creation. There is a dilemma between viewing working-class writing as a window into wider social experiences on the one hand and as an attempt to construct new meaning on the other. Despite the growing recognition of 'interior development' this remains an area with considerable potential.[43] Although poverty and immersion in a community made it difficult to plumb the depths of individual selfhood,[44] nevertheless we can at least identify subjective differences in working-class expression. For the nineteenth century Reginia Gagnier and Julia Swindells have explored some of the narrative strategies that writers adopted and, at times, were forced to adapt.[45] These approaches may have some common ground with sociological work, which has argued for an exploration of the ways in which working-class identities have been individualized.[46] Thus it may be possible to re-read the history of working-class educational institutions in terms of how they contributed to a sense of working-class subjectivity among participants.

By 'moving beyond' the labour movement in these various ways it is unsurprising that the agency of subordinate groups has been harder to detect in some of these accounts. In part this also arises from the nature and assumptions of such histories of social transformation. For instance, long-term objective accounts of change necessarily focus on dominant forces although, in doing so, they may also demote self-conscious workers and their movements to well-demarcated spaces outside which they have a limited impact. Conversely, the more detailed subjective accounts may underplay the relations between the individual and wider social structures and movements. Thus there is a possibility that the agency of working-class people seeps away between the cracks of these two approaches.

Commitment, Experience and Social Change

Previously many historians were bolstered by the existence of a working-class movement and its connections to adult education. It provided a context and an audience

---

[42] Examples include Ashraf, P. M. *Introduction to Working Class Literature in Great Britain*. Volumes 1 and 2. Berlin (GDR): Hauptabteilung Lehrerbildung des Ministeriums füVolksbildung, 1979. Maidment, Brian. *The Poorhouse Fugitives*. Manchester: Carcanet, 1987. Haywood, Ian. *Working Class Fiction from Chartism to Trainspotting*. Plymouth: British Council, 1997. Kirk, John. *Twentieth Century Writing and the British Working Class*. Cardiff: University of Wales Press, 2003. Neuberg, Victor E. *Popular Literature. A History and Guide*. Harmondsworth: Penguin, 1977.

[43] Ibid, 19. Vincent, *Bread, Knowledge and Freedom* and *Autobiography*.... Burnett, *Useful Toil*.

[44] Rowbotham, Sheila. "'Shush Mum's Writing'. Personal Narratives by Working Class Women in the Early Days of British Women's History". *Socialist History* 17, 2000: 1–21.

[45] Swindells, Julia *Victorian Writing and Working Women*. Cambridge: Polity, 1985. Gagnier, Regina *Subjectivities*. Oxford: Oxford University Press, 1991.

[46] Savage, Mike. *Class Analysis and Social Transformation*. Buckingham: Open University Press, 2000.

for historical work. However, as the institutional representations of these movements have weakened and changed it is a good time to reassess this body of work.

One limitation is the claim that the self-educated have always been a minority. Some identified a 'labour aristocracy' in the late Victorian period and others have suspected the self-educated working class may have been 'stupefiers' rather than enablers, of a wider cultural participation.[47] Indeed, building working-class forms of protest and self-help in the nineteenth century often necessitated skills and ways of working that conflicted with earlier forms of popular expression but were in tune with those favoured by the middle classes.[48] These claims need to be evaluated through an analysis of the roles this minority played and an awareness that similar activities may carry quite divergent meanings when refracted through the prism of social class. At different times those who were 'self-educated' may have been more numerous and actively engaged in wider communities than at other times; they might also have been quite a varied group in terms of their social composition and outlook. The focus on learning may also help to widen our lens beyond institutional and organizational boundaries.

Despite their often modest size, alternative educational cultures have been significant as sources of inventiveness and creativity—a sort of educational avant garde. For instance, the formation of cultural studies emerged, in part, from a growing ferment within adult education and an engagement between tutors and students.[49] Lawrence Goldman outlines the value of late nineteenth-/early twentieth-century Oxford not just for working-class students but also for the university, which was able to develop ideas for new courses from its extra-mural work whilst avoiding wider reforms. In fact working-class educational forms were one factor in the development of the post-1945 Labour Government—many MPs and even ministers could trace educational roots in the WEA and other initiatives of the labour movement. Thus, an issue that continually needs to be unravelled is how far alternative initiatives have served as seedbeds of mainstream activity and how far these new ideas have been only partially acted upon or transmogrified into practices that appear as alien to the original constituency.

Although there is a familiar pattern of innovative working-class initiatives gradually losing their radical edge as they become incorporated into existing forms, histories of working-class institutions remain valuable as examples of how significant organizations were constructed out of transient activities during a time of social dislocation. Such initiatives may survive for many years and persist even longer as memory. Whilst power and resources play a considerable role in the 'invention of tradition', for subordinate groups experience and memory tend to take on greater significance. This can prove difficult given that experience cannot simply be passed on but has to be re-learnt in new conditions. If we view tradition as an amalgamation of discontinuous moments that require continual remoulding rather than an unchanging and common

---

[47] Barrow, Logie *Independent Spirits. Spiritualism and the English Plebeians 1850–1910*. London: Routledge, 1986. Also Harrison, *Learning*, xiv.

[48] Vincent, *Literacy*, 20.

[49] Steele, Tom. *The Emergence of Cultural Studies: Adult Education, Cultural Politics and the English Question*. London: Lawrence & Wishart, 1997.

practice that is passed on directly through the generations, such experiences can be seen to inhabit overlapping universes out of which traditions are capable of being formed.[50] It may also be possible to identify continuing impulses to learn and express among subordinate groups.[51] For instance, in the 1970s the Federation of Worker Writers and Community Publishers would foster diverse forms of working-class expression through writing and publishing groups. With the advantage of hindsight, it is possible for us to connect the complaints of nineteenth-century editors of the working-class press about too much poetry being sent in with the contemporary profusion of popular poetry.[52] We should not write off working-class education as irrelevant from a modern perspective; it may yet connect with contemporary developments in unexpected ways.

Furthermore, many of these accounts have utilized the notion of experience as a building block for analysis although this dialogue with experience has become less popular in recent years. Critics of the concept have claimed that it essentializes subordinate cultures and falls into pitfalls of representation.[53] However, there is no umbilical cord attaching these tendencies to the notion of experience. It can be a way into understanding the contradictions and difficulties of people's lives and is an essential means of understanding those who live on the margins of society. It is more than just a starting point—rather, we must continually return to it and relate to it in constructing argument and theory. Empathy can also be a tool to aid the understanding of meaning and the dilemmas that historical actors faced. This may become more important as historical studies are widened to embrace gender, race, and other markers of inequality such as disability and sexuality. I would question the type of developmental subject histories found in cultural studies where experience is represented as an embarrassing childhood past now best forgotten.[54] Martin Jay has examined the historical lineage and continuing relevance of the concept with its capacity to carry complex meanings and stimulate ongoing debate.[55] As E. P. Thompson warned some years ago, jettisoning experience may make it easier to construct theories and arguments only to find that experience 'walks in without knocking at the door' to make us think again.[56] Thus, the experience and learning of subordinate groups remains an area from which new understandings of education and social change could still emerge.

---

[50] See Hobsbawm, E., and T. Ranger, eds. *The Invention of Tradition*. Cambridge: Cambridge University Press, 1983. Woodin, "'More Writing Than Welding': Learning in Worker Writer Groups", History of Education 34, no. 5 (2005): 561–578.

[51] For one example see Fryer, Bob. "The Challenge to Working Class Education". In Simon, *Search*, 276–319.

[52] On FWWCP see Woodin, Tom. "Building Culture"; "'More Writing ...'"; "'Chuck Out The Teacher': Radical Pedagogy in the Community." *International Journal of Lifelong Education* 26, no. 1 (2007): 89–104.

[53] Scott, Joan Wallach. "The Evidence of Experience." *Critical Inquiry* 17, no. 4 (Summer 1991): 773–97. *Gender and the Politics of History*, New York: Columbia University Press, 1988.

[54] Pickering, Michael. *History, Experience and Cultural Studies*. New York: St Martin's Press, 1997.

[55] Jay, Martin. *Songs of Experience*. Berkeley: University of California Press, 2005.

[56] Thompson, E. P. *Poverty of Theory and Other Essays*. London: Merlin Press, 1978, 201.

Clearly, accounts that take note of these factors will not lead back to a pristine golden age of working-class education but point in the direction of more complex and nuanced accounts of class. Although familiar themes and dilemmas may reappear in new guises, the context in which they operate will be fundamentally different than in the past. Class analysis can help to elucidate understanding but, when used to the exclusion of other categories, can also limit our vision. The universality attached to social class has been undermined but this need not preclude the use of class in educational histories. Having said this, class has always been a contested notion and it is not only academics who have recognized its specific, diverse and contingent forms in relation to other categories.[57] In part, the current stasis may be a reflection of the continuing re-constitution of class under capitalism. Our understanding of class has not kept up with the recent seismic shifts implicated in the processes of 'globalization' and, as a result, there may be a corresponding lull in intellectual activity focused on class. In the meantime our conceptual repertoire will continue to be considerably weakened by the absence of class until we learn to reinvigorate and adapt it to make sense of the past from new perspectives.

---

[57] Woodin, Tom. "Muddying the Waters: Class and Identity in a Working Class Cultural Organisation." *Sociology* 39, no. 5 (2005): 1001–18.

Social Change and Secondary Schooling for Girls in the 'Long 1920s':[1] European Engagements

Joyce Goodman

Robert Anderson argues that, as the nineteenth century progressed, the secondary school became a recognizably European institution as what was originally an ideal type or model turned into reality, though with significant differences of timing across European countries. The new secondary schools constituted an elite sector of education that rarely linked organically with popular schooling. Across Europe, secondary education was generally characterized by age-related classes and a teaching force that shared scholarly and scientific values and was certified by state examinations that reflected a university link. The secondary school curriculum was oriented to a school leaving examination that marked the transition to university.[2]

---

[1] The term the 'long 1920s' covers from 1918 to the early 1930s and denotes the difference from the later 1930s, as economic depression hit and intimations of war became stronger. Thanks to Tom Lawson for alerting me to the 'long 1920s'.

[2] This and the following paragraph draw on Anderson, Robert. "The Idea of the Secondary School in Nineteenth Century Europe." *Paedagogica Historica* 40, nos 1&2 (2004): 93–106.

Anderson highlights a number of factors central to the development of the 'idea' of the secondary school: conscious borrowing from foreign models as intellectuals and educational experts studied the systems of other countries; the development of 'modern' or scientific alternatives to classical education; 'age pyramids' and the sharpening of boundaries between the school and the university; cultural capital and the 'making' of elite groups, state and nation; segmentation and social mobility. While arguing that the model of the new secondary school established around 1802 became a standardized one, Anderson relates its adoption at different times in different countries to social and political factors, including state formation and nationalism, and notes that in Europe countries networks of secondary schools often formed part of state structures but were made manifest through different patterns. Pat Thane demonstrates for England that the 'state system' was built upon close cooperation between voluntary and local government apparatus and a central-state administration.[3] Under the English 'state-system' the secondary sector was composed of public, private and municipal secondary schools.[4]

Rebecca Rogers illustrates that the idea of the secondary school was a gendered phenomenon. Like Anderson, she points to the importance of industrialization and urbanization in the emergence of an integrated educational system within European countries. She also highlights aspects of the 'grammar' of schooling pointed up by Anderson. Rogers argues that because these educational changes happened at the same time that middle-class women gained access to higher education they challenged ideas that women's minds and bodies made them unfit for certain positions and responsibilities in the working world. Despite these increasing opportunities, however, scientific developments and sexist and racist ideologies combined at certain historical moments and within specific countries to produce discourses on women's place in society that harked back to earlier periods and impacted on girls' schooling and learning possibilities. Rogers points to a dialectic between education as a conservative force and a force for change as learning assigned women to certain roles, particularly within the family or as mothers and wives, but also as a means that opened doors for them to acquire new roles and responsibilities within the public sphere by giving them access to degrees and qualifications. Furthermore, while lessons about what it meant to be a 'good' girl, wife, mother and worker were transmitted within Europe and beyond to empire, education for domesticity was situated within a cultural nexus that highlighted new and more powerful roles for women and mothers

---

[3] Thane, Pat. "Women in the British Labour Party and the Construction of State Welfare, 1906–1939." In *Mothers of a New World: Maternalist Politics and the Origins of the Welfare States*, edited by Seth Koven and Sonya Michel. New York Routledge, 1993: 343–377.

[4] The term 'public' school originally included the nine 'Clarendon' schools. By 1900 'public' schools included schools whose heads were members of the Headmasters' Conference. These became known as 'independent' or 'private' schools, where fees were paid by parents and guardians, in contrast to 'maintained' schools supported from rates and taxes. Aldrich, Richard. "Introduction." In *Public or Private Education? Lessons from History*, edited by idem. London: Woburn Press, 2004: 5.

within British protestant evangelicalism, in the German movement around Froebel and in French Catholicism.[5]

Rogers argues that while a combination of factors interacted to bring girls from all social backgrounds into classrooms throughout Europe, change in girls' education always carried a political dimension. The political dimension came to be voiced more openly with the development of the feminist movement after the 1850s and was evident in the European effort to export models of female schooling to the colonies. By the second half of the nineteenth century, the reform movement for girls' education testified to a small but growing international feminist movement that shared information on other school systems and enabled feminists and educational reformers to challenge national stereotypes regarding women's more fragile minds or constitutions through examples of countries where adolescent girls studied 'masculine' subjects with no apparent harm. The result was that, by the second half of the century, most Western European countries had begun to develop networks of girls' schools whose relationship to a system of boys' education was increasingly under debate.

In her historiographical overview of education for girls in Europe, Rogers notes that the history of girls' education in Europe from 1700 to the present is relatively under-studied, despite the centrality of education in forging gender roles. The only monograph to take girls' education in Europe as its focus remains Phyllis Stock's *Better than Rubies*, published in 1978.[6] Although a considerable literature on girls' secondary education in England was published from the 1980s onwards,[7] only a small but significant body of scholarship locates secondary education for English girls within the wider context of debate and development of girls' education in Europe. Publications on French and English girls' schools by Rogers and by Christina de Bellaigue, and Rogers's work on English girls in French schools, provide an important comparative backdrop to the development of girls' schooling and the professionalization of

---

[5] This paragraph and the next draws heavily on Rogers, Rebecca. "Learning to be Good Girls and Women: Education, Training and Schools." In *The Routledge History of Women in Europe Since 1700*, edited by Debbie Simonton. London: Routledge, 2006: 94.

[6] Stocks, Phyllis. *Better Than Rubies: A History of Women's Education.* New York: G. P. Putnam's Sons, 1978. A recent edited collection on girlhood is: Maynes, Mary Jo, Birgitte Soland, and Christina Benninghaus. *Secret Gardens. Satanic Mills. Placing Girls in European History, 1750–1960.* Bloomington: Indiana University Press, 2005.

[7] Bryant, Margaret. *The Unexpected Revolution: A Study in the History of the Education of Women and Girls in the Nineteenth Century.* London: University of London Institute of Education, 1979; Burstyn, Joan. *Victorian Education and the Ideal of Womanhood.* London: Croom Helm, 1980; Fletcher, Sheila. *Feminists and Bureaucrats: A Study in the Development of Girls' Education in the Nineteenth Century.* Cambridge: Cambridge University Press, 1980; Dyhouse, Carol. *Girls Growing Up in Late Victorian and Edwardian Britain.* London: Routledge, 1981; Gorham, Deborah. *The Victorian Girl and the Feminine Ideal.* London: Croom Helm, 1982; Hunt, Felicity. *Lessons for Life: The Schooling of Girls and Women, 1850–1950.* London: Blackwell, 1987; Hunt, Felicity. *Gender and Policy in English Education.* Hemel Hempstead: Harverster Wheatsheaf, 1991; Purvis, June. *A History of Women's Education in England.* Buckingham: Open University Press, 1991; Tamboukou, Maria. *Women, Education and the Self: A Foucauldian Perspective.* Basingstoke: Palgrave Macmillan, 2003.

teaching for women that pushes back the chronology of change in girls' education prior to the rise of the reform movements in 1850s England.[8] Recent work focuses on British women as educator activists working increasingly in a European context. Researchers are beginning to look at how issues of feminism and internationalism played out in ideals of citizenship in English girls' schools and in discussion with schoolgirls around European disarmament and peace. A small body of scholarship discusses women educationists' involvement with the Spanish Civil War and with Belgian refugee women and children in England.[9] The most sustained analysis of girls' secondary education in Europe is James Albisetti's broad sweep of European sources on girls' secondary education, which locates secondary education for English girls in both a European and a transatlantic perspective.[10]

The following section examines the internationalization of women's and teachers' organizations, which provided a context for leading English women educators to test and discuss their ideas of the girls' secondary school within European transnational networks.

---

[8] De Bellaigue, Christina. "Behind the School Walls: The School Community in French and English Boarding Schools for Girls, 1810–1867." *Paedagogica Historica* 40, nos 1&2 (2004): 107–22; Idem. "'Educational Homes' and 'Barrack-like Schools': Cross-Channel Perspectives on Secondary Education in Mid-Nineteenth-Century England and France." In *Educational Policy Borrowing: Historical Perspectives*, edited by David Phillips and Kimberly Ochs. Didcot: Symposium Books, 2004; Rogers, Rebecca. "French Education for British Girls in the Nineteenth Century." *Women's History Magazine* 42 (2002): 21–29; Idem. "Boarding Schools, Women Teachers and Domesticity: Reforming Girls' Secondary Education in the First Half of the Nineteenth Century." *French Historical Studies* 29 (1995): 153–81.

[9] Watkins, Christopher. "Inventing International Citizenship: Badminton School and the Progressive Tradition between the Wars." *History of Education* 36, no. 3 (2007): 315–338; Goodman, Joyce. "Working for Change Across International Borders: The Association of Headmistresses and Education for International Citizenship." *Paedagogica Historica* 43, no. 1 (2007): 165–80; Roberts, Sian. "'In the Margins of Chaos': Francesca Wilson and Education for All in the 'Teachers' Republic'." *History of Education* 25, no. 6 (2006): 653–68; Myers, Kevin. "The Hidden History of Refugee Schooling in Britain: the Case of the Belgians 1914–18." *History of Education* 30, no. 2 (2001): 153–162; Storr, Katherine. "Belgian Children's Education in Britain in the Great War: Language, Identity and Race Relations." *History of Education Researcher* 72 (2003): 84–93.

[10] Albisetti, James. "Unlearned Lessons From the New World? English Views of American Coeducation and Women's Colleges, c.1865–1910." *History of Education* 29, no. 5 (2000): 13–34; Idem. "The French Lycés de Jeunes Filles in International Perspective, 1878–1910." In *Educational Policy Borrowing: Historical Perspectives*, edited by David Phillips and Kimberly Ochs. Didcot: Symposium Books, 2004; Idem. "European Perceptions of American Coeducation, 1865–1914: Ethnicity, Religion and Culture." *Paedagogica Historica* 37, no. 1 (2001): 123–38; Idem. "The Feminization of Teaching in the Nineteenth Century: a Comparative Perspective." *History of Education* 22, no. 3 (1993): 265–75; See also Essen, M. van. "Strategies of Women Teachers 1860–1920: Feminization in Dutch Elementary and Secondary Schools from a Comparative Perspective." *History of Education* 28, no. 4 (1999): 49–62; van Drenth, Annemieke and Mineke van Essen. "'Shoulders Squared Ready for Battle with Forces that Sought to Overwhelm': West-European and American Women Pioneers in the Educational Sciences, 1800–1910." *Paedagogica Historica* 39, no. 3 (2993): 263–84.

The 'Long 1920s' and Internationalization

In the aftermath of the First World War, the changing position of women in England was an issue of debate. A perceived blurring of gender lines occasioned by the war's upheaval, heightened by the partial enfranchisement of women in 1918, led many to seek the re-establishment of sexual difference as a way to re-create a semblance of order. There was a framing of 'new feminist' demands shaped around a conviction that sexual difference characterized the 'natural' relationship between men and women, rather than the strictly egalitarian position of 'old feminist' demands.[11] Yet, as Seth Koven and Sonya Michel argue, only some of women's various social movements were feminist. Furthermore, while women's social movements changed women's relationship to each other, to men, to the state and to society, women did not necessarily possess the political power to refashion the state according to their own vision.[12] There were shifts away from the earlier 'dual aims' of a liberal education oriented to fitting girls for life at home or work without compromising their femininity, to the 'divided aims' of a gender-differentiated curriculum.[13] The result, as Penny Summerfield demonstrates, was a re-working of class and gender that played out in girls' secondary education in England in complex ways.[14]

Growing world economic interdependence and the threat to peace posed by the nationalist politics of the imperialist European powers engendered a desire for international cooperation and global understanding during the interwar years that Eckhardt Fuchs argues resulted in internationalism becoming one of the key words in the international intellectual and political debates in Europe and beyond.[15] The pursuit of world peace in the aftermath of the First World War led to an increase in international organization on the part of women. Karen Offen and Leila Rupp illustrate how the internationalism that characterized many women's organizations was strongly oriented towards the maintenance of peace and disarmament and worked to promote the engagement of women with the League of Nations.[16] The Association of Headmistresses (AHM) and the Association of Assistant Mistresses (AAM), both of which included members working in the secondary sector, linked to the International Women's Suffrage Alliance, the International Council of Women, the Women's International League for Peace and Freedom and the International Federation of University Women (IFUW). Teachers' organizations and educational organizations

---

[11] Kent, Susan Kingsley. *Making Peace: The Reconstruction of Gender in Interwar Britain*. Princeton, NJ: Princeton University Press, 1993: 99–100, 117.

[12] Koven and Michel, "Introduction", 203.

[13] Hunt, Felicity. "Divided Aims: The Educational Implications of Opposing Ideologies in Girls' Secondary Schooling, 1850–1940." In Hunt, *Lessons for Life*, 20.

[14] Summerfield, Penny. "Cultural Reproduction in the Education of Girls: A Study of Girls' Secondary Schooling in Two Lancashire Towns, 1900–50." In Hunt, *Lessons for Life*, 149–70.

[15] Fuchs, Eckhardt. "Educational Sciences, Morality and Politics: International Educational Congresses in the Early Twentieth Century." *Paedagogica Historica* 40, nos 5&6 (2004): 757–58.

[16] Offen, Karen. *European Feminisms 1700–1950*. Stanford, CA: Stanford University Press, 2000: 346–50; Rupp, Leila. *Worlds of Women: The Making of an International Women's Movement*. Princeton: Princeton University Press, 1997: ch. 7.

also looked towards international organization. Both the AHM and the AAM were networked through the international committee of the Joint Committee of the Four Secondary Associations (the Joint Four), and the Bureau international des Fédérations nationales du personnel de l'Enseignement secondaire public (BIFSP). [17]

The IFUW, established in 1919,[18] placed education as central to the development of the international understanding it regarded as necessary for world peace. The objects of the IFUW included cooperation with national bureaux of education, the promotion of understanding between university women of different countries and the exchange of lecturers and scholars from different universities.[19] Caroline Spurgeon, IFUW president and Professor of English Literature at the University of London, told delegates attending the first IFUW conference in London in 1920 that the IFUW wanted to help the development of education in two ways. First, 'as regards definite and special problems of education—questions where we may learn from each other's experience, and by exchange of opinions; or by discussing and resolving on certain action in education which may be applied internationally'. A central element of her vision was the exchange of university students and teachers, which was to assist the IFUW's second object: 'the internationalism of learning, the pooling of knowledge, so as to extend it and stimulate and enrich it'.[20] Virginia Gildersleeve, Dean of Barnard College, Columbia University, New York, and IFUW vice-president, stressed that the IFUW was keen not to overlap the work being done by governments or by official bureaux of education in various countries. In view of the socioeconomic and politically disadvantaged position of women, the IFUW wished to give women a chance to participate on more equal terms.[21]

Spurgeon's approach to change in the IFUW was communicative,[22] based on her wish to 'weav[e] together individual strands of friendship to form indestructible bonds ... to bind people together the world over'.[23] This communicative approach was linked with an 'international' frame of change based on a system of discrete and sovereign nation-states that recognized national points of difference. The IFUW congresses, held in cities across Europe, worked to construct an international community of university-educated women. Rupp argues that conflict and community within the international women's organizations were part of the same process by

---

[17] Goodman, "Working for Change Across International Borders."

[18] IFUW. Report of the First Conference July 1920, 3, 10. Delegates at the first conference in London were from America, France, Italy, Spain, Belgium, Holland, Denmark, Norway, Sweden, Czecho-Slovakia, India, Canada, Australia, South Africa.

[19] IFUW. Report of the First Conference, 1920, 3. IFUW and BFWG reports were consulted at the Sybil Campbell Collection, University of Winchester.

[20] "Address by Professor Caroline Spurgeon." IFUW. Report of the First Conference, 1920, 14.

[21] "Address by Dean Virginia Gildersleeve." IFUW Report of the First Conference, 1920, 19.

[22] For congresses and communicative approaches to social change see Van Gorp, Angelo, Marc Depaepe, and Frank Simon. "Backing the Actor as Agent in Discipline Formation: An Example of the "Secondary Disciplinarization" of the Educational Sciences, Based on the Networks of Ovide Decroly (1901–1931)." *Paedagogica Historica* 40, nos 5&6 (2004): 591–616.

[23] "Address by Professor Caroline Spurgeon", 11.

which women came together across national borders to create a sense of belonging around broadly defined goals of equality and international understanding.[24] In noting that IFUW women spoke a 'common language' and that they shared understandings, traditions and ideals as a result of higher education,[25] Spurgeon highlighted the Bourdieusian distinctions through which like-minded individuals recognized each other and class, professional and elite status was constituted. Gildersleeve stressed that while the IFUW women were organizing separately from university men, they did not wish anyone to believe that they were 'separatists and ultra feminists'. Neither did they wish to force the ideas of the women of the English-speaking peoples on other countries. She told delegates that both Britain and America had much to learn from the women of other nations of the world.[26] But as Rupp notes, the degree to which key women's organizations embraced internationalism was tempered by their leadership, with influential positions remaining in the hands of a small circle from a limited number of countries.[27] In its early days British and American women, and then women from Western Europe, largely dominated the leadership of the IFUW.

Education was seen as a key instrument of international solidarity and intellectual cooperation by many organizations during the 'long 1920s'. An unprecedented explosion of activity in education was the result.[28] Fuchs charts a range of international teachers' unions and professional associations that were established and met in congress. The BIFSP, founded in Paris in 1912, aimed to form bonds of international friendship and solidarity between members of the BIFSP; to contribute to the progress of secondary education; to improve the material and intellectual conditions of staff; to cooperate in the international intellectual movement in conformity with the principles of the League of Nations, of the League of Red Cross Societies and of the World Federation of Education Societies; and to facilitate exchange of pupils, students and teachers, holiday tours and courses.[29]

Fuchs points to ways in which the internationalization of national teachers' associations was founded on material interests rather than the professional development of the teachers. While teachers' international associations aimed to foster teaching for international goodwill, concerted action on the part of international organizations representing teachers in state schools remained problematic, partly because change was impossible without the agreement of national governments, and linked to this

---

[24] Rupp, *Worlds of Women*, 6, 69.

[25] "Address by Caroline Spurgeon", 10.

[26] "Address by Dean Virginia Gildersleeve", 19.

[27] Rupp, *Worlds of Women*, 6, 69.

[28] Hofstetter, Rita, and Bernard Schneuwly. "Introduction. Progressive Education and Educational Sciences. The Tumultuous Relations of an Indissociable and Irreconcilable Couple? (Late 19th–Mid 20th Century)." In *Passion, Fusion, Tension. New Education and Educational Sciences*, edited by Rita Hofstetter and Bernard Schneuwly. Bern: Peter Lang, 2006: 12.

[29] By 1931, federated national federations of secondary school teachers included Belgium, Bulgaria, Czechoslovakia, France, Great Britain, Latvia, Luxembourg, Netherlands, Poland, Portugal, Romania, Kingdom of the Serbs, Croats and Slovenes and Spain. The League of Nations. *Supplement to Handbook on International Organisations*. Geneva: League of Nations, 1931: 87.

because internationalism and internationalization constituted historical phenomena bound to the development of modern nation-states. Fuchs argues that the degree of internationalism achieved by teachers' organizations was further tempered because internationalism was a Western enterprise embedded in a social-political context that differentiated between a 'civilized Europe' and a 'barbaric rest', in which European ideals of education were viewed as universally valid methods of teaching'.[30]

The following sections explore how investigation and discussion in Europe of English girls' secondary schooling circulated via the IFUW and the BIFSP. It did so in relation to political, professional and educational fields that were structured both by shared aspects *and* by qualitatively different dynamics. Analysis is placed within a transnational frame that focuses on 'networks of influence and understandings that transcend national boundaries and recognise the interdependence of people'.[31] From a transnational perspective, attention is given to the 'broader field of interactions between peoples and movements'[32] and 'ways in which the traditional borders of education are ... transversed by new developments which cross geographical or conceptual borders'.[33] At the same time, the transnational is seen to shape the national.[34] Transnationalism, transnational practices and transnationalities ('the meanings and practices that produce linked and specific cultural formations in late capitalism') are always situated and historical.[35]

Edward Said indicates that as ideas and practices circulate across national borders they are transformed in transit, for entry into a new space involves processes of representation and institutionalization that 'complicates the transplantation, transference, circulation and commerce of theories and ideas',[36] in the process complicating centre–periphery notions of change.[37] Readings of educational ideas and practices in

---

[30] Fuchs, "Educational Sciences, Morality and Politics", 766–69, 757–58.

[31] Curthoys, A. "Does Australian History have a Future?" *Australian Historical Studies* 118 (2002): 140–52; Lake, A. "'White Man's Country: The Transnational History of a National Project." *Australian Historical Studies* 122 (2003): 346–63. Both quoted in Whitehead, K. "'The Insufficiency of the Low Grade Teacher': A Transnational Matter." Paper presented at the American Educational Research Association, Montreal, 2005. Trethewey, L., and K. Whitehead. "Beyond Centre and Periphery: Transationalism in Two Teacher/Suffragettes' Work." *History of Education* 32, no. 5 (2002): 547–60.

[32] Mayall, L. A., E. Nym, P. Levine, and E. C. Fletcher. "Introduction." In *Women's Suffrage in the British Empire: Citizenship, Nation and Race*, edited by L. A. Mayall et al. London: Routledge, 2000: xviii.

[33] Lawn, M. "Borderless Education: Imagining a European Education Space in a Time of Brands and Networks." In *Fabricating Europe*, edited by Antonio Novoa and Martin Lawn. Dordrecht: Kluwer 2002: 20.

[34] Lawn, Martin. "Reflecting the Passion: Mid-century Projects for Education." *History of Education* 33, no. 5 (2004): 512.

[35] Grewal, I., A. Gupta, and A. Ong. "Introduction: Asian Transationalities." *Positions* 7, no. 3 (2000): 653.

[36] Said, Edward. "Travelling Theory." In *The World, the Text and the Critic*. London: Vintage, 1991: 226.

[37] McCulloch, Gary, and Roy Lowe. "Introduction: Centre and Periphery—Networks, Space and Geography in the History of Education." *History of Education* 32, no. 5 (2003): 457–459.

transit are located in membership of communities sharing foundational assumptions and interpretive strategies[38] that play out in what Bourdieu terms *fields*. A *field* for Bourdieu is a 'structured system of social positions held by people and institutions ... structured internally as a set of power relations'.[39] Bourdieu links *field* to *habitus*, 'a system of dispositions in which agents engage in certain behaviours in ....social spaces'.[40] Various forms of *capital* (social, cultural and economic) provide the currency of exchange in the *field* to enable actors to position and re-position themselves. As the following section illustrates, women's ability to debate secondary schooling for English girls in the context of Europe was circumscribed by the location of particular women's and professional organizations within wider political, professional and educational fields

The International Federation of University Women and Girls' Secondary Schooling

The IFUW Christiania conference in 1924 demonstrated the interest of national federations in secondary schooling for girls. The AHM delegate to the Christiania conference was Reta Oldham, headmistress of Streatham Hill High School, a Girls' Public Day School Trust school within the elite fee-paying secondary day school sector that served a minority of girls at this period.[41] Oldham had a longstanding interest in women's occupational mobility. From 1910 she convened the Association of Headmistresses (AHM) Committee To Enquire into Openings for Educated Girls and Women in the Colonies,[42] linking this committee with the Central Bureau for the Employment of Women and through the Central Bureau with the Students' Careers Association. She was involved in the organization of women's emigration as an executive member in the Colonial Intelligence League for Educated Women.[43] She gave evidence to the Royal Commission on the Civil Service on behalf of the AHM. At the close of her AHM Presidency (1917–1919) she became increasingly involved with European educational issues, via an AHM committee to provide teachers for Romania and Italy.[44] In 1920 she joined the British Federation of University Women (BFUW), was co-opted to the executive in 1923 to establish closer relations with the AHM, and from 1924 she chaired the BFUW's Joint Committee on Interchange of

---

[38] Livingstone, David. N. "Science, Text and Space: Thoughts on the Geography of Reading." *Transactions of the Institute of British Geographers* 30 (2005): 395.

[39] Gunter, Helen. *More Leadership?* Inaugural Lecture, University of Manchester, March 2005: 33.

[40] Ibid.

[41] The GPDST did strive to cross class barriers but their schools reached only a minority of pupils.

[42] AHM Executive Minutes, 12 November 1910. AHM records were consulted at the Modern Records Centre, University of Warwick.

[43] Goodman, Joyce. "'Their Market Value Must be Greater for the Experience they had Gained'. Secondary School Headmistresses and Empire, 1897–1914." In *Gender, Colonialism and Education: The Political Experience of Education*, edited by Joyce Goodman and Jane Martin. London: Woburn, 2002: 182–83.

[44] AHM Executive Committee Report, 10 June 1912; 10 May 1919.

Secondary School Teachers.[45] When the BFUW approached the AHM to appoint representatives to the IFUW conference to be held in Christiania, the AHM appointed Oldham.

Delegates at the Christiania conference discussed a range of issues pertaining to secondary education for girls. These included secondary school teacher exchange, the development of girls' schooling in various countries[46] and papers on girls' secondary schooling.[47] In response to a resolution by the Austrian Verband der Akademischen Fräen Oesterreichs (Federation of University Women) a committee was appointed for The Interchange of Information on the Secondary School Curriculum and Organisation.[48] By the 1925 IFUW Council Meeting in Brussels, this committee had received 20 replies from national organizations (including the BFUW) to a detailed questionnaire asking about national systems of secondary schooling for girls, the position of women teachers and the extent of the curriculum.

Summarizing the responses to the questionnaire and additional material on examinations and curricula that had been submitted, the Committee's first convenor, Dr Germaine Hannevart (Belgian Federation of University Women), told the IFUW Council meeting in Brussels in 1925 that the replies demonstrated the different meanings of secondary education held by different countries.[49] Responses showed that in most countries women could teach in girls' schools and in coeducational schools, where they existed, but in very few countries were women appointed to school boards or the inspectorate, except for subjects taught chiefly or exclusively to girls. In some countries (Italy and Switzerland) men headed girls' schools. Dr Hannevart noted that the number of schools for girls had increased simultaneously with the spread of women's emancipation and this increase, in its turn, strengthened the women's movement. She suggested that the IFUW should recommend to the administrative authorities in all countries the appointment of women as principals of girls' schools, inspectors and members of secondary school boards. She also thought that the responses demonstrated that timetables were too full, and school subjects and homework were increasing, leaving pupils worn out and bereft of initiative and critical reasoning. Part of the remedy, she thought, lay with teacher

---

[45] BFUW, Annual Report 1921–22; 1922–23, 6; 1925–26, 17.

[46] IFUW Report of the Third Conference, 1924. See University Women of Other Countries. "China", 42; Reports of National Federations, including "British Federation", 43, "Czecho-Slovakian Federation", 46, "New Zealand Federation", 55.

[47] IFUW Report of the Third Conference, 1924. Hannevart, Dr. G. "School Preparation for the Universities", 82; Jenkins, Mary. "The Interchange of Teachers", 84; Larsen-Jahn, Martha. "The International Mind in School", 88. Papers on girls' secondary education continued to be included at IFUW conferences. See, for example, Graftdyk, Dr I. M. "Higher and Secondary Education." IFUW Report of the Fourth Conference—Amsterdam 1926, 41.

[48] IFUW Report of the Third Conference, 1924, 96.

[49] Replies were received from Australia, Austria, Belgium, Bulgaria, Canada, Czecho-Slovakia, Denmark, Finland, France, Great Britain, Holland, India, Ireland, Italy, New Zealand, Norway, Sweden, Switzerland, United States. IFUW. "Report of the Council Meeting Brussels, July 1925", 43.

training, which should include temporary work either in the home country or abroad.[50] Her conclusions led to two strategies of change. The first, located within the IFUW's 'international' frame of change that recognized national points of difference within a system of discrete and sovereign nation-states, was a comparative investigation of girls' schooling across Europe, organized via the committee that she convened.

The 1926 Amsterdam IFUW conference agreed to appoint a researcher to collect, analyse, collate and centralize information on girls' secondary schooling in various countries. She was to be competent to deal with educational questions, know French, English, German and Italian, Spanish or a Slav language and be in a position to devote two years to the task. The Hungarian Ministry of Education granted a two-year paid sabbatical to Amﬁe Arato from Budapest, the IFUW paid her travel expenses and national societies provided hospitality during her visits to 200 schools in 25 European countries.[51] In her comparative survey, Arato investigated types of secondary schools and their divisions and whether girls' education was conducted in single-sex or coeducational settings; intellectual education, hours of schooling, curricula, examinations and organization of lessons; physical education; health and hygiene; preparation for future roles; teacher training; women teachers; women head teachers; women inspectors; associations for former pupils; parents; and the contemporary position of women. While collecting her data from girls' secondary schools in England Arato spent a period in residence at Crosby Hall (the BFUW's women's international hall of residence and headquarters).[52] The results of her survey were reported via the BFUW Committee on International Relations and were available in

---

[50] "Report of Committee on Exchange of Information Regarding Secondary Education." IF-UW, Report of the Fourth Conference, 1926, 54. This was formalized at the 1927 IFUW Council Meeting in Vienna. IFUW. Report 1927, 60. Discussion of school girls and overwork at the 1932 conference was led by Studiendirektorin Anna Schöborn, Vice President of the German Federation of University Women and Principal of the Uhland-Oberlyzem, Berlin. Schöborn, Anna. "Is the Schoolgirl in Secondary Schools Overworked?" IFUW Sixth Conference, Edinburgh, 1932, 41. For Hannevart's conclusions, see "Committee on Secondary Education." IFUW Report of Council Meeting in Brussels, 1925, 43 and "Report of Committee on Exchange of Information Regarding Secondary Education." IFUW. Report of the Fourth Conference, 1926, 53.

[51] "Report of Committee on Exchange of Information regarding Secondary Education." IFUW. Report of the Fourth Conference, 1926, 53; "Standing Committee for Exchange of Information Regarding Secondary Education." IFUW. Report of Council Meeting in Vienna, 1927, 20. "Report of the Committee for Exchange of Information Regarding Secondary Education." Sixth Conference, 133. She visited England, Germany, Austria, Belgium, Bulgaria, Denmark, Estonia, Finland, France, Greece, Holland, Hungary, Ireland, Italy, Latvia, Lithuania, Luxemburg, Norway, Poland, Romania, Russia, Sweden, Switzerland, Czechoslovakia and Yugoslavia.

[52] She visited Grey Coat School, Honor Oak School, Aspen House Open Air School, George Green School, St Paul's Girls' School, Convent of Our Lady of Sion in London, Roedean, Girls' Public Day School Trust Schools in London, Francis Holland Church of England School, plus the London Day Training College and Furzedown Training College

England to BFUW members at Crosby Hall,[53] where a library was established in 1927 for international women students.[54]

Teacher exchange, the second strategy adopted at Christiania, was based on the IFUW communicative approach to social change. It was overseen by a Committee on the Interchange of Secondary School Teachers convened by Reta Oldham.[55] Oldham demonstrates Bourdieu's contention that to enter a field to play the game it is necessary to possess both the habitus that predisposes entry to the field and the minimum amount of knowledge, or skill or 'talent to be accepted as a legitimate player'. In place' at Christiania as the AHM delegate, Oldham's symbolic capital was recognized in her appointment as convenor of this IFUW committee.[56]

Oldham was convinced of the influence of teachers on the thought and character of their nation and the value to pupils of the insight into the life and history and aspirations of other peoples gleaned by teachers during a period of work overseas.[57] She considered the selection of 'suitable' teachers the key to successful exchange and recommended to the 1925 IFUW Council meeting in Brussels that teachers sent abroad should be university graduates, well qualified to represent their countries, be extremely good teachers, should remain longer than one year, should have a sufficient knowledge of the language of the country visited and should, as a rule, teach only their own language, or subjects such as gymnastics or handicrafts.[58]

Oldham's reports to the IFUW in 1926 and 1927 picked up on a number of practical difficulties that exchange engendered, including finance and exchanges with 'small' countries. But the steadily increasing list of interchanges facilitated by the BFUW, and reports coming from the Board of Education's Department for Special Inquiries, demonstrate that an (albeit limited) mobility for teachers in girls' secondary schools in England was fostered in the period. Significant for teachers in England were changes to the Teachers' Superannuation Act permitting absence for a limited time without loss of pension.[59] In 1927 Oldham indicated that the Board of Education had extended the arrangements already operating with the British Dominions to the wider interchange of teachers and that a number of local education authorities, including the London County Council, had agreed to employ teachers selected under approved systems of interchange.

---

[53] BFUW. Annual Report 1929–30, 52; 1933–34, 29.

[54] The Library was named the Sybil Campbell Library in 1965 in remembrance of Sybil Campbell, first woman stipendiary magistrate in Britain and secretary of the BFUW 1921–33.

[55] IFUW, Report of the Third Conference, 1924, 87; AHM, Executive 10 May 1924; 12 July 1924; 11 October 1924.

[56] Johnson, Richard. "Pierre Bourdieu on Art, Literature and Culture." Editor's introduction in Bourdieu, Pierre. *The Field of Cultural Production.* Cambridge, Polity Press, 1993, quoted in Gunter, *More Leadership?*, 34.

[57] "Interchange of Secondary School Teachers." IFUW, Report of the Fourth Conference, 1926, 55–56.

[58] "Committee on Secondary Education." IFUW Report of Council Meeting in Brussels, 1925, 44.

[59] "Interchange of Secondary School Teachers." IFUW, Report of the Fourth Conference, 1926, 55–56.

In congratulating Oldham on her success, Dr Winifred Cullis, Professor at the London School of Medicine for Women, pointed to the importance of the changing political situation for women. She stressed the fact that the Board of Education 'now had a woman, the Duchess of Atholl, as Parliamentary Secretary and that her influence, as well as that of Miss Fawcett on the London County Council' had probably assisted 'the admirable and persevering work which Miss Oldham had performed in putting the case for interchange to these bodies'.[60] While Cullis viewed this from a feminist standpoint, other factors were also at play. Widening teacher exchange formed one of the agendas of the Board of Education's Office of Special Inquiries[61] and the League of Nations' Committee of Intellectual Co-operation at Geneva was also working to facilitate exchange.[62] Oldham was operating in an educational field in England where gendered and international relations were undergoing shifts.

The Bureau international des Fédérations nationales du personnel de l'Enseignement secondaire public and Girls' Secondary Schooling

Discussion of girls' secondary schooling at the BIFSP demonstrates strategies that contrast with those of the IFUW. Girls' secondary schooling formed a focus for discussion at BIFSP congresses in Luxemburg (1922) and Prague (1923) with a mix of well-trodden views over whether the education of girls was a pedagogical or a social issue and whether girls should have access to the same education as boys in terms of equality, or receive an education oriented to their future roles as mothers and wives.[63] The 1929 Hague congress took single-sex education for girls and coeducation as its focus. Delegates from a range of European countries responded to a questionnaire compiled for the conference by Z. Degen-Slosarka, head of the girls' secondary school in Warsaw, Poland. Part 1 of this questionnaire solicited factual information concerning the organization of secondary schooling: single-sex or mixed and the proportions; differences between programmes for girls and boys, in mixed schools, and in separate classes, and differences in methods of teaching boys and girls; teachers in boys', girls' and mixed schools; and rights to enter university or other institutions of higher education through leaving examinations. Part 2, which sought national societies' views on the best arrangements for secondary education, considered single-sex or mixed secondary schooling, or coeducation; whether girls' secondary schooling should be

---

[60] "Standing Committee for Interchange of Secondary Teachers." IFUW, Report of Council Meeting in Vienna, 1927, 21.

[61] See account of this development in Board of Education. *Education in 1932*. London: HMSO, 1933 (Cd 4364): 79.

[62] See Interchange of Teacher File Correspondence with the British National Committee on Intellectual Cooperation, League of Nations Archive, Geneva, Box r2283, 5B/37366.

[63] "Suggestions formulés par M Pecqueuer Professeur àl'Athné de Liege, Au Congrès de Luxembourg 1922." And "Arguments Préentes par M Ch Becker, Professeur àEchyternach (Grand Duce de Luxembourg), Au Congrès de Luxembourg 1922." Both in *Bulletin International* 25, June 1929: 53–54.

adapted to a future role in the family and in society; material to be added to the girls' curriculum and redundant curricular areas; whether girls' schools should be staffed exclusively by women and headed by a woman; whether it was possible to reconcile in mixed schools the 'particularities' and 'differences' in programmes and materials and methods of secondary schooling for boys and girls; and the rights for young women entering higher education.[64]

Four of the 11 British delegates to the BIFSP Hague congress were women. These included Una Gordon Wilson, secretary to the AAM and an experienced secondary school teacher. Her teaching career, like that of Oldham, had been spent in the secondary schools that taught the minority of girls. These included Dame Alice Owen's School London, St Saviours and St Olave's Girls' Grammar School London and Aigburth Vale High School Liverpool.[65] Nonetheless the report on girls' secondary schooling was provided to the congress by the Incorporated Association of Assistant Masters in Secondary Schools (IAAM). The IAAM was founded in 1891 as a professional association to protect and further the interests of assistant masters in secondary schools.[66] In 1921, the IAAM federated with the Incorporated Association of Head Masters, the AHM, and the AAM into the Joint Four.[67] Despite this federation, the IAAM evidence provided a masculinist slant on the question of girls' secondary schooling grounded on material and gendered interests amongst professional teachers in England and their national associations.

Ostensibly equivocal over single-sex or coeducation, the IAAM noted the existence of a great variety of opinions. On the one hand were those who believed that it was necessary to provide different methods of teaching boys and girls 'because the power of assimilating intuitively amongst young girls and the masculine logic of intelligence were strongly marked'; on the other were those who thought that 'the two types of intelligences were reciprocal and that there was advantage for them to develop in contact, with each intelligence gaining strength from the contact with the other'. The IAAM's view that coeducation was unsatisfactory was based on the evidence of masters, while the views attributed to women teachers about girls' education were simply estimated. Many of the IAAM statements demonstrated gendered provision and practice, but were treated as unproblematic. The IAAM found it appropriate for men to head mixed schools with a senior mistress in charge of the discipline, special educational requirements and interests of the girls,[68] a stance that was opposed by

---

[64] "L'enseignement secondaire des jeunes filles." *Bulletin International* 18 July (1929): 12–13.

[65] Liste des membres du Xe congrès international de l'enseignement secondaire Angleterre. League of Nations archive, Geneva, Box 2270; *The Directory of Women Teachers, 1927.* London: HFW Dean and Sons, 1927: 170.

[66] Quoted in Gosden, P. H. J. H. *The Evolution of a Profession: A Study of the Contribution of Teachers' Associations to the Development of School Teaching as a Professional Occupation.* Oxford: Basil Blackwell, 1972: 10.

[67] Available from http://www.archives.lib.soton.ac.uk/guide/MS67.shtml; INTERNET [cited 4 December 2006].

[68] "Great Britain", 39.

women teachers.[69] Their report, based on a supposed difference between boys and girls, also proposed that girls' particular attitudes towards aesthetic and scientific thought should be taken into account and that, at certain periods of 'crisis' in girls' physical and mental development, pressures on girls needed to be relaxed, whereas boys needed a firm hand.[70] Their evidence reflected many of the views expressed to the Board of Education's Consultative Committee deliberating the *Differentiation of the Curriculum* and supported the claims of men teachers within the teaching profession.

How this was received by the female delegates of the AAM at the congress remains a matter of speculation, as does the question of whether the topic of girls' secondary schooling was marginalized by delegates. Monsieur Pelt, the League of Nations' delegate, questioned the importance of the congress itself in an internal memorandum on his return to Geneva. The organization of the congress by the BIFSP gave the congress a seriousness in his eyes. But as Monsieur Pelt noted, a large number of delegates appeared to have little knowledge of the subjects under discussion, and when it came to voting on resolutions, they passed without debate or challenge.[71]

While English women were involved in international organizations that discussed aspects of secondary schooling for English girls, debate at the BIFSP illustrates that gender carried different amounts of symbolic capital in different contexts and was related to the wider political, professional and educational fields in which the AAM was located.

Conclusion

Transnational analysis of discussion and investigation of girls' secondary education via the IFUW and the BIFSP demonstrates the international dimension to the professional identities of English women educationists as they moved through European social space. It is notable that the English delegates to the IFUW and BIFSP conferences included women whose symbolic capital accrued from careers spent in the secondary schools that taught the minority of girls in England. Within the IFUW, the

---

[69] See, for example: AHM. *Mixed Secondary Schools Under the Headship of a Man.* Memorandum of the AHM, 1912.

[70] "Great Britain." *Bulletin International* 18 July (1929): 39. Many of the IAAM's comments on 'difference' resonate with the Board of Education Consultative Committee's *Report on the Differentiation of the Curriculum.* London: HMSO, 1923.

[71] 2nd Council Meeting of the Bureau International d'Education, 13 July 1931, League of Nations Archive, Box 2181 5A/8186 viii; Memorandum on the X1e Congrès International de l'enseignement secondaire La Haye Juillet 1929, League of Nations Archive Box r2270. In 1935 the BIFSP was renamed the Fédération Internationale des Professeurs de l'Enseignement Secondaire Officiel (FIPESO). For the history of international teacher organizations see: Simon, F. and H. Van Daele. "The International Teachers Organisations Until World War II." In Onderwijs, opvoeding en Maatschappij in de 19ste Eeuw, edited by M. Depaepe and M. D. Hoker. Leuven: Acco, 1987: 141–152.

experience of higher education provided the shared understandings, traditions and ideals through which Bourdieusian distinctions of class and professional and elite status were constituted. Analysis of debate demonstrates ways in which gender carried different amounts of symbolic capital in different contexts in relation to wider political, professional and educational fields. This, in turn, shaped the possibilities for English women to enter European debate and to bring about change, as is evidenced by the marginalization of AAM delegates as evidence-givers at the BIFSP and the possibility that the topic of girls' education was treated with less seriousness by the BIFSP than it deserved.

Both the IFUW and the BIFSP were, however, implicated in similar ways in constructing the idea of girls' secondary schooling through transnational networks. The IAAM evidence to the 1929 BIFSP congress at The Hague formed part of a wider approach to collecting comparative evidence. Each congress organized by the BIFSP focused on a key topic, with national delegates preparing responses in advance by means of a questionnaire. This formed part of a wider method propagated by the International Bureau of Education at Geneva of constructing educational policy on the basis of trends that were to be identified by questionnaires. As Robert Cowan illustrates, this formed part of a long history of the concept of action within comparative education, based on the concern to identify 'best practices' on the basis of international experience. Both the BIFSP questionnaire and the more wide-ranging IFUW survey used similar units of comparison. Both demonstrate Cowan's contention that comparative surveys are based on analytical frameworks in which factors may well exist before a 'fact' is collected.[72] In the case of the IFUW and the BIFSP, both surveys picked out ideal-type versions of common elements in categories that mesh with Anderson's description of the idea of the secondary school that emerged in Europe. The adoption of comparative method, as a result, worked to validate the 'idea' of the girls' secondary school.

Comparative method in the IFUW and the BIFSP incorporated historically located assumptions about social change. Pertinent here is Cowan's argument that comparative frameworks based on factors that exist before a 'fact' is collected result in a particular conceptualization of time that produces a 'linearity' which assumes the same future social time and an infinitely malleable social present. Cowan argues that as an approach to social change, 'linearity' lacks a serious account of political and cultural contexts and of significant individual actors and social movements. As a result, 'linearity' oversimplifies what he terms 'contextual time' by ignoring the cultural, biographical and political contexts in which educational systems have their longue durée. [73]

Bourdieusian field analysis within a transnational frame illustrates how comparative methodologies in the IFUW and the BIFSP operated in the context of fields within which particular structures and struggles around continuity and change operated. This was manifest as cultural, biographical and political aspects derived

---

[72] Cowan, "Moments of Time", 417, 420.
[73] Ibid.

from the English national context played out in the IFUW and the BIFSP in social spaces across Europe. At a time when the shifting position of women was an issue of debate in England, when increasing numbers of English women were enfranchised, when feminist demands in England included those of 'old' and 'new' feminism, and English feminist and non-feminist women and teachers increasingly pursued world peace through international cooperation, struggles within fields meant that secondary schooling for girls in England continued to operate as both a conservative force and a force for change for women in English society during the 'long 1920s'.

Thinking Education Histories Differently: Biographical Approaches to Class Politics and Women's Movements in London, 1900s to 1960s

Jane Martin

Introduction

It has only been relatively recently that gender has come under scrutiny in the history of education. Some 40 years ago, the sex/class binary supported an approach to the history of mass compulsory schooling that frequently subordinated questions of gender to questions of class. Among historians of women's education this assumption manifested itself in a largely separate history of the education of elite and middle-class girls. And yet, by the late 1970s feminist-inspired work had begun to redress the imbalance. Education, as Carol Dyhouse pointed out, was a public arena where women achieved a measure of status and authority, making it a 'good area in which to explore the social history of sexual politics and that of sex and gender generally'.[1]

---

[1] Dyhouse, Carol. "Miss Buss and Miss Beale: Gender and Authority in the History of Education." In *Lessons for Life. The Schooling of Girls and Women, 1850–1950*, edited by F. Hunt. Oxford: Basil Blackwell, 1987: 23.

The literature has now expanded greatly, challenging historians to shift the emphases of the 'master' narrative both to include women and to use gender as a lens through which to examine the past. This paper forms part of a recent trend that aims to bring together the scattered evidence and use biographical research to make available to new generations the experience of past girls and women and simultaneously to contribute to the writing of a more inclusive education history sensitive to the operation of gender.

Recognition that personal and private lives have political meanings grew out of the Women's Liberation movement in the early 1970s. Collective memory was crucial to feminists seeking to establish a legitimizing tradition, a heritage to impart. Conscious-ness-raising groups were set up to pool collective knowledge and begin to answer questions about the politics of women's situation. There was a desire to reclaim feminist foremothers, to explore interruption and silence in the historical record, to address the question of whether they were the first generation of women to feel and think as they did in a male-dominated society. And yet, rediscovering the words and actions of their predecessors prompted questions of another kind. As Dale Spender says, 'the comfort of finding so many women of the past began to give way to the discomfort of wondering about the present.... What was the process by which women were erased; and was it still in operation?'[2] Knowledge of women's past can be a source of strength, of guidance and of inspiration. There was a concern to render women visible and offer an explanation for women's disappearance. It is in this sense that we have a history of praxis with the emphasis on the meaning of experience and gender as a division of power. Put another way, the notion of what Nancy Miller has called 'the authority of experience' also made it possible to see that 'the personal is part of theory's material'.[3]

To the extent that one of the original premises of 1970s feminism was a concern with making women visible, it is hardly surprising that the interaction of personal and historical pasts has become a staple of feminist scholarship. Written at the intersec-tions of biography and autobiography, case-history and social history, psychoanalysis and oral history, Carolyn Steedman's classic feminist study, *Landscape for a Good Woman*, suggested a subversion of central cultural norms based on a nuanced under-standing of a differentiation between narratives as purely chronological accounts and stories as emplotted narratives. Interweaving elements of her own and her mother's biography, she was intent to recast the interpretive devices of working-class autobiog-raphies to find a place for working women's lives in the male narratives. In so doing she developed a political perspective on women's private lives as she sought to illumi-nate the wider social history from the particular circumstances of 1920s Burnley and South London in the 1950s. Steedman signalled the need to move beyond traditional historical class perspectives, for it is often too easy to fall into the trap of accepting

---

[2] Spender, Dale. *Women of Ideas and What Men Have Done to Them*. London: Routledge & Kegan Paul, 1982: 4–5.

[3] Miller, Nancy. *Getting Personal. Feminist Occasions and Other Autobiographical Acts*. London: Routledge, 1991: 14, 21.

central cultural narratives because they are 'made out of metaphors that look as if they describe nothing at all, but rather simply *are* the way the world is'.[4] She concludes with a counterpoint that captures the tension between coming in from the margins and not wanting to see the hitherto neglected voices 'absorbed by the central story'.[5] Touching on the danger of a patriarchal component in the dominant view, Steedman signifies how autobiographical memory is dialogic. In turning her childhood memories into texts she brought the concepts of social memory and collective memory clearly into view.

These themes also surface in Liz Stanley's writing. She uses the analytic idea of auto/biography, 'a term which refuses any easy distinction between biography and autobiography, instead recognizing their symbiosis',[6] to encompass a range of methods drawing on individual memory, both biographical and autobiographical. Stanley likens auto/biographical work to looking through a kaleidoscope—with each shake you see something different, even if the configurations remain the same. More recently, she has made auto/biographical practices (including the written, oral and visual), the object of study, to reinforce the point that we are always creating and presenting stories about the self across a range of social and cultural practices.[7] Auto/biographical practices provide a window through which to conceptualize dialectical and contingent social practices that underscore aspects of the age-old structure–agency debate conducted within sociology. For Harold Rosen, the practice of using the term auto/biography instead of or alongside the term autobiography on the grounds is not helpful. His preference is to map the landscape of autobiographical discourse, written and oral, and to 'raise questions of contiguity, overlap, and identity of discursive resources at the appropriate moment.... A blurred boundary is still a boundary, as dialect cartographers found out a long time ago.'[8] But, to my mind, the insertion of a 'slash' in the terms 'auto/biography' and 'auto/biographical practices' can be seen as performing a number of functions. First, by reminding us that the relation between, say, the individual and collective is contingent and dialectical, it can facilitate a critical awareness of binaried language. Second, it can underscore that this is an attempt to capture in the written form the essentially elusory quality of what we are theorizing about, namely the complex reality of lived experiences. Finally, it can caution us that this is not to imply a sense of compulsion when thinking about the production of self-narratives. Rather, it is to portray the sense that we are continuously involved in this process of negotiation in a public presentation of self, aspects of

---

[4] Steedman, Carolyn. *Landscape for a Good Woman: A Story of Two Lives.* London: Virago, 1986, 76–77.

[5] Op. cit., 144.

[6] Stanley, Liz. *The Auto/biographical 'I': The Theory and Practice of Feminist Auto/biography.* Manchester: Manchester University Press, 1992: 127.

[7] Stanley, Liz. "From 'self-made women' to 'women's made-selves'? Audit selves, simulation and surveillance in the rise of public woman." In *Feminism and Autobiography. Texts, Theories, Methods,* edited by Tessa Cosslett, Celia Lury and Penny Summerfield. London: Routledge, 2000: 40–60.

[8] Rosen, Harold. *Speaking from Memory: A Guide to Autobiographical Acts and Practices.* Stoke on Trent: Trentham Books, 1998: 8–9.

which are conscious (such as decisions about what to wear on a particular occasion), others that are part of our very being but of which we may be completely unaware (certain mannerisms for instance), that may send particular messages to some about our classed, ethnic, gendered and national identities.

In sum, this perspective provides a way of evoking the politics of experience. It involves rethinking the discursive constructions of concepts of selfhood and identity in relation to the emphasis on performance and simultaneously using this analysis to explore the links between gendered practices and discourses and personal action through the cultural mappings of a particular time and space. The social practices by which we construct and negotiate social identities is something raised by Morwenna Griffiths. Her metaphor of a 'web of identity' allows for the notion of agency and creativity (as the individual spins her/his own web), but not in circumstances of her/ his own making. Just as webs are 'made in a temporal and social context', so the processes of construction and maintenance that express the ideas of becoming and agency 'take place throughout a person's life and leave their traces on future selves'.[9] The metaphor of a web helps to make the unfamiliar understandable by tackling the issues of identity, autonomy and self-creation as if analogous to a familiar process. The notion of invisible bonds provides a powerful image of the structural properties of social relations and a means of considering social practice as it relates to gender relations within and between immediate situations and organizing structures. Stanley and Steedman both emphasize the need to pay close attention to the social contexts in which the speaking and writing and picturing of 'selves' takes place. However, the narration of a life or self can never be confined to a single, isolated subjecthood. The ways in which the self is framed and created by the social can be seen in the concept of intersubjectivity. So the narration of a life can never be confined to a single, isolated subjecthood. As Stanley notes, 'no person is an island complete of itself; and an approach informed by feminist sociology and cultural politics should recognise that social networks are a crucial means of enabling us to get a purchase on other lives'.[10] Social network analysis concentrates attention on the complex association between structure and agency, captured in Pierre Bourdieu's notion of the habitus as 'both structured and structuring, a product and producer of social worlds'.[11] Although some feminists have been hesitant in appropriating the insight and analysis of pre-eminent male theorists like Bourdieu who had little to say about women or gender, the work of scholars like Diane Reay and Beverley Skeggs amply demonstrates the richness of his theory for contemporary feminism.[12]

---

[9] Griffiths, Morwenna. *Feminism and the Self. The Web of Identity*. London: Routledge, 1995: 176.

[10] Stanley, Liz. *The Auto/biographical 'I': The Theory and Practice of Feminist Auto/biography*. Manchester: Manchester University Press, 1992: 10.

[11] Crossley, Nick. "From Reproduction to Transformation: social movement field and the radical habitus." *Theory, Culture and Society*, 20, no. 6 (2003): 43.

[12] See for example Adkins, Lisa, and Beverley Skeggs, eds. *Feminism after Bourdieu*. Oxford: Blackwell, 2004; Reay, Diane. "It's all becoming a habitus': beyond the habitual use of habitus in educational research." *British Journal of Sociology of Education* 25, no. 4 (2004): 431–44.

Individual life histories can be used to unpack the political meanings of everyday experience. Education historians can use biographical enquiry as a lens through which to explore the origins of ideas, to discover the existence of social possibilities and alternatives, to consider the relation between education and social change. In the words of Barbara Finkelstein, biographical studies 'provide a documentary context within which to judge the relative power of material and ideological circumstances, the meaning of education policy, the utility of schooling, the definition of literacy and the relationship between teaching and learning and policy and practice'.[13] From this overview there emerges a set of themes and propositions when thinking about feminism and auto/biography in the field of history and history of education today. Let me list them:

- relations between mainstream/tributaries/margins;
- relations between the individual and social movements;
- relations between the individual and collective practice;
- relations between knowledge and power
- relations between gender and social capital
- positioning as 'different'—positive, negative, affirming, source of strength?
- theorizing intersubjectivity: how do we deal with the contradictions in all of this?

Currently I am addressing some of these questions as part of a three-year research project exploring the changing relation of work, social identities and action over the last 100 years.[14] The focus is on three occupational sectors: teachers, bank workers and the railway industry, and two main geographical regions—the North West and South East England.

Methodology

The project uses the methods of life-story work. We analyse a range of material from written accounts, to oral and visual testimony on working lives. In examining the working lives of those active in the early twentieth century we depend on autobiographies, on biographies and on 'accessories to a life story' including diaries, letters, obituaries, photographs, possessions (Ken Plummer calls these 'objects of biography'), press interviews and sites of commemoration.[15] In addition to this, the project examines fictional representations of work, looking at a range of writing from the nineteenth century through to the present; and we examine how work and the workplace are constructed through a range of visual material. Central to the study are the

---

[13] Finkelstein, Barbara. "Revealing Human Agency: the uses of biography in education studies." In *Writing Educational Biography: Explorations in Qualitative Research*, edited by Craig Kridel. London and New York: Garland Publishing, 1998: 59.

[14] This work in part emerges out of an ESRC project 'Does Work Still Shape Social Identities and Action?'. Part of the Economic and Social Research Council Social Identities and Action programme, award number RES 148 25 0038.

[15] Plummer, Ken. (2001) *Documents of Life 2*. London: Sage Publications, 2001: 48–77.

120 work-life histories carried out with respondents from the three main occupational sectors. However, the primary focus of this paper is how we might address and engage with written and visual texts, approached as narratives, to reconstruct the 'interior cultures'[16] of a couple of educator activists, Charles and Florence Key, who started their working lives in the 1900s. The intent is to show the possibilities of auto/biography for the study of community defined as 'a fluid network of social relations that may be but are not necessarily tied to territory'.[17] The examples of community considered here relate to working-class aristocracies on the one hand and communities of women on the other, being particularized in time and space.

The observations on what is now a well-established feminist literature that I set out in my introduction led me to conceptualize the remainder of this paper in terms of the following aims. First, to present an analysis of educator activists in twentieth-century England that connects, rather than separates, the domains of education, labour history and politics. Second, to contribute to a redefining of history/histories of education which, instead of relegating gender to the margins, integrates this perspective into its mainstream conceptual frameworks and third, to use auto/biography (with an emphasis on the reconstructive nature of memory, of history) to connect the field of theorizing with the field of empiricism. The intent is to examine the circumstances that make class politics grounded in gendered and occupational identities possible, showing the way in which the politics of place works as an active influence at a range of scales (community, city and locality). Here the auto/biographical practices of Charles and Florence Key will be used to light up the larger questions of the intersection of biography and history, the distinction between lived experience and historical experience, the link between generation and social change.

Olive Banks[18] highlights the need to acknowledge the importance of change over time and the main unit of analysis in her study of the social origins of the 'first wave' of modern feminism is a cohort or generation based on year of birth. Banks's sample consists of 98 women and 18 men and four cohorts are designated to illuminate the link between generation and social change. Taking each in turn, cohort 1 consists of those born before 1828, cohort 2 of those born between 1828 and 1848, those in the third cohort were born between 1849 and 1871 and those in cohort 4 between 1872 and 1891. This group represents the last generation of 'first-wave' feminism and it includes Florence Key. Indeed, the militant face of the Edwardian suffrage movement provided the subjective experience that shaped her political beliefs and campaigns. Paid employment as an elementary school teacher may have provided a sounding board for civic engagement but it will be argued that her primary identity came from membership of a community of feminist women. All of this makes Karl Mannheim's classic treatment of generations a particularly appropriate framework for interpreting

---

[16] Finkelstein, Barbara. "Redoing urban educational history." In *The City and Education in Four Nations* edited by Ronald K. Goodenow. Cambridge: Cambridge University Press, 1992: 183

[17] McDowell, Linda. *Gender, Identity and Place: Understanding Feminist Geographies*. Cambridge: Polity Press, 1992: 100.

[18] Banks, Olive. *Becoming a Feminist*. Brighton: Harvester Wheatsheaf, 1986.

this material.[19] As Mannheim points out, members of any one generation can only participate in a temporally limited section of the historical-social process. Charles and Florence Key are similarly located in terms of their common experience in history, belonging to the same actual generation in terms of the wider criterion of a community of location. Historical time understood as individual time, family time and community time[20] provides the context for their active roles. On a political and personal level the effect of their participation in historical conflict and change means they fall into a separate generation unit within the actual generation. It follows that they share some elements of identity including an original and distinctive consciousness reflecting the codes of an established generational culture or 'entelechy'. The contingency of all this will be illustrated by drawing attention to their common identity as socialists of the 'War Generation' despite the fact that as a man and a woman they experienced the First World War differently. Indeed Florence embedded and articulated that difference in her suffrage identity. Auto/biography as method has the capacity to integrate macro-historical themes with a network of meanings emerging from the work-life histories and shot through with conflicts, contradictions, ambiguities and doubts. There is the potential to map historical changes and provide pointers to the analysis of motivating force.

Here the emphasis is on the social networks formed by educator activists who became professional politicians from working-class backgrounds. Auto/biographical practices are used as a means of understanding their different strategic approaches and effects. Focusing on the individual as the main unit of analysis, I concentrate attention on the lived connections between personal and political worlds. To map this terrain is to examine the ways in which individuals display self-knowledge through the creation and presentation of stories about the self across a range of social and cultural practices—both public and private. It will be argued that the legacy of Bourdieu can be used to provide a framework that can connect individuals, networks and structures.

The Making of Teacher Politicians: Mapping Exposure to Oppositional Ideas

Florence Ellen Key (né Adams) was a native of Wapping, London, and the daughter of a licensed victualler. At the time of writing no further details are known of her early life beyond the fact that sometime in the First World War she accepted a teaching post in the girls' department at Dempsey Street Elementary School, Stepney. There she met her future husband and political partner, Charles William Key (1883–1964), the son of a brick worker, whom she married before he joined the Royal Garrison Artillery. The ceremony took place on 8 April 1917 at St Matthias Church in

---

[19] Mannheim, Karl. "The Problem of Generations." In *Studying Aging and Social Change*, edited by Melissa Hardy. London: Sage Publications, 1997: 22–65.

[20] T. K. Hareven (1982) *Family Time and Industrial Time* cited in Vincent, John. "Understanding generations: political economy and culture in an ageing society." *British Journal of Sociology* 56, no. 4 (2005): 579–99.

Canning Town, an industrial and residential area dating from about 1850 and built to house the labourers in Victoria Docks, the coal wharves and the shipbuilding works on Bow Creek. The witnesses were Florence's brother Harry, a baker and confectioner, and fellow elementary school teacher Helen Dedman. Helen's father, Arthur Dedman, was also a schoolmaster, suggesting she might have been born into an established teaching dynasty.[21] Born in the village of Chalfont St Giles, in rural Buckinghamshire, Charles witnessed extreme and grinding poverty after the death of his father (of consumption) before he was six years old. His mother became an applicant for poor relief and once a week he missed school to accompany her to collect their dole. To make ends meet his mother worked as a char and took in lodgers, one of whom showed an interest in Charles's future welfare. With this patronage 15-year-old Charles moved to London and became an apprentice pupil teacher. The London School Board was one of the leading authorities in the development of pupil-teacher centres and Charles spent up to half his time at the Mile End Centre in Stepney and the other half in his practice school in Hackney, as a teacher. He subsequently won a Queen's scholarship and trained at Borough Road College from 1903 to 1905. On completion of his teacher training Charles accepted a post as assistant master at the aforementioned Dempsey Street Boys' School. Only after his marriage did he become a citizen of the metropolitan borough of Poplar, which consisted of the subdivisions of Bow and Bromley, as well as the Isle of Dogs and Poplar itself. Having returned from army life to a brief spell of teaching at the Dempsey Street elementary school, he was promoted to a headship, first in Mile End and then in Hoxton and Poplar.[22]

To begin to disentangle the 'interior cultures' of this couple I will be working with a 'social' definition of culture, to look at the meanings and values implicit and explicit in a particular way of life, which expresses certain meanings and values. This analysis draws on Bourdieu's conception of the habitus since habitus provides a way of theorizing durable dispositions focused around the lived connections between personal and political lives. Bourdieu understands the social world as made up of different but overlapping 'fields of power' which function according to their own tacit logic or set of rules. Acceptance as a legitimate player of the game within a specific field of action is achieved by access to different types of capital—economic, social, cultural and symbolic.[23] If and when the different forms of capital are accepted as legitimate they take the form of symbolic capital. Field positions are constituted in social relations and through social practice, while the habitus is formed through the

---

[21] Marriage certificate Charles William Key and Florence Ellen Adams, 8 April 1917; 1901 census for England, Ilford, Essex.

[22] *Evening News*, 28 September 1944; 'Ald. C.W. Key, M.P.', *East End News*, 22 August 1947; 'Why I have fought for better conditions' by C. W. Key, Minister of Works, Labour candidate for Poplar, press cuttings Tower Hamlets Local History Library.

[23] Economic capital refers to income, wealth, financial inheritances and monetary assets. Cultural capital, defined as high culture, can exist in three forms: embodied cultural capital, objectified cultural capital and institutional cultural capital. The last is the product of investment in formal education. Social capital is the product of sociability, which speaks of investment in culturally, economically or politically useful networks and connections.

process of internalization of capitals. Learned more by experience than by teaching, habitus relates to a way of seeing and being within the world, enabling us to concentrate on cultural and symbolic, as well as economic axes. These include distinctions of class, gender and ethnicity manifest in ways of taking up space, ways of speaking, styles of dress, besides dispositions, attitudes and tastes. Habitus inscribes the individual with a repertoire of practices, with a history, which are themselves generative of enduring (although not entirely fixed) orientations to action. To bring these dimensions into view I will focus on small face-to-face social contexts and processes. I will map exposure to oppositional ideas with sensitivity to London's East End and the locality of Poplar as distinctive sociocultural, psychosocial environments. The examples of community considered here relate to the political culture of the locality on the one hand and women's communities on the other. We start with the place where Florence and Charles Key spent most of their married life—living in what was described as a workman's flat at Wellington Buildings, Poplar, over the Bow district railway and opposite the home of the Labour leader, George Lansbury, and his wife, Bessie.

Late Victorian Poplar was revealed and anatomized by Charles Booth in the 1880s. In his 17-volume survey of poverty, industry and religion, Booth described the predominantly working-class area as:

> A vast township, built, much of it, on low marshland, bounded in the east by the River Lea and on the south by a great bend in the Thames. In North Bow and the outlying parts there is a great deal of jerry building ... among the early troubles of these streets are fevers....[24]

Poplar was (and is) an assemblage of localities shaped by street patterns and the passage of canals, roads and railways, as well as successive waves of immigrants over the centuries. Varied districts and quite different communities meshed and intermeshed with various manufacturing areas associated with the processing or manufacturing of chemicals, dyes and paint, along with cabinet-making, match-making and tailoring. Like other riverside developments in the capital city, Poplar had its own maritime identity derived from long experience of loading and refitting ocean-going vessels, even before the opening of the first enclosed docks. Booth's social survey achieved a good deal of publicity. Among other things it showed chronic unemployment, poor housing and extremes of poverty and social deprivation were endemic in Poplar. Similarly, David Widgery's many-voiced work *Some Lives! A GP's East End* provides the contemporary reader with a strong sense of déjàvu when peeling away the record of 10 years of 'urban renewal' by the London Docklands Development Corporation in the 1980s.[25]

By the early twentieth century, the East End and the lives of its two million inhabitants had received considerable attention from writers and journalists. In respect of the language used to map the characteristics of the area and the people who

---

[24] Booth, Charles, ed. *Life and Labour of the People of London, I: East, Central and South London* (1892): 71.
[25] Widgery, David. *Some Lives! A GP's East End*. London: Simon & Schuster, 1991: 31.

lived there, it should be clear that this was the era of the colonial empire and the politics of 'social imperialism'.[26] Corresponding ideas about racial or cultural difference articulated in a way that served to 'distance' working-class city life so that, for example, parallels were drawn between the localities labelled slums and colonies in geographically distant parts of the world. Just as the treating of non-Western cultures as Other played a crucial role in organizing ideas of 'race' and 'civilization' so the new representational taxonomy of what can be termed 'domestic colonialism' operated at two interconnected levels: the depiction of impoverished neighbourhoods as 'dark' and 'hostile' places and the representation of sections of the urban poor as 'primitive tribes', 'savages' or 'races' apart. This 'East End' was a city of 'darkness' that was seen in stark contrast to the city of 'light' and enlightenment that was London's West End. In this context, Social-Darwinistic terminology provided a strong referent for those who feared the city as an incubus of public disorder, whilst new techniques of social investigation fed into the construction of particular out-groups as social 'problems'. Hence the theme of a metropolis at risk became an important part of London's political culture.[27]

The Keys were among those who believed in the potential of education to change society. Both socialists, they can be counted among the second generation of apostles touched by the 'religion of socialism', a term in common currency in the 1880s and 1890s. Their political journeys were rather different, however. For Florence the trajectory was teacher politics and municipal activism, whereas Charles moved from the local into the national political field, following his friend and mentor, George Lansbury, as MP for Poplar, Bow and Bromley (in 1940) and subsequently Minister of Works (in 1947). Looking back, Charles the mature politician used the child-figure (remembering himself as a child) to explain his actions in press interviews. On these occasions he would recall the promise he made to his mother when he was nine, 'that he would go into Parliament and try to put an end to the misery that she, and a great many others had endured through the Poor Law'.[28] Moving toward adulthood he recalled there were stirrings of political consciousness in debating contests for pupil teachers organized by volunteer workers at the middle-class university settlement, Toynbee Hall, on the Commercial Road, in Whitechapel. In 1905–1906 he joined the Independent Labour Party and appeared on public platforms in the Limehouse district of London shortly after. Charles was one of 39 Labour candidates swept to power on Poplar borough council in November 1919. Two years later he was deputy mayor and at the centre of the Poplar Rates Rebellion of 1921 when 30 Labour councillors (including George Lansbury) were sent to prison for their refusal to collect Poplar's poor rate.

Faced by a rating system that discriminated heavily in favour of the wealthy boroughs Poplar's Labour councillors argued that the burden of poor relief should be

---

[26] See: Hobsbawm, Eric. *The Age of Empire 1875–1914*. London: Cardinal, 1987: 56–83.

[27] Feldman, David, and Gareth Stedman Jones. *Metropolis London: Histories and Representations since 1800*. London: Routledge, 1989.

[28] *East End News*, 28 February 1947.

spread more evenly within London as a whole. Charles did not go to jail but was prominent in the campaign to secure the release of those who did, writing the pamphlet *Guilty and Proud of It* (1922) to explain their actions. The pamphlet argued against the treatment of poverty as a crime and observed: 'in Poplar it is well understood that the poor are poor because they are robbed, and they are robbed because they are poor'. In defending his working-class community Key spoke a language of protest accessible to the people he represented:

> The workers of Poplar, who have to live there, provide the means for the pleasures and amenities of life enjoyed by others. What is their reward? To be lampooned as shirkers and loafers, to be the butt of every foul innuendo from the mouths of the very people who live upon their labour.[29]

Opinion was divided. Whereas some celebrated Poplar's heroic stand against central government policy as an example of the 'local road to socialism', others were more censorious. In answer to their critics, Lansbury wrote a foreword to Key's contemporary account, *Red Poplar*, published in 1925:

> We have nothing to apologise for.... We all graduated in the school of experience and hard work and can claim that we belong to those who having seen the light never turned back or longed for the flesh-pots of office.[30]

This was socialism in action. Poplarism became synonymous with a 'participatory form of politics' that sought to inform and consult the local community and included the spectacle of street melodrama.[31] Emulating Dick Whittington, Charles was thrice Mayor of Poplar (1924, 1928, and 1933) and contemporaries recorded the people 'loved him almost as much as they loved George Lansbury'. They made much of his nomenclature as the *Architect* told its readers in the 1940s: 'to men of all parties he is "Charlie" just as he was to the citizens of Poplar when he was "His Worship the Mayor"'.[32] This teacher-politician spent 42 years in the classroom. His working life in the political field ended only with his death in 1964.

Although she also belonged to the Labour Party, Florence chose to commit herself to feminism rather than socialism. A feminist when she married, in the years before the First World War she joined the Women's Freedom League, which began as a breakaway from the Women's Social and Political Union, the prime mover of suffrage militancy. Secretary of its East London branch, for her, class politics was grounded in other identities. Poplarism was 'deeds not words' but this was also one of the slogans used by feminist teachers who decided to form their own separate union that would put women first. The National Union of Women Teachers (NUWT) began as an Equal Pay League (in 1904) formed within the largest teaching union, the

---

[29] Key, Charles. *Guilty and Proud of It!*, London: Poplar Board of Guardians, 1922: 22.

[30] Key, Charles W. *Red Poplar*. London: Labour Publishing Co., 1925: 4.

[31] Rose, Gillian. "Locality, Politics and Culture: Poplar in the 1920s." *Environment and Planning D: Society and Space* 6 (1988): 151–68; Rose, Gillian. "Imagining Poplar in the 1920s: Contested Concepts of Community." *Journal of Historical Geography* 16, (1990): 425–37.

[32] *East London Advertiser*, 2 January 1922; "Minister in Spats." *The Architect*, 7 March 1947.

National Union of Teachers (NUT). In 1909 the League changed its name to the National Federation of Women Teachers. Support grew and 10 years later the London section joined with the Women Teachers' Franchise Union to split from the NUT. Never numerically very large (by 1920 there were 21,000 members) the women who turned to the new organization united in demonstrations and deputations, lobbying and public statements, seeing their struggle as an intrinsic part of the wider women's movement for full political, social and economic parity with men. The NUWT published its own journal (the *Woman Teacher*) and communicated its ideas through a column in a general educational journal, *The Schoolmistress*, which claimed to have the largest circulation of all educational magazines among women teachers.

Florence and her close friend Helen Dedman were among the leading members of the new union. First Helen and then Florence held the post of president of the London Unit, in 1926 and 1927 respectively, and they both joined the central council in 1927. While Florence had an unbroken record of service lasting until 1951, Helen stood down in 1929 before returning to serve a further 16 years between 1931 and 1947. By the 1930s Florence was in the vanguard of a number of pressure groups which acted to ensure that women's rights were constantly brought to the attention of Parliament: notably the Six Point Group which took as its motto 'Equality First' and another new organization formed in the 1920s, the Open Door Council. In these years her 'Watching Brief' occupied a regular slot in the *Woman Teacher*. Consistently arguing the case for the full inclusion of women in all areas of public life, it offers the reader a running commentary on social policy besides numerous examples of patriarchal domination in public life. In these circumstances she urged women teachers to stand together with the wider women's movement in the struggle for equality.[33] Directly challenging the subordination of women she argued they would never achieve full political equality unless women voters use the opportunities available to them and 'wake up to the fact that, if they want more women in Parliament, they must be prepared to finance and work for them'. Stung to reply, Conservative MP, Joan Davidson, disagreed. She thought the lack of women MPs reflected 'their home responsibilities … plus a lingering though dying prejudice against women in Parliament on the part of some Selection Committees'.[34] As time went by the separatist women's union found difficulty in recruiting new members. A tendency to nostalgia accelerated after the Second World War and Florence was among the pioneers to reminisce about past struggles, besides writing obituaries of deceased members in a heroic effort to rally the rank and file.[35]

The ex-Mayoress of Poplar was elected union president in 1932. The *East London Advertiser* carried the full text of her presidential address delivered at the annual conference at Southend-on-Sea. After a stinging attack on Conservative attempts to

---

[33] *Woman Teacher*, 16 February 1934: 406.
[34] *Woman Teacher*, October 1958: 3–4; March 1959: 74–75.
[35] National Union of Women Teachers, London Unit Minute Books 1918–1937/8; Pierotti, A. M. *The Story of the NUWT*. London: Publishers for the NUWT, 1937: 83–85.

cut education spending during the Depression, she argued that political activity was crucial:

> Just as true religion does not manifest itself merely in Sunday observance and occasional emotional revivalist meetings, so politics, which are an extension of our duty towards our neighbours, should not be a matter of wild excitement during election campaigns and of apathy and indifference at other times.[36]

It was the responsibility of women teachers to become activist citizens. To this end they must form a new habit, 'the conscious use of political power', to secure resources for state schools. Local religiosity was an element of Poplar's political culture and she ended with a heartfelt plea to women teachers. 'The world to-day has need of earnest thought; we teachers must do our part and our resolve must be one with Blake's—"I will not cease from mental fight, nor shall my sword sleep in my hand, till we have built Jerusalem in England's green and pleasant land"'.[37] Helen shared her outlook. Five years later she, too, accepted the union presidency.

Generations and Social Change: Work and Community for Women Teachers

The presidency of Florence Key coincided with the onset of change in the NUWT. Many of the suffrage generation were nearing retirement and there was a felt need to reinvigorate the message to address a new audience of younger women teachers. The *Woman Teacher* was re-launched with a new editor and a new volume and a message from the president clearly designed to include both groups. In it, Florence re-stated union goals, which she distilled into two main aims. The first was unified professional standards. This meant *one* salary scale for all teachers irrespective of sex or geographical location and *one* principle of promotion, 'namely that the *best* person fill the post irrespective of sex, religion, politics or any other irrelevance'.[38] The second goal toward which they worked was 'an educational system in which *all* children shall have an equal chance of the best education the community can provide, irrespective of the social status or financial standing of their parents'.[39] Not surprisingly, she rejected arguments for mixed unions, reminding readers that though the NUT membership was 70 per cent female, that figure was not reflected in the composition of its committees and deputations. Neither did the NUT safeguard the interests of women teachers. This was demonstrated in two ways. First, she pointed to the double standards the union displayed in its sympathetic stance toward the entry of unqualified women into the profession for the purpose of teaching the under-fives, which was very different from the forthright opposition to the use of unqualified men. Second, she highlighted its practice of advertising promotion posts for men in the union journal, with reference to current policy of amalgamating infants' and junior departments

---

[36] *East London Advertiser*, 2 January 1922.
[37] Ibid.
[38] "From the President." *Woman Teacher*, 7 October 1932: 5.
[39] Ibid.

under one head. This linked to her critique of the Burnham Committee, set up in 1919 to agree nationally negotiated salary scales. The National Federation of Women Teachers was responsible for securing some form of equal pay for teachers, such as equal minimum salaries and equal increments from the local authorities, in such areas as outer London and South Wales, where it had organized particularly strongly.[40] This advance was lost when the Burnham scales were introduced in 1920 and in searching for an explanation she was quick to point to the committee's composition— 40 men and five women in 1919, 42 men and six women in 1941.[41] Florence became particularly active in campaigns for equal pay and equal opportunities and against the marriage bar, though the policy did not affect her personally since the London County Council did not sack those married women teachers already in their employ when the ban was introduced. Here I will take just a few examples from her speeches to read them with an eye to the way in which the vocabulary and metaphors reinforce/ subvert gendered practices and discourses.

Poplar's Labour council promoted equal pay and in May 1924 Charles Key addressed a mass meeting in Trafalgar Square supported by an alliance of societies, associations, unions and other professional, social and political organizations organized by women or for women. Enlarging on a thinly veiled critique of another NUT breakaway, the National Association of Schoolmasters, formed specifically 'to safeguard and promote the interests of men teachers', the then Mayor of Poplar expressed surprise that its members did not support the principle of equal pay since it would protect men teachers from women's competition. Castigating his male colleagues for suffering from 'elephantiasis of the inferiority complex' he proclaimed he was there 'in no spirit of chivalry' but because he recognized the danger of cheap labour:

> So long as women teachers take lower pay, competition between men and women was unfair, because it was based on factors not relative to their respective ability. "What care I how fair you be? If you be not fair to me?" he extemporised, amid laughter and applause.... He concluded by saying that he believed in Equal Pay for women with men in the community at large. There would be an equal call on the abilities of all and with the winning of equal pay women would most readily respond to this call for public service, to the betterment of our social order. He hoped that men teachers would quickly learn their folly in opposition and that they would join the women and help them to win.[42]

In her speeches on the subject Florence made the link between socialist and feminist arguments to promote equal pay. In 1929, for example, she 'pointed out that the dilution of women's labour by the employment of unqualified women as teachers increased the proportion of women teachers to men and thus artificially strengthened the argument of supply and demand'.[43] Debating equal pay at the 1931 NUWT

[40] Oram, Alison. *Women Teachers and Feminist Politics 1900–39.* Manchester: Manchester University Press, 1996: 124.

[41] NUWT London Unit Minutes, Annual General Meeting, 8 November 1941.

[42] "Equal Pay for Equal Work Trafalgar Square Demonstration, an Army with Banners!" *Woman Teacher*, 16 May 1924: 250–51.

[43] *Woman Teacher*, 15 February 1929, 134.

conference she recalled past victories with the warning 'political freedom was no use without economic freedom'.[44] Two years later she threw doubt on the competence of male teachers who felt threatened by the woman teacher or inspector who sought authority over a man. In her opinion:

> A man whose mind was so obsessed by sex that he could not think of a woman except in terms of sex and could not regard her as a colleague and work with her or under her, was totally unfit to have dealings with little children and the sooner such men left the profession the better.[45]

Little wonder that east Londoners wrote of her determination of character, whilst friends and colleagues in the London Unit spoke of her 'well known logical and forceful manner' in reporting her work on the campaign platform.[46]

Approached as narrative, Florence's political rhetoric on the question of married women teachers is revealing of a number of themes. On the one hand, she constantly reiterated her belief that the freedom of the married woman was the crux of the feminist position. 'Every woman required freedom in order to develop herself and to give her best in the world.' She stressed also the importance of economic independence. Far from married women workers being a danger to the community, in her eyes 'the real menace lay ... in that section which led luxurious lives on unearned incomes'.[47] On the other hand, she showed considerable reluctance to positively defend the position of spinster teachers tending, instead, to stress the value of marriage. In 1924, for instance, 'Marriage was an experience which was valuable to a woman and would have a valuable reaction on the children under her care'.[48] During the 1931 conference debate on married women teachers in Dartmouth she criticized a school atmosphere dominated by unhappy teachers: 'It was a wicked thing that women should by a public authority have to give up marriage... Enforced celibacy made unhappy teachers and this had an unhappy effect on the children.'[49] And again, in September 1932, 'The beneficial psychological outlook which marriage gave a woman was never considered. The whole situation had, in fact, almost reached this position: should a woman marry? Not should a married woman work?'[50] Our final example comes from a 1933 conference speech, in which she turns soothsayer: 'By compelling people who wish to marry to remain celibate, a great social problem was being created.'[51] Much of this political rhetoric is couched in terms that would seem to imply that spinsterhood was an undesirable way of life. Her position may be characterized by the following extract from yet another NUWT speech, this time in Canterbury, when she reiterated the point that 'we were training human beings and

---

[44] *Woman Teacher*, 20 January 1933: 66.
[45] Ibid.
[46] *Woman Teacher*, 11 September 1931: 282; 22 January 1932: 117.
[47] *Woman Teacher*, 23 September 1932: 302.
[48] *Woman Teacher*, 18 January 1924: 22.
[49] *Woman Teacher*, 16 January 1931: 95.
[50] *Woman Teacher*, 23 September 1932: 302.
[51] *Woman Teacher*, 20 January 1933: 61.

therefore she considered that the school should reflect the outside world. We wanted all kinds of teachers in our schools, not spinsters and widows only.'[52] Adopting a more strictly equalist position on the issue of women's employment and financial inequality, she ended: 'It was a question of freedom but we did not want freedom only for spinsters, for we demanded the rights of every woman to go forward on her own feet with equal opportunities.'[53]

It would seem that to some extent the feminist politics of Florence Key took on aspects of the negative attitudes towards unmarried women that gained an additional inflection after the First World War, through the pathologizing of spinsters' sexuality. We can only surmise as to whether her religious beliefs informed these views. But, above all else, she was driven by the struggle for social justice. As she told conference in 1934, she supported the right of married women to earn because she 'wished to insist on the adult status of women, that they must order their own lives and not have them ordered for them by every Tom, Dick and Harry who found himself on a public body'. This was the kind of interference that made her 'blood boil'. She agreed with a previous speaker 'that there are no peculiarly "manly virtues," and she considered that sturdy independence and self reliance were as admirable and desirable in a woman as in a man'.[54]

In 1937 Florence resigned from her secure and now pensionable post as assistant teacher at Dempsey Street Girls School to become a full-time official of the NUWT, for some years undertaking both the secretaryship of the Legal and Tenure Committee and editorship of the *Woman Teacher*. The London Unit adopted her as their candidate for the 1940 county council elections but war intervened. By the time of the next elections both she and the union were in a very different time–space. Her continued commitment to feminism was expressed in her decision to stand as a Labour candidate in the Putney division of Wandsworth. But there is evidence that it was considerably harder to get NUWT election workers than it had been in the 1920s when another past NUWT president, Agnes Dawson, stood successfully as a Labour candidate in the safe seat of Camberwell. A sense of the frustration she felt underscores the tone of her progress reports to union activists. Explaining the need for a party candidate and to choose a party whose policy most nearly approached NUWT ideals she said 'no party was 100 per cent feminist and it was very necessary to have a member on the London County Council who could watch the interests of women teachers and the children and voice their desires'. Moving on, she urged election workers to come forward, 'to go into the constituency after school and on Saturdays at any time'[55] for the three-week campaign. But it was all to no avail: she lost the contest for the Putney seat.

---

[52] *Woman Teacher*, 10 January 1930.
[53] Op. cit., 99.
[54] *Woman Teacher*, 19 January 1934: 361.
[55] NUWT London Unit Minutes, Annual General Meeting, 5 November 1945, 21 January 1946, 31 January 1946.

Municipal activism and a bout of ill health notwithstanding, in September 1946 she was one of two British delegates to the meeting of the Open Door International for the Emancipation of the Woman Worker in Denmark. Despite setbacks, her feminism was undimmed. In May 1947, she wrote a hard-hitting piece for the *Woman Teacher* entitled 'Are you a real feminist?'. In it, she made a plea for NUWT members to renew their lapsed subscriptions for the Open Door Council. Founded by Lady Rhondda (Six Point Group), Elizabeth Abbott (National Union of Societies for Equal Citizenship), Emmeline Pethick-Lawrence (Women's Freedom League) and Virginia Crawford (St Joan's Social and Political Alliance) in May 1926, it had the aim of opposing what was termed 'protective' employment legislation in the face of Labour government proposals to extend those regulations which had the effect of excluding women, not men, from the better-paid jobs in industry. As far as Florence was concerned, real feminists would not confine themselves to questions of professional self-interest only, for, 'the individual teacher widens her own interests and gives more fully to the women's cause by being a member of a feminist organisation which includes *all* women workers'.[56] This principle was close to her heart. Like a high proportion of women politicians Key had no children and in later life she directed her formidable energies toward the attempt to rejuvenate the Open Door Council and place it once more at the forefront of the movement for the right of married women to work. She applauded the efforts of the international committee to ensure women got a 'square deal from the United Nations and are not relegated to some sub-human category when human rights are under consideration', besides the continued fight for equal pay and removal of all restrictions on women's work.[57]

Conclusion

Used as a means of understanding the couple's different strategic approaches and effects, the auto/biographical practices of Charles and Florence Key show the importance of intersectionality. Working with the personal history documents one can see the relative value of this couple's capitals (to use the language of Bourdieu) as realizable and able to be converted in the political field. The articulation of class consciousness, educational achievement and the work of teaching created empowering identities that were of enormous strength to these professional politicians from working-class backgrounds. There was an affinity of ideas between husband and wife. For both of them, classrooms and teaching were intimately connected with the world outside.

Media representations make it clear that the definition and practice of teaching was crucial to the production and consumption of their public identity. On the one hand, a *Star* reporter said of Charles, 'if I am asked where this new type of London statesman and leader had got it all from, I can only say that for many years he was a London

---

[56] "Are you a real feminist?" *Woman Teacher*, 9 May 1947.
[57] Ibid.

schoolmaster'.[58] On the other, the *Woman Teacher* quotes a journalist on the *East London Advertiser* reaffirming local pride in the achievements of Florence Key. The writer emphasizes how she completely confounded the 'schoolmarm' stereotype with her 'high spirits and joyous disposition'.[59] It would seem reasonable to suggest a particular white working-class gendered habitus was of benefit to Charles in following the path from pupil teacher to professional politician, and eventually entering the House of Commons. Speaking on past struggles he explained the debt he owed the young Florence Adams:

> Who for some unknown reason made him her husband and a resident of Poplar? Had she not done that, what Charles Key would have been now, nobody knows…. Thanks are due to her for the forbearance she showed to the absences from home which the giving of time to local government inevitably involves.[60]

The silences provide an interesting feature in this picturing of selves. One would never suppose that his had been a political partnership with a feminist trade union leader who had herself led a very full and active public life in teacher politics and the women's movement. It is noteworthy that Charles never lost sight of the debt he owed the Poplar councillors who went to prison for their beliefs, consistently stressing 'he had been the agent of other planners and the expounder of policies originated by others'.[61] And yet, in this very public account of their political partnership, given on the occasion of his accepting the Freedom of the Borough of Poplar in 1953, Charles Key relegates his wife to a supporting role. In death, it is he who has a site of commemoration, the Charles Key Lodge, a home for people with physical disabilities.

It is my contention that educational and political evaluations suffer from a preoccupation with successful organizations, leaderships and ideologies. This is not, however, an argument for alternative heroes and heroines. It is, rather, an argument for new ways of seeing the same historical space. In her lifetime Florence Key had not created the new world for women that she had thought possible. Nonetheless, a reading of her political practice combined with the collective practice of the NUWT establishes that teachers were indispensable to 'first-wave' feminism both as leaders and as followers. We get a sense of this cultural milieu and influence in her answer to the rhetorical question 'what is conference'? This is what she wrote:

> It is a great gathering of kindred spirits at which we not only declare our faith and affirm our creed, but where we also renew our spirit. In short, it is a religious experience, but, like all other religious experiences it is of no use unless its reality penetrates our daily lives. We must *live* our faith. It is all very well to enjoy Conference but what are we going to *do* about it? In other words, we promised not only to give lip-service to our creed, but to act as

---

[58] "Charlie Key of Poplar." *The Star*, 4 January 1941.

[59] *East London Advertiser*, 15 May 1953; *East London Advertiser* cited in *Woman Teacher*, 22 January 1932: 117.

[60] *Daily Herald*, 11 February 1947.

[61] *East London Advertiser*, 15 May 1953.

missionaries. How can we? The present writer would like to suggest that we must have Faith, Work and Courage.[62]

Here she makes visible a particular political mobilization of spirituality and morality. For Florence and her supporters, the NUWT was feminism in action. Like Poplarism, its legacy was a strongly assertive political tradition. Like Poplarism, also, the space it occupies is on the margins of history. But in examining the auto/biographical practices of a relatively unknown couple of classroom teachers we see here the possibilities of biographical studies to produce a historical ethnography of political spaces that connects, rather than separates, the stories of lives in educational settings with those of political and social movements.

---

[62] *Woman Teacher*, 27 February 1931: 145.

Higher Education and Social Change: Purpose in Pursuit?

Harold Silver

In 1956 the vice-chancellor of the Queen's University of Belfast wrote categorically that 'educational institutions are not the pace-makers for social change (much as they like to think they are): they are drawn along, often reluctantly, in the wake of social change'.[1] The relationships of British higher education institutions with their communities and the processes and outcomes of social change have been considerably reshaped since the 1950s. The landscape of British higher education itself has become almost unrecognizable, and the pressures for change both in higher education and in its social and political environments have increased both steadily and on occasion dramatically. And yet a study of relationships between 'a traditional civic university and its regional community' could argue equally categorically that even up to the 1990s 'it has not been a habit for the city or the region to seek expert help from the university or for the university to engage in a significant way with the city and the region in its work'.[2] A new vice-chancellor at another civic university found when he

---

[1] Ashby, Eric. "Function and Survival in British Universities." *University of Toronto Quarterly* 25, no. 2 (1956): 22–29.

[2] Wedgwood, Marilyn, and Brigitte Pemberton. "The University of Sheffield's Regional Office: Forging Relationships between a Traditional Civic University and its Regional Community." In *Universities and the Creation of Wealth*, edited by Harry Gray. Buckingham: Open University Press, 1999: 141.

arrived in 1986 that 'there was a lot of work already being done by staff on an individual level linking the University with the community, but the institutional role he was looking for was not there'.[3] The aim here, therefore, is to consider some historical questions concerning changes in higher education and whether or in what ways these may have influenced social change, as well as being influenced by it. For the literature on higher education this has generally involved focusing on such issues as expansion, patronage, diversification and the very concept and mission of a 'university' or 'higher education', including, for example, structures, curricula and contribution to the local and national economy. For social change this has been a question of defining 'social' and 'society' in breadth or more narrowly in terms of community and economy—'the city and the region in its work'—and the concept as interpreted by the increasingly interventionist state.

The Long Story

This relationship over the centuries has been treated by historians overwhelmingly in terms of the functions of the university with regard to its dominant environments:

> Our main question is how far the universities were influenced by, or themselves influenced, the society of which they formed part. From the thirteenth century to the early sixteenth, the universities were professional schools catering for the needs of the sub-society, the church.

In sixteenth-century England, Kearney here argues, the universities of Oxford and Cambridge were royally supported to help secure 'religious, political and social orthodoxy', and thenceforward the universities 'became institutions that catered for laymen as well as clerics' and the subjects they taught 'bore the marks of the Renaissance and the Reformation for a long time'. Their identities became a focus of debate from the early nineteenth century.[4] At all stages up to and including the nineteenth century the new institutions were enmeshed with outside agents and environments—the church, the city, employers and patrons, the professions and communities that sought them and their qualified and expert products. Histories of Oxford and Cambridge have traced their beginnings and some of the continuities in these contexts[5]—though most frequently with their internal features as the focus. Histories of the nineteenth-century foundations place their beginnings in community and wider contexts, but concentrate thereafter mainly on eminent figures, buildings, subjects and student life with the external world intruding only in the shape of, for

---

[3] Harrop, Sylvia. *The University of Liverpool 1981–1991*. Liverpool: Liverpool University Press, 1994: 95.

[4] Kearney, Hugh. "Universities and Society in Historical Perspective." In *Present and Future in Higher Education*, edited by R. E. Bell and A. J. Youngson. London: Tavistock Publications, 1973: 1–5.

[5] Cf. notably *The History of the University of Oxford*. General editor T. H. Aston. Oxford: Oxford University Press, vol. 1, 1984. *A History of the University of Cambridge*. General editor C. Brooke. Cambridge: Cambridge University Press, vol. 1, 1988.

example, war or shifts in government policy. There are exceptions, with attention paid to the university in interaction with Manchester, or the involvement of such cities as Hull or Leicester in the funding, expansion, student accommodation and curriculum development of their university.[6] There is difficulty, however, in most of this literature in locating a sustained interest in university–society interaction at an institutional level. In some general historical literature on higher education there is more frequently attention to a relationship with industry and the economy, incorporating also the history of university resistance to training other than for the most traditional professions of the church, law and medicine. The relationships of old and new universities and colleges in the nineteenth century and the outcomes of the industrial revolution have been the subject of historical scholarship,[7] although the economy as direct beneficiary of university expansion does not indicate a direct and intended impact on social change interpreted more broadly. Restructuring university curricula and pedagogy in order to meet the demands of changing professions and the creation or status of new ones may have implications for social change, but reaction to external changes and the supply of personnel for the professions do not necessarily suggest university intentions to effect change or to recognize responsibility for stimulating it.

The 'long story' is not, however, just about 800 years of 'universities'. The history of the new 'higher education' of the twentieth century has had to address developments out of alternative traditions. There were the universities created and in many cases re-created from the twelfth to the early twentieth century, adapting or developing alternative core models. There were new generations of higher education, many with ancestries in the technical and other institutions of the nineteenth century, converted from the mid-twentieth century into regional colleges, colleges of advanced technology, polytechnics and universities. Teacher education contributed the colleges that had begun life on the margins of or totally beyond what was understood as higher education until the mid-twentieth century. It is not easy to relate this complex picture of higher education after the Second World War to the rapid social changes that influenced or shaped higher education and looked to it for solutions to social and economic problems. The colleges of advanced technology were part of the response to postwar pressures for an increased supply of engineers and other technologists. The championing of 'sandwich courses' by these colleges and the National Council for Technological Awards (NCTA) that oversaw them aimed directly to shape one corner of the employment market. From the early 1970s the polytechnics further helped to influence technological and professional employment, and with the Council for National Academic Awards (CNAA), which awarded their degrees,

---

[6] Pullan, Brian, with Michele Abendstern. *A History of the University of Manchester 1951–73.* Manchester: Manchester University Press, 2000. Bamford, T. W. *The University of Hull: The First Fifty Years.* Oxford: Oxford University Press, 1978. Simmons, Jack. *New University.* Leicester: Leicester University Press, 1958.

[7] Notably Sanderson, Michael. *The Universities and British Industry.* London: Routledge & Kegan Paul, 1972.

developed degree programmes in professional, business and socially relevant interdisciplinary areas.[8] National committees and commissions and agencies, as well as the growth of higher education, brought the universities into more direct preparation for employments such as business, nursing and school teaching.

How all of these, particularly the 'old' universities and the polytechnics that were renamed universities in 1992, contributed to social change in Britain is a question not addressed simply by consulting the extensive institutional historical writing of the late twentieth and the early twenty-first century. A focus on rising student numbers and new student constituencies, the widening range and intensity of research and undergraduate and postgraduate curricula all have obvious social implications, but they tell little of the social mission of the universities. Although 'community' has often been referred to as part of universities' mission it has not generally been acted upon as a priority. The descendants of the technical institutions, of course, were intensely local in character and until the mid- to late twentieth century were under local control and influence unlike anything that applied to the universities. The colleges of advanced technology and especially the polytechnics not only offered socially important courses but also provided them for part-time, mature and employment-based students—ones that had not traditionally been the clientele of the universities. The colleges designated as polytechnics at the end of the 1960s and the beginning of the 1970s were reorganized so as to hand over much of their sub-degree work to 'further education' colleges, but they remained under local authority control until 1988. Their profiles as 'new universities' from 1992 differed considerably and their commitment to local and regional communities was balanced variously against their new position in national policy and funding frameworks. Their student recruitment remained predominantly local and regional.

The relationship between, on the one hand, the universities and the higher education system that grew in the twentieth century, and on the other hand the 'communities' in which they lived and worked, was invariably a major element in the histories written about the birth and early years of the institutions. While focusing on the internal life an occasional history might offer more than a glimpse of support by and for the local and regional economy[9] or controversial local, national and international policy issues. A chapter of a history of the University of Liverpool situated it in the Edwardian period in the context of dissolving Victorian certainties, the organization of labour and women on the march to political power.[10] The authors of a history of the University of Glasgow from 1870 indicated that 'in order to understand the

---

[8] Silver, Harold. *A Higher Education: The Council for National Academic Awards and British Higher Education 1964–89*. London: Falmer Press, 1990. Pratt, John. *The Polytechnic Experiment 1965–1992*. Buckingham: Open University Press, 1997.

[9] For example, *Aberdeen University 1945–1981: Regional Roles and National Needs*, edited by John D. Hargreaves with Angela Forbes. Aberdeen: Aberdeen University Press, 1989. Ives, Eric, Diane Drummond, and Leonard Schwartz. *The First Civic University: Birmingham 1880–1980. An Introductory History*. Birmingham: Birmingham University Press, 2000.

[10] Kelly, Thomas. *For Advancement of Learning: The University of Liverpool 1881–1981*. Liverpool: Liverpool University Press, 1981: ch. 4.

institution in the round, and to maximise the general relevance of the study, we have attempted ... to relate our evidence and interpretation to wider patterns'.[11] A history of Westminster College, Oxford was explicitly directed to 'the changing face of teacher education 1945–2001', relating the internal life of the college to the outside world of teacher education policy, local politics and decision-making, changes in higher education and demography, and relations with the Methodist Church, crossing relevantly a variety of college boundaries.[12] Most historians of institutions, however, have kept close to the internal narrative and such extensions of it as may be important to the external audience.[13] The long relationship with local authorities in the case of what became the polytechnics gave a different kind of prominence to accounts of their communities. *Degrees East*, the story of a century of 'the making of the University of East London' brought into play the local institutions from which it was created, their civic contexts, their aims and values, and the indebtedness of the changing institution to its combined ancestries.[14]

Responsiveness

The long history of the universities has been seen by historians as containing frequent evidence of responsiveness under pressure or duress. From the thirteenth to the eighteenth centuries, in Kearney's summary, 'the balance of subjects taught within the universities was dictated by the presumed needs of the sub-society they served.... The universities in short were the organs of an ecclesiastical elite.' Sixteenth-century royal endowments were 'part of a policy to secure religious, political, and social orthodoxy throughout the country ... the new regius professorships were royal nominees and the new royal colleges were visible reminders of the power and patronage of the state'. The creation of University College, London in the 1820s was seen as aiming to serve the 'middling rich', and changes at Oxford and Cambridge in the 1850s made them 'a training ground for the new breed of civil servants that came into existence as a result of the Northcote-Trevelyan report (1853)'. From then on the universities were 'the source of a new governing elite in England and in her Indian Empire'.[15] The long history (extended, modified and remodified in various ways in recent decades) has also focused on other forms of change as response, notably in the recent past, and internationally. Universities moved into the twentieth century with their directions determined increasingly by government and its appointed commissions. The Barlow

---

[11] Moss, Michael, J. Forbes Munro, and Richard H. Trainor. *The University of Glasgow since 1870.* Edinburgh: Edinburgh University Press, 2000: 3–4.

[12] Bone, Jennifer. *Our Calling to Fulfil: Westminster College and the Changing Face of Teacher Education 1951–2001.* Bristol: Tockington Press, 2003.

[13] For example, Dahrendorf, Ralf. *LSE: A History of the London School of Economics and Political Science 1895–1995.* Oxford: Oxford University Press, 1995, with its interest in the coming of age of the social sciences.

[14] Burgess, Tyrrell, Michael Locke, John Pratt, and Nick Richard. *Degrees East. The Making of the University of East London 1892–1992.* London: Athlone Press, 1995.

[15] Kearney, "Universities and Society", 2–3, 6–7.

report of 1946 on scientific manpower exemplified the tone for policy-making from the Second World War, when urging a doubling of the output of scientific graduates: 'Each University and University College in the Kingdom must be invited to consider its position and form an assessment of the way in which it can best contribute to the expansion demanded.' A regional and national system needed to be developed in order to knit together the schools, the technical colleges, the higher technical institutes, the universities and industry.[16]

The universities felt national planning and funding pressures that were to strengthen as the relationship between higher education and economic growth became dominant determinants of policy-making. The Committee of Vice-Chancellors and Principals (CVCP) talked of the universities' role after the war in terms of their 'national service'.[17] In 1945 it outlined the part the universities were playing in national life, and 'in other ways the nation turns to us'.[18] By 1970 the CVCP was pointing out the 'more central and significant role in society' of the universities than a decade previously, because of the increase in the number of professions formerly recruiting non-graduates and now turning to university-trained graduates, and the increased number of graduates being recruited for occupations that had previously recruited smaller numbers.[19] The University Grants Committee, though playing a buffer role between government and the universities, in the 1950s and 1960s shaped the latter's curricula by advising on development plans that might be 'required in order to ensure that they are fully adequate to the national needs'. Its report covering 1957–1962 dealt in this regard with its efforts, for example, on behalf of science and technology, medicine, dentistry, veterinary science, agriculture and forestry, oriental, African, Slavonic and East European studies, social and economic research, oceanography and management studies.[20] Five years later the directions on which its efforts had focused included agricultural education, area studies, business management studies, educational technology and town and country planning.[21]

There were divided views regarding the growing policy, planning and financial role of the state and its agencies, particularly as these began to invest in alternatives to the universities. Davis, in his account of the precursors of the NCTA and the Diploma in Technological Education in the 1950s, emphasized the postwar moves towards a government, 'dirigiste' approach to technological education, while Burgess and Pratt went further, seeing the NCTA as a historical breakthrough: 'For the first time in the history of higher education an institution was created specifically to respond to the requirements and demands from bodies in the outside world, and to administer an

---

[16] *Scientific Manpower* (Barlow report, Cmnd 6824). London: HMSO, 1946: 20.

[17] CVCP. A note on university policy and finance, 6 July 1946: 15. Warwick Modern Records Centre, U.G.C. No. 1, 1945–75.

[18] CVCP. Deputation to the Chancellor of the Exchequer on January 25th, 1945: 7. Warwick Modern Records Centre, U.G.C. No. 1, 1945–75.

[19] CVCP. *University Development in the 1970s.* [London]: CVCP, April 1970: 3.

[20] UGC. *University Development 1957–1962.* London: HMSO, 1964 (Cmnd 2267), ch. 7.

[21] UGC. *University Development 1962–1967.* London: HMSO, 1968 (Cmnd 3820), ch. 5.

award of national currency at first-degree level in direct response to these demands.'[22] The Organisation for Economic Co-operation and Development, in a foreword to the Burgess and Pratt study, made a general comment that is in line with much of the historical account of higher education in its social and economic setting:

> ... it is now increasingly recognized that educational systems in general, and higher educa-tion in particular, cannot adequately respond to the needs of the economy and society unless they are *subjected* to more or less profound adaptations implying equally important innovations.[23]

'*Subjected*' (emphasis added) is open to interpretation but no doubt it reflects the frequent processes and events by which historians underline the pressures and inter-nalization underlying university responsiveness over the centuries. Sanderson's account of the varied developments in industrial connections with British universities old and new in the nineteenth and twentieth centuries reinforces the point. This is a complex portrait of changes in industry, changes in the universities (including the creation of new ones) and the relationships. It traces the penetration of the sciences, economics, commerce and administrative studies into the universities and the slow change from the recruitment to industrially related courses of the children of indus-trialist and business families to a wider concern with directing graduates into indus-trial, scientific and administrative careers. There is no suggestion in the story, however, that new departures originated in the universities' own initiatives or that these were aiming to achieve any social changes other than ones already in motion with which they were requested, required or induced to associate themselves. Sand-erson suggests, for example, that at the turn of the twentieth century business atti-tudes 'were giving way to a recognition that even the non-technical businessman had to be given a higher education relevant to his future career. This task was thrown on the universities because traditional forms of business training within the firm were ceasing to be effective'. In the 1930s 'it was not only the increasingly scientific char-acter of industry ... that created a demand for graduates; it was also felt by several eminent business leaders that management was becoming more difficult and called for better educated and more intelligent minds than before'. By the early 1960s and the Robbins committee British industry itself, Sanderson emphasized, was clear that it would benefit from the expansion of higher education and was 'aware that the universities had not kept pace with the demands of industry and ...hoped that an expansion would rectify this by raising university entrance from 4 to 7 per cent of school leavers'.[24]

Sanderson is here concerned exclusively with those university developments relating to industry and business. We have seen also through the eyes of the CVCP

---

[22] Davis, Martin. "Technology, institutions and status: technological education, debate and pol-icy. In *Technical Education and the State since 1850: Historical and Contemporary Perspectives*, edited by Penny Summerfield and Eric J. Evans. Manchester: Manchester University Press, 1990; Burgess, Tyrrell, and John Pratt. *Technical Education in the United Kingdom*. Paris: OECD, 1971: 49.

[23] OECD, Foreword to Burgess and Pratt, *Technical Education in the United Kingdom*, 5.

[24] Sanderson, *Universities and British Industry*, 185, 245, 363 and passim.

how 'the nation turns to us' and through those of the UGC how it undertook to pilot the universities in particular directions. We have sampled only a small number of changes in university behaviours under external pressure and stimulus, and these have indicated some relationships between higher education and segments of the outside world. Little of the literature of higher education treats historically the nature of the community relationship, and certainly with regard to the twentieth and twenty-first centuries what has been most highlighted has been the impact of social change on higher education, not vice versa. Much attention has been paid internationally to the effects on higher education or categories of higher education of the requirements, policies, funding arrangements, blandishments and temptations adopted by governments and their agencies. Sporn's study of US and European university adaptation to changing socioeconomic environments, for example, describes 'how different environmental changes are impacting demands of access, quality, costs, and effectiveness of education at colleges and universities'. It covers comprehensively 'the changing role of the state, the autonomy status of institutions, new funding mechanisms, and globalization of scholarship ... increased competition and challenges universities are facing in their "core business"'.[25] The massification of higher education has itself produced changes in mission, structures, processes, the roles of new technologies and close engagement with transferable skills and preparation for employment. Differences have only partly been associated with the distinction between 'old' and 'new' universities, since basic changes once unwelcome have taken place—not without reluctance—in the former as they have recognized the power of external agencies scrutinizing their practices, procedures and outcomes. They have had to worry about competition for financial support and students in the marketplace, prepare for detailed external scrutiny and be seen to be achieving high standards, newly defined.[26]

Higher education has therefore had to respond to interrelated economic and social changes embodied in policy shifts affecting the system, as well as the expectations of community and political and increasingly interventionist constituencies. The greater scale and restructuring of institutional administration and resource allocation have meant greater oversight of procedures. Curriculum change has responded to student preferences—themselves in part shaped by age, gender, ideological pressures and expectations of the labour market. Pedagogical change has been driven by teachers' ability to manage new structures, as well as student numbers and assessment, the use of new technologies and expected learning and its explicitly defined outcomes. To what extent, therefore, have institutions sought to influence or succeeded in influencing the social changes that in recent decades have had such considerable external and internal impacts on them? Is it possible even to pose the question when types of institutions have historically addressed change with different emphases and transformational or

---

[25] Sporn, Barbara. *Adaptive University Structures.* London: Jessica Kingsley, 1999: 6–7.

[26] For a detailed international discussion see Brennan, John, Peter de Vries and Ruth Williams (eds). *Standards and Quality in Higher Education.* London: Jessica Kingsley, 1997.

defensive attitudes? Even within institutions responses have been hugely kaleidoscopic, as they have faced an essential paradox:

> Changes in the world at large, particularly in high technology, information-rich, post-industrial societies, constitute an environment common to all universities ... in many ways culturally alien to the traditional university, both British and continental European. At the same time it opens up new and large opportunities ... as the need for highly skilled and frequently updated labour shows itself.[27]

The paradox has been presented as positive, since 'if higher education has been and is about anything it is about exploiting and realizing the potential of the world around us and understanding it better'.[28] It has also been presented as intensely negative, with students having become 'customers', heads of departments 'line managers', many vice-chancellors 'chief executives', lecturers no longer teaching but 'delivering the curriculum'. Financial cuts have become 'efficiency gains', staff are not made redundant but simply removed as the result of 'downsizing'. Understanding 'is being replaced by "competence"' and education is being transformed into 'a mass commodity to be bought and sold in the market place'. The future of the country is in terms of an industrial model—'UK plc'.[29]

Universities with histories in technical and further education have had the most clearly definable relationships with their external contexts. Redbrick, provincial universities had beginnings and missions strongly influenced by their location. New 1960s universities were able to pursue changes in their social and curriculum structures. Oxbridge had long established, characteristic and deeply cherished commitments. Monotechnic institutions preparing for technological, fine arts, teaching and other professions had features they struggled to maintain independently or when amalgamated into comprehensive institutions. Within institutions specific units often had remits to serve community needs—particularly in the case of what have been termed extension, adult or continuing education units, or other forms of outreach. Research related to and could be conducted with or financed by external commercial, industrial or governmental bodies. One account of the trajectory of these issues from the vantage of the early 2000s placed the book's origins in 'the increasingly instrumental direction of higher education, the growing idolatry of market forces, and higher education's seeming dislocation from a contribution to sustaining deliberative democracy in the broader society'.[30]

It is arguable that all of the institutions in which these various features could be found were in fact *created in order to respond*. Occasional visionaries within higher

[27] Duke, Chris. *The Learning University: Towards a New Paradigm?* Buckingham: Open University Press, 1992: 7.

[28] Holland, Geoffrey. "Foreword." In *Universities and the Creation of Wealth*, edited by Harry Gray. Buckingham: Open University Press, 1999: xii.

[29] Coffield, Frank, and Bill Williamson. "The challenges facing higher education." In Coffield and Williamson, (eds), *Repositioning Higher Education*. Buckingham: Open University Press, 1997: 1.

[30] Walker, Melanie, and Jon Nixon, eds. *Reclaiming Universities from a Runaway World*. Maidenhead: Open University Press, 2004: 1.

education institutions might look to achieve social impacts in the arts or education, science or technology, but this has not necessarily been the case at institutional level. Institutional makeovers producing colleges of advanced technology or polytechnics might achieve changes in scale, mission and status, but though adaptation and purpose were closely linked, the purpose might point to responses in various directions, not to the *initiation* of change. The introduction of new subjects—environmental, business related and others—in the polytechnics, for example, provides examples of awareness of social change, not of its instigation. Modularization or new forms of outreach to disadvantaged communities are examples of other forms of social awareness, which come close to influencing social change, but still are not clear forms of its instigation. The conclusion is that higher education has often acted to *confirm* and *extend*, not to initiate, and much of its impact has been indirect. The teaching of more and different students clearly has a social effect that is long term but not necessarily directed towards the institution's own search for social change. This does not mean that British experience of systemic and institutional restructuring and its curricular and pedagogical components has been without significance or benefit. What it does mean is that Ashby's description of British higher education in the mid-twentieth century has continued to be reflected in institutions not acting as conscious and explicit change agents.

The argument can be clarified by comparing attempts by some American higher education institutions to take on the role. Sociologist Adam S. Weinberg in 2002 addressed the issue in a paper entitled 'The university: an agent of social change?'. The question was whether it was true that 'universities never act as agents of progressive social change', and Weinberg adduced four examples of institutions that were in fact doing so. Loyola University had established a Center for Urban Research and Learning, enabling faculty and students to use research experience 'to provide political power to local community groups fighting poverty, racism, and other major urban problems'. Trinity College had 'publicly embraced the role of social change agent within the city of Hartford, and reconstructed itself internally to meet this commitment ... to a revitalization initiative' for a major area surrounding the college. Colgate University had created 'a free-standing nonprofit organization ... to support the implementation of a multi-year based planning process', diverting existing resources and obtaining state and other grants. Georgetown University operated a number of programmes through a Center for Social Justice, Research, and Service, including a collaborative programme with two Washington communities that had been named 'empowerment zones'. Involvement with local communities, Weinberg points out, was not new. The novelty in these cases arose from the university having altered its normal operating principle, elevating social change from 'a by-product of some process to a core product'. From a service provision model the institutions had developed new models of 'changing the community by empowering it in relevant political arenas'.[31]

---

[31] Weinberg, Adam S. "The university: an agent of social change?" *Qualitative Sociology* 25, no. 2 (2002): 263–72.

Crucial to these examples is their *explicit* commitment to some form of social change. These examples obviously have to be seen in relation to aspects of the institutional decisions and resources and the histories of American university–community relations. It is not possible to say how many institutions have gone in this explicit direction, though service learning and donor involvement have histories back to the 1960s, in particular.[32] It is well to remember, however, that there are widespread and very different judgements about American higher education and its purposes. Astin, one of its major interpreters, concluded in 2004 that higher education plays a central role in 'shaping civic life' by educating 'each new generation of leaders in government, business, law, medicine, the clergy, and other advanced professions'. The position, nevertheless, was that, 'like it or not, American higher education is sanctioned and supported by that society, and has in turn pledged itself to serve that society'.[33] Shapiro, former President of Princeton University, in 2003 described 'the two most crucial characteristics that public and private universities share: they serve society as both a responsive servant and thoughtful critic'.[34] Neither Astin nor Shapiro (and many other commentators) goes beyond service or critique to the kind of initiative-taking in Weinberg's examples. The comparison with these American initiatives, however, helps to highlight the 'by-product', inexplicit nature in Britain of any institutional interest in social change. It would be impossible to discuss, for example, Enterprise in Higher Education, sandwich courses and work-based learning or continuing education as comparable with these American strategies, and there are, of course, major differences between the positions of institutions in the two systems. British institutions' responsiveness across the twentieth century might be described as 'induced action' or 'commissioned innovation'.

'Engagement'

It is worth reflecting on directions taken by higher education around the turn of the twenty-first century, and the fragments of comment and analysis available to future historians. By the turn of the century definitions of the relationships between higher education institutions and their communities were being fashioned anew. In old vocabularies, higher education was having to review its connections with the local and regional community, if only to reaffirm its position as a (often *the*) major local employer. New vocabularies also emerged, however, asserting directions linked to older traditions, the most clamorous and debated being in the

---

[32] Boyer, Ernest L. *College: The Undergraduate Experience in America*. New York: Harper & Row, 1987, ch. 13, "Service: getting involved".

[33] Astin, Alexander W. "Exercising Leadership to Promote the Civic Mission of Higher Education" (address at Campus Compact's Presidents' Leadership Colloquium, 2004). Available from http://www.compact.org/2004PLC/Alexander_Astin_PLC_Talk.pdf; INTERNET (accessed 14 April 2006).

[34] Shapiro, Harold T. "A Larger Sense of Purpose: Higher Education and Society." Available from http://www.pupress.princeton.edu/chapters/s8022.html (accessed 14 April 2006).

United States, but taken up in the UK and widely in Europe. For some American contributors the record of higher education's social responsibilities simply needed reinvigorating. A Kellogg Forum committed itself from 2001 to enhancing the level of public understanding about 'the contribution higher education makes to the improvement of our lives, the defence of our freedoms and the practice of democracy in a diverse society'. The public did not understand that 'colleges help society as a whole, and that more people benefit than the graduates themselves'. A national campaign was being launched to promote 'a new national dialogue on the social compact between higher education and society'.[35] Universities were also returning to nineteenth-century definitions of their role as 'trustees for the public interest' and the 'public mission of higher education', reviving vocabularies as old as American college education itself. What was new was what Burton Clark had placed on the agenda in 1998 with his survey of some European (including British) 'entrepreneurial universities'.[36] This concept surfaced in British policy on higher education in terms of dangers that had emerged in the late twentieth century: 'Over the last two decades, various social critics and leaders worldwide have noted a disturbing trend in higher education: the collective or public good, historically an important component of the charter between higher education and society, is being compromised....'.[37] 'Public mission', 'public trust', 'charter between higher education and society' were prominent American vocabularies, alongside 'campus compact' and 'civic mission', probed comprehensively by Astin in 2004. Apart from higher education's historic mission to educate new generations of leaders in prominent 'advanced professions', it also exerted 'important societal influences through the scientific, technological, and cultural knowledge produced by their faculties'. Nevertheless, 'the quality of civic life and engagement' was in decline. Attempts to take civic responsibilities more seriously were reflected in 'the rapid growth of the Campus Compact and the involvement of many of our leading higher education associations in initiatives to foster greater attention to civic engagement'.[38] All such concerns, in Britain as well as in the US, were encapsulated in the vocabulary of 'engagement'.

Debate in Britain was confined to increased partnerships between higher education institutions and economic entities, encouraged by national policy interests. The American debate was about protecting or resurrecting something in the American college dream and basic concerns regarding American democracy, civic responsibility and society. British concerns focused essentially on higher education and 'social'

[35] Kellogg Forum on Higher Education for the Public Good, 2001. Available from http://www.thenationalforum.org/goals.shtml (accessed 21 April 2006).

[36] Clark, Burton R. *Creating Entrepreneurial Universities: Organizational Pathways of Transformation.* Oxford: Pergamon Press, 1998.

[37] Kezar, Adrienna. "Compromising the Charter between Higher Education and Society." *International Higher Education,* Spring (2003). Available from http://bc.edu/bc_org/avp/soe/cihe/newsletter/News31/text010.htm (accessed 15 April 2006).

[38] Astin, "Exercising Leadership".

change, where 'social' still most frequently meant 'economic'. The vocabulary of 'engagement' underpinning the British development did parallel the intensive American developments in aiming to take higher education further away from the reality or the mythology of the ivory tower. A discussion paper from a British university began by describing national policy as seeking 'to encourage engagement between universities and society that ensures the assets and resources of universities, particularly the intellectual assets that the country has invested in, contribute to economic growth'. The analysis was grounded in the latter:

> Universities/HEIs, with their rich range of subject disciplines and intellectual resources have the capacity to contribute to these various aspects of economic productivity.... Each HEI, through their core activities of teaching and learning, research and knowledge transfer ... has a particular, and relatively distinctive contribution to make, based on its strengths, assets and missions, its culture, history and traditions.[39]

This 'Third Stream Funding' (that is, supplementary to the teaching and research 'streams') was essentially a product of engagement or productive partnerships. From the late 1990s the goal in the UK was to ensure that all higher education institutions 'are committed to making an active and effective contribution to improving the performance of the UK's knowledge base, and the overall innovation performance of the economy for the social and economic benefit of the UK'.[40]

Over the nineteenth and twentieth centuries a contribution to the economy was a possible choice for a higher education institution, for its founders and patrons. Policy-makers had, however, come to diagnose a pervasive weakness in the casual or reluctant nature of higher education's relationship to the economy, and by the beginning of the twenty-first century engagement with the economy had become a dirigiste, policy-directed imperative. It was no longer enough in the UK and across Europe for institutions with technological or industrially directed histories and missions to be the prime movers in economic competition and innovation. The search was for means of enabling or requiring *all* higher education institutions to participate in partnership in the primacy of the economy as the engine of social change. Historians of this period will have to determine the relative strengths of the motivations and the directions taken, in the different cultural, 'étatiste' and funding positions of different countries, including the finger pointed accusingly at institutional irrelevance. The authors of a contribution to an American 1998 book on *The Responsive University* described many educational institutions as having 'gates, well-manicured lawns, shrubs and flowers, walls and trees to buffer the campus from the outside world. The academy does not often believe and act as though the campus is

---

[39] Wedgwood, Marilyn. "A Quality Framework and Metrics for HEIF3: A Discussion Paper from Manchester Metropolitan University", 2003. Available from http://www.mmu.ac.uk/externalrelations/papers/quality.pdf (accessed 21 April 2006).

[40] "Third Stream Funding: Funding Universities for Engagement in the Third Millennium." Paper submitted to the AVCC on behalf of the New Generation Universities, 2005. Available from http://research.vu.au/ordsite/ThirdStreamFunding.pdf (accessed 15 April 2006).

the world and the world is the campus.'[41] It was to counter such perceptions in the UK that the CVCP commissioned a report published in 1994 on *Universities and Communities*. Universities, pointed out the CVCP Chairman, 'are not ivory towers, despite the popular misconceptions in some quarters. They are living organisations which draw their vitality from the world around them.' The report itself was a rounded account of the economic and other social impacts of the universities in their localities. It covered the kinds of local contribution institutions made in research and training, the availability of amenities and examples of types of community service.[42] It will serve historians of the period as a valuable database but, as we have stressed, the contribution of the institutions may be one of partnership and service but not necessarily one of leadership and initiative. This was clearly implied by the vice-chancellors' organization Universities UK in 2006, when issuing a statement on 'Universities: engaging with local communities', beginning:

> Universities have a massive impact on their locality, not only as a result of the—often large—movement of people at the beginning and end of terms. Their social and cultural impact is felt through their provision of sports facilities, art galleries, cinemas and theatres, while as employers, and providers of skilled graduates, universities contribute to their local economies…. One of the core aims of UK higher education has been to meet the needs of the wider community, and the expansion of higher education has meant an increasing impact on that community.[43]

The details of the universities' mission and impact are in these terms quite different from any conception of leadership in social change. What historians will no doubt have to consider will be the outcomes of the processes of 'engagement' as a product of the complex interaction of expansion and 'impact' resulting from national policy, community pressure and institutional response.

On the Run?

The main aim of British higher education institutions in this connection has been one of *support*, either of the status quo or of externally determined change. It produced the eighteenth-century gentleman, the nineteenth-century administrator, the twentieth-century professional. Higher education endeavours were focused on appropriate supply and improvement. Individual academics (whether Oxbridge dons, founders and leaders of new universities, or higher education teachers of all kinds) have sought to bring about curricular or pedagogical changes that might—largely through the beneficent effect of new generations of students—influence the aims and behaviours of engineers, teachers, doctors or academics. Major disturbances to established

---

[41] Braskamp, Larry A., and Jon F. Wergin. "Forming New Social Partnerships." In *The Responsive University: Restructuring for High Performance*, edited by William G. Tierney. Baltimore, MD: Johns Hopkins University Press, 1998: 62–63.

[42] Goddard, John, et al. *Universities and Communities*. London: CVCP, 1994: ii and passim.

[43] Universities UK. "Universities: Engaging with Local Communities." Available from http://bookshop.universitiesuk.ac.uk/downloads/students_communities.pdf (accessed 9 June 2006).

patterns of provision have come from public demands for more understanding or communicative doctors, more socially conscious professionals of many kinds, or a more technically competent workforce. Higher education has made responses to known external social forces and demands with much, little or no enthusiasm, depending on an institution's history and status, its expectation of loss or gain, and its willingness or otherwise to confront internal support or dissent. Higher education has been a target for constantly changing expectations, for calls to help to mediate change of many kinds and overcome time lag in the achievement of social change promoted from other directions. These are not unworthy roles for higher education, and indeed in relation to the civic universities, the colleges of advanced technology or the polytechnics they have been an important means of enabling external changes to find a location for expression and continuity.

The effect of major contextual pressures, policies and changes on higher education has been a focus of research and analysis, including by sociologists, specialists in higher education and concerned participants. There is as yet, however, no historical agenda to elucidate such issues, whether recent or across the twentieth and twenty-first centuries. The history of the lack of 'social purpose', in Pippard's words in 1973, has not attracted sustained historical interest. He was responding to an Oxford don's reservations about universities or any extensive part of higher education 'acting as the intellectual powerhouse of social control and change, as problem-spotter and solution-seeker at all social levels, from the most sophisticated planning bureaux to the most mundane grassroots'.[44] Pippard, Cavendish Professor of Physics at Cambridge, thought that social purposes were in search of higher education rather than the reverse:

> Higher education as we were brought up to think of it, is on the run with social purpose rampantly in pursuit, and we are now having to face up to the fact that the institutions of higher education are the creation of government in response to the will of the people.

The latter, he emphasized, included the students. Student demand was 'for something having moral and social content, and not for the exclusive pursuit of knowledge divorced from action. I do not believe we can ignore this pressure—I don't believe we ought to.'[45] Eric Ashby had underlined in 1956, as we saw at the outset, that education institutions were 'not the pace-makers for social change', they were drawn along 'in the wake of social change'.[46] Mackinder had commented in 1903, the year in which he became director of the London School of Economics, that in the mid-nineteenth century Oxbridge was penetrated by a variety of external pressures, and 'as a natural result of this invasion of the territory of higher education Oxford and Cambridge were compelled to an effort of defensive energy'.[47] A complex historical

---

[44] Weinstein, W. L. "Social Purposes in Search of Higher Education, or Higher Education in Search of Social Purposes?" In *A National Purpose for Higher Education*, edited by David Warrant Piper. London: University of London Institute of Education, [1973]: 20 (typescript publication).

[45] Pippard, Brian. "Comment". In *A National Purpose*, 27.

[46] Ashby, "Function and Survival".

[47] Mackinder, H. J. "Higher Education". In *The Nation's Need: Chapters on Education*, edited by Spenser Wilkinson. London: Archibald Constable, 1903: 238.

account is needed to explore the details of higher education, its sectors and institutions, following in the wake of social change or being on the run with social purpose in pursuit. Oxbridge's 'defensive energy' has had its historians, but the phrase is applicable to a historical thread in higher education that has been barely explored. Investigation of higher education's impact on or contribution to British social change has been meagre—and by historians virtually non-existent.

Disability, Education and Social Change in England since 1960

Felicity Armstrong

Disability and disabled people are under-represented in the history of education. The exclusion of disabled children from ordinary schools, which occurred routinely in England until the late twentieth century, is mirrored in the way disability and difference have been largely ignored in formal historical work.[1] Richard Altenbaugh has argued that disability has not been treated in the same way as social categories such as race, class and gender and historians have 'generally neglected disability itself as a mark of inequality'.[2] It could be argued that this neglect is underpinned by an understanding of impairment as being a *natural* or implicitly justifiable reason for marginalization, in contrast to inequalities experienced by other social categories.

The history of the relationship between education and disability in England in recent years has been marked by struggles over participation, social attitudes and rights within a period of rapid social and economic change. Dominant assumptions regarding impairment, the experience of disabled people and their social roles have

---

[1] For example, In *A History of English Education from 1760,* first published in 1947, with a 2nd edn in 1966, Barnard devoted approximately three pages out of 334 to special education. See Barnard, H. C. *A History of English Education from 1760.* London: University of London Press, 1947.

[2] Altenbaugh, Richard J. "Where are the disabled in the History of Education? The Impact of Polio on Sites of Learning." *History of Education* 35, no. 6 (2006) 705–30.

been increasingly challenged by the disability movement and disability scholars, and within human rights debates and organizations. Legislation such as the Disability Discrimination Act (1995) and the Special Educational Needs and Disability Act (2001) have attempted to remove some of the barriers to access and participation in education, the environment, employment and ordinary social life, marking an apparent cultural shift in official assumptions, expectations and opportunities. However, the effects of discriminatory structures, attitudes and practices are still deeply rooted as evidenced, for example, by the numbers of children identified as having 'special educational needs' attending segregated schools or units in England,[3] the economic status of disabled people and the low levels of participation by disabled people in higher education and employment.

The aim of the first half of this paper is to outline some of the key developments that have taken place in the field of education and disability, particularly since 1944, with some reference to changes in the social and intellectual context since 1960. These changes have included a critical re-evaluation of existing historical work and the emergence of new approaches that recognize subjectivity, multiple levels of experience, the micro-politics of power, and the centrality of discourse in the study of social relationships. The second half of the paper is concerned with the historiography of education and disability and considers some of the different approaches that have been adopted to historical analysis in the field in the recent period.

'Education and the Handicapped, 1760–1960'— on the Cusp of Change

D. G. Pritchard's major work[4] *Education and the Handicapped, 1760–1960*, published in 1963, marks a transition stage in terms of historical enquiry in the field of disability and education. It provides a useful starting point for a discussion of some subsequent and contrasting developments, both in the history of education and provision for disabled students, and in the ways these have been researched and written about. Pritchard's work is an example of a 'modernist' approach in which historians engage in a 'quest for revealed truth' involving the 'discovery, identification of hidden structures, and the 'digging up of clues'.[5] The challenge to historians of the period was not to explore different 'realities' or 'interpretations' of the world from different perspectives, in which the 'voices' of insiders are regarded as key in constructing different narratives, but a rational and empirical search for 'truths' in a knowable, researchable world. The modernist tradition was 'part of a conservative commitment to realism that theory is unnecessary, epistemology and methodology being largely a matter of

---

[3] *Segregation trends—LEAs in England 2002–2004*. Bristol: Centre for Studies on Inclusive Education, 2005; Department for Education and Skills First Release. *Special Educational Needs in England, January 2006*. Department for Education and Skills, National Statistics, SFR 23/2006.

[4] Pritchard, D. *Education and the Handicapped 1760–1960*. London: Routledge & Kegan Paul, 1963.

[5] McCulloch, G., and W. Richardson. *Historical Research in Educational Settings*. Buckingham: Open University Press, 2000: 30.

common-sense'.[6] It is this 'common-sense' tradition which has been challenged, if not trounced, by new, fundamentally different approaches to historical enquiry that reflect the changing cultural understandings and sociopolitical struggles over the past 45 years.

The material in Pritchard's book provides a detailed account of structures, pedagogies and practices in the education of disabled children over a period of 200 years. The author's sources were extensive and included legislation, official reports, conference proceedings, books and articles. It is an example, perhaps, of what Foucault referred to as 'history as that which transforms documents into monuments'.[7] I will return to Pritchard's work in the second half of the paper.

The work of Foucault, also referred to later in this paper, made a key contribution in refocusing attention away from 'grand narratives' featuring prominent historical figures, legislation, and notions of 'evolution and recurrence' which were part of the dominant social-historical paradigms.[8] Foucault's 'genealogical' approach recognized 'the events of history, its jolts, its surprises, its unsteady victories, and unpalatable defeats—the basis for all beginnings, atavisms, and heredities'. O'Brien describes this approach as appearing:

> ... deceptively simple: recognizing and juxtaposing differences in search of the manifesta-
> tion of power that permeates all social relations. Power is a complex phenomenon that
> challenges positivist assumptions. Foucault's method allows us to perceive how societies
> function. Studying power through discourse allows us to perceive the moment when new
> technologies of power are introduced.[9]

This understanding, which is in profound contrast with Pritchard's approach, is relevant to some of the work that has been carried out in recent years in the field of disability, which explores critically the role of professionals and the discourses and power relations invested in their 'expertise', and involves systems of categorization and labelling,[10] or 'regimes of truth'.

Another important influence on the way history has been re-conceptualized in seeking to understand social and historical change relates to the cultural explorations of social historians such as E. P. Thompson and Natalie Davis in the early 1970s, which sought to 'give voice and life to the peasants, workers, and artisans they studied'.[11] The emergence of this kind of work reflects the political and social 'egalitarian' upheavals of the 1960s and a growing awareness of social inequalities. It challenged

---

[6] Parker, C. *The English Historical Tradition since 1850*. Edinburgh: John Donald, 1990: 199–200, cited in McCulloch and Richardson, ibid.

[7] Foucault, M *Archaeology of Knowledge*. London: Tavistock, 1972.

[8] O'Brien, P. "Michel Foucault's History of Culture." In *The New Cultural History*, edited by Lynn Hunt. California: University of California Press, 1989.

[9] O'Brien, P. Ibid, 38.

[10] Billington, T. *Separating, Losing and Excluding Children: Narratives of Difference*. London: RoutledgeFalmer, 2000.

[11] Desan, S. "Crowds, Community, and Ritual in the work of E. P. Thompson and Natalie Davis." In *The New Cultural History*, edited by Lynn Hunt. California: University of California Press, 1989.

the historical silencing of working-class people, and of marginalized groups, and opened up new ways of exploring social history and legitimized new kinds of material. This is also relevant to some of the more recent work in the history of education and disabled people, which focuses on the importance of 'voice' and narrative histories and will be returned to.

In tracing an outline of some of the key developments that have taken place in the field of education and disability in the following section, I adopt an economical and linear approach in providing some key features and facts, rather than a more textured, critical and analytical account. It is precisely this kind of teleological 'writing of history' that is critiqued in the second part of this paper, and which is now regarded as very limited in terms of understanding historical and social change. However, some kind of 'historical background' is required and it is not possible, in the space available, to cover such a large period and complex subject matter in a way that recognizes subjectivity, contradiction, multiplicity and the richness and diversity of human experience. The account in the next section is, therefore, only a bare skeletal, surface account of the development of education and disability, and gives no insight into the social and cultural relations and struggles that have underpinned it. In the second part of this paper, I will discuss some alternative approaches to exploring the historical development of education and disability.

Disabled Children, Education and Legislation—a 'Linear' Account

The setting up of educational structures for children with impairments can be traced back to the eighteenth century in England, although there were many earlier examples of institutions established by religious orders, and later examples set up by lay voluntary associations funded by charities[12] and philanthropists. Prior to the 1870s, many disabled children from poorer families were sent to workhouses, reformatory or industrial schools[13] where they sometimes received basic education and training. There were also the lunatic asylums where children and adults diagnosed as insane or 'mentally defective' were placed, and where they sometimes received education and training,[14] but the residential special schools, which were located in asylums controlled by doctors, psychiatrists and philanthropists, were detached from the education sector and the influence of educationists.[15] The dominance of the early history of special education by medicine and psychiatry has had a profound and long-lasting influence

---

[12] Sutherland, G. "The origins of special education." In *The Practice of Special Education*, edited by Will Swann. Oxford: Basil Blackwell, 1981: 94.

[13] Hurt, J. S. *Outside the Mainstream: A History of Special Education*. London: Batsford, 1988.

[14] One example of this was the Starcross asylum near Exeter, which was later developed as a residential special school. See Dale, P. "Tension in the voluntary–statutory alliance: 'Lay professionals' and the planning and delivery of mental deficiency services, 1917–1945." In *Mental Illness and Learning Disability since 1850: Finding a Place for Mental Disorder in the United Kingdom*, edited by P. Dale and J. Melling. London: Routledge, 2006.

[15] Dale, P. "Special Education at Starcross before 1948." *History of Education*, 36, no 1 (2007): 17–44.

on perceptions of disabled children and the kind of provision made for them which has been characterized by care, control, therapy and remediation.

Formal education structures designated for disabled children began to develop following the introduction of elementary education through the education acts of 1870, 1876 and 1880. The *Report of the Royal Commission on the Blind, the Deaf, the Dumb and Others of the United Kingdom* (The Egerton Report), published in 1889,[16] was underpinned by a pragmatic and moral commitment to providing elementary technical education for blind people rather than 'support them through a life of idleness'.[17] These twin projects—that of economic rationalism and the moral imperative of productive labour—have dominated the history of responses to disability and the provision of education and training in England.

The burgeoning of the medical and therapeutic professions,[18] the interest in eugenics[19] and the refining of categorizations of defects and deficiency, as well as the increasing involvement of the state in social welfare and education since the late nineteenth century, fostered the growth in special education. It was also influenced by a number of other, sometimes conflicting, factors, including contemporary humanitarian values, a growing societal commitment to formal education, the need for a literate and manageable workforce, and the development and strengthening of local education authorities. These all played a part in the development of the network of structures which made up the special education system that developed during the first half of the twentieth century.

The 1944 Education Act (UK) introduced 11 'categories of handicap' and guidance concerning provision for each category and degree of impairment. It widened access to formal state education by drawing large numbers of disabled children into the education system for the first time and gave Local Education Authorities (LEAs) responsibility for their education. Significantly, the 1944 Education Act decreed that each child, with the exception of those deemed to be 'uneducable', should receive 'efficient full-time education suitable to his age, aptitude and ability either by regular attendance at schools or otherwise'. Subsequently, the Education (Handicapped Children) Act (1970) made local education authorities responsible for the education of *all* children, bringing every child into the education system, regardless of impairment or learning difficulty.

---

[16] *Report of the Royal Commission on the Blind, the Deaf, the Dumb and Others of the United Kingdom* (The Egerton Report). London: HMSO, 1889.

[17] Quoted in Tomlinson, S. *A Sociology of Special Education*. London: Routledge & Kegan Paul, 1982: 13.

[18] Potts, P. "Medicine, Morals and Mental Deficiency: the contribution of doctors to the development of special education in England." *Oxford Review of Education* 9, no. 3 (1983): 181–96.

[19] Barker, D. "How to Curb the Fertility of the Unfit: The Feeble-minded in Edwardian Britain." *Oxford Review of Education* 9, no, 3 (1983): 197–211.

The Warnock Report (1978)[20] challenged dominant assumptions that there were 'two types of children, the handicapped and the non-handicapped' and that the categorization of impairment was a justification for 'special' provision. It argued that the term 'handicapped' provided no information about *educational* need, marking an important change of emphasis. Disabled children were not to be seen as the recipients of therapy and care, but as learners with an entitlement to education. The 1981 Education Act which followed enshrined the term 'special educational needs' in legislation, ostensibly replacing the categories of impairment encoded by the 1944 Education Act. Provision was made for the introduction of statutory assessment of learning difficulties to establish whether a child had special educational needs, introducing the new label 'SEN', and what these needs were. 'Statements' of special educational needs, stipulating the nature of the 'needs', how they should be met and the resources required were drawn up for some children as an outcome of multi-professional assessment procedures. These procedures themselves had important implications in terms of educational provision and resources and engendered a massive rise in the number of professional assessments carried out. Paradoxically, although the term special educational needs focused on educational needs rather than individual impairments, it became a globalizing category denoting difference or learning difficulty which coexisted with the established categories of impairment, and alongside new ones.

More recently, legislation such as the Special Educational Needs and Disability Act (2001) adopted a change of emphasis in establishing a duty to educate children with special educational needs in mainstream schools, but this duty remains contingent and provisional as it applies only if 'it is compatible with the wishes of the parent' and the 'provision of efficient education for other children'. These are some of the 'bare bones' of key legislative changes in the development of special education in England. They say little about the wider social contexts in which they occurred and nothing about the experiences of disabled children.

Special Education and Social Change

Special education, its structures, practices and purposes are embedded in wider cultural values and social change. For example, the collusion of eugenics with humanitarianism and the growth in the power of the state at the end of the nineteenth century and the during the first part of the twentieth century were the architects of the growth and character of special education and these influences

---

[20] Department of Education and Science. *Special Educational Needs. Report of the Committee of Enquiry into the Education of Handicapped Children and Young People* (Warnock Report). London: HMSO, 1978.

were played out in debates and policy developments throughout the twentieth century.[21]

Changes in social life brought about by war have also influenced perceptions concerning impairment and disabled people and, in turn, have influenced the development of special education. During the Second World War the infrastructures of ordinary schooling, special education and residential institutions, were profoundly affected by the blitz, the evacuation of children from the cities, the widespread disruption in education services and a massive reduction in human resources and basic amenities. In 1941, for example, the number of disabled children attending special schools in London was reduced by 50% and many attended ordinary schools. These changes and the growing belief that special schools should be brought into the general education system paved the way for the 1944 Education Act. The postwar period marked a shift in emphasis in terms of the power and responsibility of different agencies in the governance of social life. Thus, in the postwar period medical officers have no longer been the designated decision-makers regarding diagnosis and educational placement. The local education authorities took on the role of coordinating the assessment process and making the final decision regarding special education placements, although medical professionals have continued to play an important role in assessment procedures and outcomes.

The growth of the welfare state during the postwar period, with the provision of services which were seen as a common social good—rather than a national economic drain on resources signalling economic and social dependency—also marked changes in perceptions of disability. As in the cases of illness, poverty and housing, rather than being a purely private and personal problem impairment and disability came, to some extent, to be regarded as a *social* issue legitimately requiring state support and

---

[21] This is well expressed in C. W. Hutt's *Crowley's Hygiene of School Life*. London: Methuen, 1910: 16–17. 'The newer views and outlook upon life which this opening century has brought, the increased development of social consciousness and of communal responsibility, together with the publication of the results of investigations by various observers, have ... served to arouse and even alarm the public. In addition, the great fact is steadily becoming admitted that these conditions of defective physique are the results of causes ... capable of removal and therefore to be removed.' Insight into the eugenicist thinking of the time can be found in C. W. Saleeby's book *The Progress of Eugenics*. London: Cassell, 1914: 208–09. 'For the greater number of cases where the principle of negative eugenics apply, permanent care or segregation of the individual is the remedy, if only because the individual would require such treatment even were he sterile, or were his defect not hereditary. No problem arises, therefore, except to silence stupid legislators. Nor does the question of possible sterilisation arise, for there is no such need where the individual will be permanently cared for. But the case is entirely different when we consider, (a) the "impure dominant" and (b) the "recessive", whose defect, such as deafness, does not need segregation on individual grounds, and whole segregation on eugenic grounds cannot be seriously contemplated. In some types of case, if sterilisation without mutilation or personal injury be found perfectly feasible, the choice between segregation and such sterilisation—a far more humane and less severe measure—might conceivably be offered to the individual. But I should be inclined to rely far more upon the spread of eugenic knowledge, upon the creation of a eugenic conscience, and upon the self-control which we might hope such individuals would exercise.'

intervention. At the same time, the legacy and continual refinement of systems and procedures concerning the diagnosis, categorization and medicalization of impairment and the important role played by professionals in these processes led to a continued pathologizing and othering of disabled children in the education system. It is against this background that changes in special education and educational responses to disability need to be understood.

The 1960s were characterized by a spirit of optimism and openness in terms of social values and the need to address social inequalities in education. The Newsom Report (1963)[22] was indicative of this mood, revealing vast differences in the quality of education received by children, according to class and social location. It recommended the raising of the school leaving age from 15 to 16, calling for action to address inadequacies of the system such as overcrowding and poor facilities, and for research into teaching methods to overcome environmental and linguistic deficiencies. However, the vision underpinning the Newsom Report did little to challenge educational divisions based on the outcomes of education, as it was primarily concerned with providing education that would prepare children and young people for their future roles in society, which were largely defined by class and existing perceptions of ability.[23]

The Labour government Circular 10/65 (1965) invited all un-reorganized LEAs to submit plans for the introduction of comprehensive schools and an end to selection at the age of 11, but did not make this obligatory. The 1944 Education Acts, the Newsom Report, the development of comprehensive education and the implementation of the 1970 (Handicapped Children) Act were all precursors to debates on the integration of disabled children into ordinary schools. Other changes were taking place in society during the 1960s and 1970s. For example, the numbers of children with conditions such as congenital heart disease, tuberculosis of the joints, rheumatic fever, spina bifida and cerebral palsy had decreased dramatically over the previous 20 years. Advances in medical knowledge and surgical techniques made more children less dependent on care and management, and more likely candidates for 'education'.[24]

There were a number of key factors that influenced developments in special education during the period between the 1970s and early 1980s, including the growth in self-advocacy groups and parent pressure groups.[25] Research began to raise questions about the quality of education provided by special schools and there emerged a critical debate regarding the categorization and 'labelling' of children.[26] The development

---

[22] Report of the Minister of Education's Central Advisory Council. *Half Our Future* (The Newsom Report). London: HMSO, 1963.

[23] McCulloch, G. *Failing the Ordinary Child? The Theory and Practice of Working-class Secondary Education.* Buckingham: Open University Press, 1998.

[24] Hurt, ibid.

[25] Jones, Neville J. "Policy Change and Innovation for Special Needs in Oxfordshire." *Oxford Review of Education* 9, no. 3 (1983): 241–54.

[26] For example, Swann, W. *The Practice of Special Education.* Oxford: Basil Blackwell/Open University Press, 1981.

of 'resource bases' attached to mainstream schools led to a gradual blurring of the boundaries between some mainstream and special schools, and the presence of children identified as having special educational needs or a disability became increasingly 'natural'. These factors, and the emergence of a 'critical literature' in sociology of education, which developed a critique of the notion of 'special needs' and special education, signalled a widespread re-evaluation of the principles of segregated special education. In many respects, these issues reflected wider social change and social movements in support of civil rights, participation and political struggles around identity and self-realization.

However, the global movements of the 1960s and 1970s, which claimed civil rights and equality of treatment, focused in particular on inequalities based on class, opportunity and discrimination on the grounds of race, gender and sexuality. During the social changes and political and cultural upheaval that occurred in the 1960s disabled people remained on the outside in terms of recognition. Tom Shakespeare[27] links the liberation struggles of the 1960s to the politicization and growth of the disability movement but, as Karen Hirsch observes in relation to the USA, 'compared with the impact on historical studies of the Black freedom movement and the women's movement ... the disability rights movement has had little effect on historical scholarship'.[28]

The development of the disability movement, and its fight to make visible the oppression of disabled people and campaign for the full participation of disabled children in mainstream education, have been crucial in the ways in which perceptions about disability and rights have been transformed. At the forefront of these struggles in England has been disabled people's organizations such as the Integration Alliance, Young and Powerful, and others such as the centre for Studies on Inclusive Education (CSIE), all of which have campaigned for the recognition of the rights of disabled children and for their 'voices to be heard'. At the same time, theorizations around the role of the 'experiential' and the notion of voice have become increasingly important in the research literature, particularly in support of a human and civil rights agenda.[29]

Education, Disabilities and Social Change

Debates about whether 'history' is concerned with constructing accounts of 'what happened' through the collection of 'facts', or whether history can only be understood as an infinite array of multiple experiences and perspectives, rest on differences that

---

[27] Shakespeare, T. "Disabled people's self-organisation: a new social movement?" In *Overcoming Disabling Barriers: 18 years of Disability and Society*, edited by L. Barton. London: Routledge, 2006.

[28] Hirsch, K. "Culture and Disability: the role of oral history." In *The Oral History Reader*, edited by R. Perks and A. Thomson. London: Routledge, 1998.

[29] Moore, M., S. Beazley, and J. Maelzer. *Researching Disability Issues*. Buckingham: Open University Press, 1998; Shakespeare, T. "Rules of engagement: doing disability research." *Disability and Society* 11, no. 1 (1996): 115–19.

are both theoretical and political. As Mary Fuller observes in the Preface to her book on Historical Theory:

> ... all history writing inevitably entails taking a stand on key theoretical issues, whether or not the historian is aware of these—and many practising historians are not. There is no escape from having a theoretical position, whether explicit or implicit.[30]

Such debates open up useful routes into approaches to the history of education and disability developed over the past 40 years. Differences in theoretical approaches in this field are closely linked to contrasting positions on the way the notion of disability has been theorized and represented. The embracing of the social model of disability,[31] regardless of which particular interpretation is adopted, has profound implications for the way the purposes of education are understood, and the way histories are written.

The traditional divide between sociology and history has, until recently, been largely followed in Disability Studies—heavily weighted in favour of the sociologists— and 'education' has not been the first concern of academics in the field. Articles on issues related to education and disability appear relatively rarely in the sociological journal *Disability and Society* and, although more general historical articles are published fairly frequently, these rarely explore *educational* histories. Anne Borsay notes that 'history is a missing piece of the jigsaw in disability studies',[32] and she explains this in terms of the 'formative influence' of sociology in disability studies and the 'alien nature' of historical methodology to social scientists. Furthermore, the 'late arrival of social history as a specialism within historical scholarship' and, she argues, the reproduction of the social discrimination experienced by disabled people in academic discourse have also contributed to the scarcity of historical work in Disability Studies. However, increasing numbers of researchers in disability and education have turned to historical texts and engaged in historical enquiry and critique of their own as a prerequisite to an exploration of current themes.[33] Patricia Potts, for example, has explored the categorization of children and the way their needs are defined by professionals on the basis of perceived impairment, through a historical study of the involvement of doctors in special education and their role in diagnosis

---

[30] Fuller, M. *Historical Theory*. London: Routledge, 2002: ix.

[31] The 'social model' of disability stresses the social construction of disability in contrast to the 'medical model', which focuses on individual impairment. See Hahn, H. "Adjudication or empowerment: contrasting experiences with a social model of disability." In *Disability, Politics and the Struggle for Change*, edited by L. Barton. London: David Fulton, 2001.

[32] Borsay, A. "History, Power and Identity." In *Disability Studies Today*, edited by C. Barnes, M. Oliver and L. Barton. Cambridge: Polity Press, 2002.

[33] See Hall, J. T. *Social Devaluation and Special Education: The Right to Full Mainstream Inclusion and an Honest Statement*. London: Jessica Kingsley, 1997; Copeland, I. *The Making of the Backward Pupil in Education in England*. London: Woburn Press, 1999; Race, D. G., ed. *Learning Disability—A Social Approach*. London: Routledge, 2002; Armstrong, D. *Experiences of Special Education: Re-evaluating Policy and Practice through Life Stories*. London: RoutledgeFalmer, 2003; Armstrong, F. *Spaced Out: Policy, Difference and the Challenge of Inclusive Education*. London: Kluwer, 2003.

and labelling.[34] Jane Read and Jan Walmsley have explored documentary evidence from the public and private domains in an attempt to reinterpret historical accounts of special education. They were particularly interested in uncovering the 'authentic voice of disabled children and parents in the past', but observed that they were unable to find the 'voices of recipients of early forms of special education. The historical record is documented only in the professional voice'.[35]

There have been many approaches to describing and analysing history in relation to policy, experience and marginalized groups in education over the past 40 years. For example, Kevin Myers and Anna Brown have explored the historiography of mental deficiency in relation to special school leavers in Birmingham in the first part of the twentieth century.[36] They identify three broad categories of historical studies of special education. The first adopts:

> ... the perspective of the policy maker and the administrator ... as problems emerge and solutions develop. Individuals feature prominently and, in the older histories in particular, are lauded for the warmth of their humanity and the wisdom of their vision. Progress follows from the noble and benevolent intentions of voluntary effort....

Myers and Brown critique this approach on the grounds that it has:

> ... little or no conception of the structural relations that impact upon the perception and resolution of particular educational 'problems'. It effectively silences the voices of the people deemed mentally deficient or in need of special schooling.[37]

Their second broad category of historiography in relation to special schooling is 'sociologically and analytically based', and focuses on 'production' and the way in which historically special schooling (and in particular the category of 'mental deficiency') legitimized and reproduced 'a given social order'. While, in general, this approach adopted a 'macro level of analysis', Myers and Brown recognize the permeability of the macro and micro levels at which structures and social practices merge, citing Foucault's 'micro-physics of power' which is embedded in 'local conditions and practices'. They critique this approach on the grounds that it rendered children and their families entirely passive. They appeared rarely and only as problems— educational, medical or administrative—to be solved or as objects to be disciplined.[38] In contrast, their third category of the historical study of 'the national system of schools to accommodate the newly identified deficient' focuses on the local context, the micro-politics of mental deficiency, and the effects which policies and practices had on individuals and families.

---

[34] Potts, P. "Medicine, morals and mental deficiency: the contribution of doctors to the development of special education in England." In *Oxford Review of Education*, 9, no. 3 (1983): 181–96.

[35] Read, J., and J. Walmsley. "Historical Perspectives on Special Education, 1890–1970." *Disability and Society*, 21, no. 5 (2006): 455–69.

[36] Myers, K., and A. Brown. "Mental Deficiency: The Diagnosis and After-care of Special School Leavers in Early Twentieth Century Birmingham (UK)." *Journal of Historical Sociology*, 18, nos 1/2 (2005): 72–98.

[37] Ibid., 73.

[38] Ibid., 73.

The first category maps on to other ways of describing historical approaches such as the 'modernist' approach in which developments are located in 'facts' such as social and economic change, legislation, the ideas of reformers and developments in scientific knowledge. The second can be interpreted as relating to a number of different strands, including Marxist approaches. The third, which is concerned with micro-politics and lived experience, relates to 'micro-history' and owes much to oral history, anthropology and an exploration of local culture and experience.[39]

Foucauldian analyses have strands that connect to both 'social production' models and to approaches rooted in explorations of power relations, cultures, discursive practices and the management of difference.[40] The following sections focus on five distinctive historical approaches to the history of disability and education: the 'modernist' tradition, the 'functionalist', the 'Marxist', the 'Foucauldian' and 'oral history'. Such broad categorizations should not be taken to mean that these represent unitary concepts.

Disability, Education and the Writing of History

D. G. Pritchard's book *Education and the Handicapped 1760–1960* is, as we saw earlier, fundamentally modernist and teleological in approach, and might be categorized as contributing to the 'grand narrative' of an increasingly humane and progressive world. Nevertheless, the detailed material it contains throws light on the unpredictable nature of developments in education, as well as providing a coherent account of their history. It also allows us to challenge later assumptions embedded in education policy. A study of this text reveals, for example, that the idea that children identified as having special educational needs should attend their local schools was not, as is often assumed, an 'invention' of the 1981 Education Act or the Warnock Report (1978)[41] on which it was based, but was included in the 1944 Education Act. The Education Act of 1921 had provided education for disabled pupils only in special schools or 'certified special classes' but the 1944 Act instructed LEAs to:

> ... provide for the education of pupils in whose case the disability is serious in special schools appropriate for that category, but where that is impracticable, or where the disability is not serious, the arrangement may provide for the giving such education in any school maintained or assisted by the local education authority.[42]

Pritchard commented:

---

[39] Burke, P. *What is Cultural History?* Cambridge: Polity Press, 2004.

[40] See, for example, Copeland, I. *The Making of the Backward Pupil in Education in England*. London: Woburn Press, 1999; Armstrong, F. *Spaced Out: Policy, Difference and the Challenge of Inclusive Education*. London: Kluwer, 2003.

[41] Committee of Enquiry into the Education of Handicapped Children and Young People, *Special Educational Needs* (Warnock Report). London: HMSO, 1979.

[42] Pritchard, op. cit., 209.

> ... unfortunately the wording of the Act allows authorities to evade their responsibilities. The evasion, in so far as it exists, is not so much in the provision of special schools, as in the lack of provision of special educational facilities in the ordinary schools.[43]

Rather than writing a purely descriptive account of the unfolding of legislation and the construction of systems, Pritchard provides a commentary and critique of policy, which challenges suggestions that history is concerned only with 'the facts' or that the subject matter should be treated in a clinical, deterministic way. In this sense, although the 'voice' of the author is obscured, the 'analytical self' is not entirely absent.

In Pritchard's book, little attention is paid to the lived experience of disabled children. At the time such an approach would be seen as 'subjective' and not, therefore, a legitimate source of information. While it was recognized that history is complex and uneven, the idea that there could be 'multiple' histories, rather than one unfolding narrative, was not considered. This mirrors the historical dominance of positivist research at the time in which 'facts', and observable, measurable data were privileged over qualitative approaches to educational research. It is important, therefore, to avoid critiquing the work of historians such as Pritchard from the vantage point of the more recent intellectual context in which the values and insights and constructions of historical knowledge are very different from those which framed historical work half a century ago.

'Functionalist' History

The 'functionalist' perspective[44] is based on the premise that disabled children have particular needs as a result of their impairments which require specialist provision, often including separate structures and the involvement of specialist professionals. The response to impairment is understood in terms of the policies and adaptations put in place, which are seen as being necessitated by the impairments and difficulties of the individual child. The roots of the 'functionalist' approach are diverse, with branches arising from the proliferation of medical and technical responses to impairment and the emergence of powerful groups of professionals with their particular interests in and perspectives on the needs and requirements of disabled children—a process which began in the eighteenth century and gained momentum so that by the early part of the twentieth century diagnosis and treatment was a massive industry. This can be seen as part of a wider project in the increasing management and control of the population—linked to the growth of interest in eugenics and the humanitarian concerns of social welfare.

The underpinning assumption of functionalist approaches is that an impairment is something that is 'wrong' with the child and which needs fixing or ameliorating; efforts are made to introduce techniques, equipment and teaching strategies tailored

---

[43] Ibid., 209.
[44] Barnes, C., G. Mercer, and T. Shakespeare. *Exploring Disability: A Sociological Introduction.* Cambridge: Polity Press, 1999.

to the particular impairment to offset its effects. It is essentially a normalization project in which the 'problem' to be addressed is seen as situated within the child. Since the early part of the twentieth century, and particularly since the 1960s, there has been a massive growth in literature with a functionalist orientation intended to provide solutions to or offset the detrimental effects of impairment—especially in relation to what is described as 'the autistic spectrum'—and related areas such as 'attention deficit hyperactivity disorder' and 'emotional and behavioural difficulties'. Work derived from the activities of the Peto Institute in Hungary is an example of a functionalist approach to impairment, popular in the 1980s, which sought to teach children with physical impairments to stand upright and walk, through a strict regime of physical exercise and therapy. In general, such functional accounts of impairment are based on a traditional 'deficit' gaze, which has 'concentrated upon individual limitations as the principle cause of the multiple difficulties experienced by disabled people'.[45] Again, the experiences of children themselves are absent.

There are some very different examples of work which adopts a functionalist perspective. The Open University textbook *The Disabled Schoolchild*[46] by Anderson, first published in 1973, is concerned with the integration of 'physically handicapped' children in ordinary schools, the possible educational and social problems which may arise, and how these may be managed. Although the book is conceptualized around the notion of 'handicap', the book was radical at the time in advocating 'integration' in situations where the child can be 'satisfactorily educated in an ordinary school'. *Mental Subnormality*[47] by Heaton-Ward, published in 1975, focuses on the diagnosis, typology, grading, treatment and management of 'mental subnormality' with an emphasis on training rather than education. In contrast, Cole's book, *Apart or A Part? Integration and the Growth of Special Education*,[48] published in 1989, constructs the history of special education in terms of a humanitarian response to individual deficits and impairments.

'Marxist' Historical Analysis and Disability and Education

Ideological struggle and power relations are largely missing from discussion in both modernist and functionalist historical accounts. In contrast, 'neo-Marxist' interpretations see the history of responses to disability, and the development of special education, as part of a wider system of oppressive social control informed by dominant ideologies and values (e.g. Tomlinson, 1982).[49] Finkelstein[50] was among the

---

[45] Ibid.

[46] Anderson, E. M. *The Disabled Schoolchild: A Study of Integration in Primary Schools*. London: Methuen, 1973.

[47] Heaton-Ward, W. A. *Mental Subnormality*. Bristol: John Wright and Sons, 1975.

[48] Cole, T. *Apart or a Part? Integration and the Growth of British Special Education*. Milton Keynes: Open University Press, 1989.

[49] Tomlinson, S. *A Sociology of Special Education*. London: Routledge & Kegan Paul, 1982.

[50] Finkelstein, V. *Attitudes and Disabled People*. New York: World Rehabilitation Fund, 1980.

first to analyse the relationship between disability and society from a historical materialist perspective. For Finkelstein—and other Marxists—the problems created by impairment relate to questions of usefulness and productivity and the ability to compete in the labour market and contribute to the creation of surplus value. Just as production became industrialized, so did the management and containment of disabled people in institutions. Scull's historical study of the growth and role of asylums, *Museums of Madness*,[51] shows how their development mirrored the growth and scale of capitalist modes and structures of production with institutions for the old, insane, disabled or destitute similar in size and assembly-line organization to the vast factories that emerged during the same period. Marxist approaches, provided by sociologists and historians, are well represented in disability studies. In his analysis of the history of 'integration' and education, Oliver argues:

> The production of disability in one sense … is nothing more nor less than a set of activities specifically geared towards producing a good—category disability—supported by a range of political actions which create the conditions to allow these productive activities to take place and underpinned by a discourse which gives legitimacy to the whole enterprise.[52]

Historically, therefore, schools have been, and continue to be, part of the capitalist 'means of production' which (re)produce social groups through processes of categorization and labelling, and the necessary labour force, to support the continuation of the capitalist system. The placement of disabled children in segregated schools prepared them for a life of marginalization and inactivity. In the broader education system curricula, systems of assessment and pedagogy are all harnessed to the reproductive task.

The Influence of Foucault

There is a close relationship between traditional approaches to historical research and writing on the history of education, 'special educational needs' and disability, and the embeddedness and persistent use of medicalized language and categories to refer to particular impairments and to disabled people themselves.

There has recently been a strong critique in the literature of social practices which are underpinned by categorization, labelling and impairment-led language, from a range of theoretical or value-based positions. In particular, the history of disability has been critically examined through various Foucauldian analyses in which categorization and the 'language of special needs' are seen as conduits for the exercise of power that merge the 'pastoral' with the 'disciplinary'.[53] Others have

[51] Scull, A. T. *Museums of Madness: The Social Organization of Insanity in Nineteenth Century England*. London: Penguin Books, 1979.

[52] Oliver, M. *Understanding Disability from Theory to Practice*. London: Macmillan Press, 1996: 127.

[53] Peim, N. "The history of the present: towards a contemporary phenomenology of the school." *History of Education*, 30, no. 2 (2001): 177–90.

developed a critique of labelling as power embedded in professional knowledge and discourses[54] or have drawn on Foucault's concept of 'traditional' and 'effective' history, in challenging traditional, linear accounts of educational responses to disability and learning difficulty.[55]

Drawing on narrative documentary material, Derrick Armstrong has explored the methodological implications for historians of accepting Foucault's analysis of knowledge as 'social practice' and the 'decentring' of the individual as a 'historical agent'[56] He argues:

> When considering the history of education it is important that we ask the question: 'Whose history is being talked about?' If we ask 'whose history?' we start to realise that history is not simply a set of facts about the world but is rather a set of contested perspectives. Secondly, it becomes apparent that some of those perspectives or voices are left out of official or dominant representations of the study altogether.

Questions concerning power and voice have become increasingly central in the way the histories of marginalized groups are conceptualized.

Oral History, Autobiography and the Question of 'Voice'

The politicization of impairment, the increasing strength of the disability movement, the radicalizing effects of the implications of the social model, and the influence of theorizations and debates arising out of the women's movement have revealed different perspectives and new sociological questions concerning disability, framed by Carol Thomas, for example, as: 'How can this social phenomenon be theorized? What is its social history?'[57] Such questions have opened up debate, raising, in particular, questions about the role of the experiential in theorizing impairment and disability, and the championing of 'emancipatory research' in which the experiences and voices of disabled people, and children in particular, were drawn into the centre. Much of the work, which includes oral accounts of the experiences of disabled children, has not been written by 'mainstream' historians.[58] For example, Wilmot and Saul, family and 'local' historians, have carried out work on the history of Open-Air schools in Birmingham[59] and draw extensively on reports and other archive

---

[54] Corbett, J. *Bad Mouthing*. London: Falmer Press, 1996.

[55] Copeland, I. *The Making of the Backward Pupil in Education in England*. London: Woburn Press, 1999; Armstrong, F. "The Historical Development of Special Education: Humanitarian Rationality or 'Wild Profusion of Entangled Events'?" *History of Education*, 31, no. 5 (2002) 437–56.

[56] Armstrong, D. *Experience of Special Education: Re-evaluating Policy and Practice through Life Stories*. London: RoutledgeFalmer, 2003: 23.

[57] Thomas, C. "Disability Theory: Key Ideas, Issues and Thinkers." In *Disability Studies Today*, edited by C. Barnes, M. Oliver and L. Barton. Cambridge: Polity Press, 2002: 38–57.

[58] See, for example, Booth, T., and W. Booth. *Growing Up With Parents Who Have Learning Difficulties*. London: Routledge, 1998, and Goodley, D. *Self-advocacy in the Lives of People with Learning Difficulties*. Buckingham: Open University Press, 2000.

[59] Wilmot, F., and P. Saul. *A Breath of Fresh Air: Birminghams's Open-Air Schools 1911–1970*. Chichester: Phillimore, 1998.

material, much of which is based on narrative documentary evidence of 'insiders'. In his work on self-advocacy, Goodley,[60] a disability theorist, draws extensively on the narrative documentary accounts of people labelled as having learning difficulties, to explore the impact of self-advocacy. Murray and Penman,[61] disability activists and parents of disabled children, have gathered together narrative accounts of the experiences of families 'living with and learning about' impairment, which include narratives of the experience of education.

Oral history is an approach associated with local and anthropological historical research, and nurtured the kind of cultural history which flourished in the History Workshops, founded by Raphael Samuel, in the 1960s in which 'history' was made 'from below'. There are close links here with the development of what was referred to as a 'new genre'—that of 'micro-history' which Peter Burke describes as offering 'an attractive alternative to the telescope, allowing concrete individual or local experience to re-enter history'. Micro-history:

> .... was a response to a growing disillusionment with the so-called 'grand narrative' of progress [which] ... passed over the achievements and contributions of many other cultures, not to mention [the] social groups in the West....[62]

Micro-history allows in personal accounts as valued material through which to explore social relationships and social change.

The relatively recent interest in the 'voices' of disabled people in disability research and in the construction of histories of the experiences of disabled people is therefore both part of a wider tradition in historical and cultural studies, and part of a contemporary movement in historical research which links directly to recent developments in disability studies and activism. The contribution from feminists working in the field of disability studies has been particularly important in stressing the importance of the experiential in analysing and understanding social and historical processes.[63] The accounts of individuals are seen as making a major contribution in terms of understanding the relationship between the individual experience of impairment and the social conditions which create disabling barriers.

Conclusion

Carol Thomas, a researcher, feminist and activist, who has developed a 'social narrative' approach to exploring issues of disability, gender and power, reminds us of the importance of developing counter-narratives, and for others to take notice of them:

---

[60] Goodley, ibid.

[61] Murray, P., and J. Penman. *Telling Our Own Stories: Reflection on Family Life in a Disabling World.* Sheffield: Parents With Attitude, 2000.

[62] Burke, P. *What is Cultural History?* Cambridge: Polity Press, 2004: 43–44.

[63] For example, Morris, J. *Encounters with Strangers: Feminism and Disability.* London: Women's Press, 1996.

Perhaps the key point is that without the counter-narratives of others who challenge social 'norms' we, as isolated individuals, are trapped within the story-lines of the prevailing narratives. If we do re-write out own identities then we strengthen the counter-narrative, and the dominant and oppressive narratives begin to crumble.[64]

These counter-narratives represent a struggle against hegemonic accounts of the history of education and disabled people which focus on the legislative and technical responses to impairment. In some important respects the approaches to historical enquiry relating to disability and education have reflected changes in social values, policy and practices. The different kinds of historical work which have been carried out can be linked to differences in the way the identity and interests of disabled children have been conceptualized. It is particularly significant that historical work on education has routinely ignored disability and special education systems, or treated them as of minor, peripheral importance. History works, therefore, in hegemonic ways, implicitly sustaining the exclusion of disabled people, but history is also a 'site of contestation and conflict'[65] that mirrors wider struggles in the social world.

In reflecting on the different approaches adopted in historical research in the field of education and disability, the absence of experiential and biographical evidence[66] in mainstream historical accounts is evident. Existing work undertaken in other disciplines such as disability studies and critical policy studies, and less orthodox historical research such as narrative and 'insider perspective' research, provides fresh starting points for future research in the history of disability and education. There is an urgent need to adopt a cross-disciplinary approach to research that both complements and challenges dominant historical accounts, many of which serve to legitimize the exclusion of the historical, experiential and analytical knowledge of disabled people.

---

[64] Thomas, C. "Narrative Identity in the Disabled Self." In *Disability Discourse*, edited by M. Corker and S. French. Buckingham: Open University Press, 1999: 55.

[65] Popkewitz, T., B. M. Franklin, and M. A. Pereyra, eds. *Cultural History and Education*. London: RoutledgeFalmer, 2001: 11.

[66] Goodley, ibid.

British Historiography of Education in International Context at the Turn of the Century, 1996–2006

William Richardson

Education and Social Change: the British Historiography in the Latter Twentieth Century

In tandem with the huge growth in Britain of scholarly output in history as a whole, our understanding of the historical development of education, and its role in social change, has been transformed in scale and range over the past half century. With the exception of the history of medicine, uniquely endowed in British social history through the munificence since 1959 of the Wellcome Trust,[1] the historical development of education in Britain has become as well charted as any of the 'sub-fields' of social history that emerged in the early 1960s. In parallel with other specialist

---

[1] Hall, A., and B. Bembridge. *Physic and Philanthropy: A History of the Wellcome Trust, 1936–1986.* Cambridge: Cambridge University Press, 1986: 124, 193–97. In 2006 in Britain there were centres, units or research groups active in the history of medicine at the universities of Birmingham, Durham, East Anglia, Exeter, Glasgow, Leeds, London (Imperial College, University College, School of Tropical Hygiene and Medicine), Manchester, Newcastle, Open, and Warwick.

groups, historians of education welcomed the appearance of new scholarly journals designed to open up the scope of academic history as a whole;[2] in addition, they benefited through the broadening, from a dominant emphasis during the 1930s and 1940s on psychology, of research into education as a social process.[3] Consequently, alongside new concerns in historical research such as business, population, science and labour, historians of education more than held their own as a distinctive community during the first wave of the 'new' social history from, say, 1960 to 1980,[4] with the years 1972–1976 marking an especially energetic period for the field.[5] Over the subsequent 25 years, the landscape of social history has continued to evolve and several of the specialist genres—labour history, urban history, education history, science history, even economic history[6]—have had to face the prospect of reduced institutional momentum and the need to regroup while, at the same time, experiencing and attempting to harness the intellectual energy unleashed by feminism and postmodernism.[7]

On a broader geographical canvas, the foremost characteristic of academic history in Britain, North America and Western Europe since the 1960s may be said, at its most succinct, to comprise the ousting of traditional political concerns, centred on chronicle and the deeds of exceptional individuals, in favour of social and economic themes ('history from below'); only for these, in turn, to be eclipsed from the 1980s by a move away from sociology and the search for causation (often via quantification)

---

[2] During 1966–1976 the UK history journals providing most coverage for education were (in order): *Past and Present*; *Journal of Contemporary History*; *Journal of Ecclesiastical History*; *Medical History*; *History Today*; *Scottish Historical Review*; *Bulletin of the Society for the Study of Labour History*; and *Economic History Review*.

[3] The leading UK journal of educational research in the earlier period had been *the British Journal of Educational Psychology* (from 1931). After the war outlets for historians arising from the broadening of educational research in Britain were: *British Journal of Educational Studies* (from 1952), the *Journal of Educational Administration and History* (from 1968) and *History of Education* (from 1972). See also, Richardson, W. "Educational Studies in the United Kingdom, 1940–2002." *British Journal of Educational Studies* 50, no. 1 (2002): 9–10.

[4] Albeit a community full of institutional and professional tensions, see Richardson, W. "Historians and Educationists: the history of education as a field of study in post-war England." *History of Education* 27, no. 1 (1999): 1–30 and 27, no. 2 (1999): 109–41.

[5] Ibid., 117–23. The high water mark was, perhaps, the Royal Historical Society's conference on 'Education and its social purposes' held at Clare College Cambridge in September 1976, ibid., 124 and n. 103.

[6] Jordonova, L. *History in Practice.* London: Arnold, 2000: 202–03; Mills D, A. Jepson, T. Coxon, M. Easterby-Smith, P. Hawkins and J. Spencer. *Demographic Review of the UK Social Sciences.* Swindon: Economic and Social Research Council, 2006: 59.

[7] See for example, Halpern, R. "Oral History and Labour History: A historiographic assessment after twenty-five years." *Journal of American History* 85, no. 2 (1998): 596–610; Geary, D. "Labour History, the 'Linguistic Turn' and Postmodernism." *Contemporary European History* 9, no. 3 (2000): 445–62; McEvoy, J. "Presentism, Whiggism and the Chemical Revolution: A study in the Historiography of Chemistry." *History of Science* 35 (1997): 1–33 (including reference to the 'recent period of crisis in the history of science profession', op. cit., 24).

toward anthropology and studies centred on the social ascription of meaning, individual and collective.[8]

In parallel with these overall shifts of emphasis and interpretive frames in research, historians at the end of the twentieth century felt a continuing need to maintain some broad categories of enquiry able to lend support, bestow identity and secure the legitimacy of the undergraduate history curriculum. Thus, for Ludmilla Jordonova writing in 1999, economic history, like political, social and intellectual history, constituted 'a fundamental part of the discipline of which every student *ought* to have some understanding'. Despite the intrinsic interest of more specialist areas, these broad thematic strains, she maintained, were likely to be of more general use for students than specific sub-fields since 'there are only a limited number of such structural phenomena and they lie at the heart of history, which, as a discipline, aspires to make general statements about past societies'.[9] Similarly, when David Cannadine, as Director of the Institute of Historical Research, convened an international conference in London in 2001 to pose the question 'What is history now?' the themes chosen included Jordonova's core of social, political and intellectual history, while also admitting the history of religion, culture, gender and empire.[10]

As would be expected of a long-established and distinctive field characterized by sustained scholarly achievement, historians of education over the past decade in Britain have been influenced by, and have contributed to, these mainstream currents in English-speaking and European historiography. However, due to their position at the intersection of mainstream university history and the concerns of faculties of education, the history of education in Britain since 1945 has only briefly either held the sustained attention of academic historians,[11] or commanded a solid constituency of committed students of education.[12] Neither has been present on any scale over the last decade[13] yet historians of education in Britain have continued to enjoy significant freedom to pursue their interests, and this has ensured that research into education and social change has remained vibrant and built upon the dramatic expansion of the size and shape of their field over the previous half-century.[14]

---

[8] See D. Cannadine, "Preface." In *What is History Now?*, edited by D. Cannadine. Basingstoke: Palgrave Macmillan, 2002: viii–ix. The effects of these developments on the history of education by the mid-1990s were noted in Richardson, "Historians and Educationists", 136–37. See also below, nn. 84–87.

[9] Jordonova, *History in Practice*, 203.

[10] Cannadine, *What is History Now?*, passim.

[11] During 1967–76, see Richardson, "Historians and Educationists", 21–23, 25–26, 117–23.

[12] Mainly among practising teachers seeking higher qualifications and funded by their local government employers during the period 1970–1985, ibid., 113.

[13] Bar a small number of courses offered in established centres, see below, n. 97.

[14] This autonomy may appear less than in the past (see, for example, Lowe R., "Do We Still Need History of Education: Is it Central or Peripheral?" *History of Education* 31, no. 6 (2002): 495) but it has been stable and generous by international standards over the past two decades. Recognizing this, vice-chancellors in 2006 waged a mainly successful campaign to retain the government funding arrangements that have supported this form of academic freedom in British universities since 1986 (but see also n. 122, below).

Patterns of Expansion

What were the characteristics of that expansion?[15] First, overall scholarly output in the field in Britain as reflected in journal literature grew steadily throughout the period 1956–2005 (see Appendix I),[16] notwithstanding changes in the institutional context in which that scholarship was produced. The period of significant investment by the UK government in humanities in the universities and polytechnics during 1963–1979,[17] coupled with the government-sponsored drive to broaden the humanities base of teacher training in education departments during 1965–1979, accounts for the surge in scholarly activity from the mid-1960s.[18] Subsequently, it is notable that momentum was sustained after the severe retrenchment in funding imposed by the University Grants Committee in 1981 and the rapid erosion of a historical dimension within teacher training from the mid-1980s,[19] although a consequence of these policies was that articles in journals edited from the university departments of education fell sharply in the early 1990s relative to all such output (Appendix II), before staging a recent recovery as new academics have entered the arena and, since 2001, created a new surge.[20] A second clear finding from analysis of the journal literature is that, as with academic history more broadly,[21] research in the history of education has increasingly become concentrated on the most recent periods. Within the data summarized in Appendix III, it is evident that, over the last quarter-century, general historical journals have kept alive in Britain the study of education before 1750,[22] while those historians closest to the profession of education have, since the 1960s, been preoccupied with the period from 1750 in general, and the late nineteenth century in particular. Finally, Appendix IV contains information on thematic trends evident in the journal literature over the

---

[15] The summary that follows is based on analysis of the scale and patterning of more than 3000 articles published in UK scholarly journals covering the history of education. For justification of this method of depiction, which uses journal articles as the key proxy for the literature as whole, see n. 16.

[16] A genre that has 'become increasingly dominant in the field over the past 20 years', McCulloch G., review of R. Lowe, ed. *History of Education: Major Themes* (4 vols). London: Routledge (2000), in *History of Education* 31, no. 3: 305). In Lowe's collection, 73 of the 111 items first appeared in article form.

[17] Shattock, M. *The UGC and the Management of British Universities*. Buckingham: Open University Press, 1994: 34, 21.

[18] Richardson, "Educational Studies", 18–19, 28–29.

[19] Richardson, "Historians and Educationists", 132–33, 137–38.

[20] The introduction of national research assessment from 1986 stimulated a further wave of journal-founding, a pattern that seems now to have reached a plateau. Journal output of articles on the history of education was checked for the only time in the postwar period during the late 1990s (as the 'Robbins generation' of academics retired) before displaying further strong growth from 2001 (Appendix I).

[21] Jordonova, *History in Practice*, 202.

[22] Most notably, through a significant increase from the early 1980s of work on medieval universities and, from the mid-1990s, on the family in the ancient world.

period.[23] Here, a number of features stand out: the heavy preponderance of studies concerned with formal institutions and the role of the nation-state in education (around three-quarters of the non-historiographical articles); the particular concern of the specialist journals edited from departments of education with ideas and biography (currently resurgent), schooling and governance (currently somewhat diminished) and historiography (both in the 're-founding' phase of the field's development, the mid-1950s to the mid-1970s, and again most recently as it has caught up with the effects of postmodernism); the traditional and sustained coverage within the general historical journals of the history of universities;[24] and the recent surge in interest in these journals in the history of childhood and the family.

Overall, then, a number of 'headline' findings emerge as to the scale and patterning of research into the history of education reported in articles on education published in scholarly journals of history established or edited within the British Isles over the last 50 years. The field has grown steadily throughout the period,[25] with a majority of articles being published in the five specialist periodicals edited in the university departments of education. Studies of the recent past have become an ever-greater majority and, most recently, the dominance of formal education has lessened, as interest in the informal agencies of education has grown. To this body of literature on the history of education in Britain may be added the scores of monographs published over the period,[26] along with the many articles that have appeared in specialist journals across the world.[27] As Asa Briggs had recommended in the early 1970s,[28] the theme of education and social change has been integral to this entire literature, with perhaps the only outlying areas being aspects of the genre of administrative history

---

[23] The data in each of the tables have been calculated on the basis of each article being assigned a primary category within four chosen parameters: date of publication, journal provenance, chronological range and thematic focus. In Appendix IV there is a particular difficulty in identifying with consistency and accuracy the primary characteristic (thematic focus) but the attempt has been made to categorize the substantive aspect of education under study while allowing also for the categories of 'bibliography', 'historiography' and 'overview' articles. For the difficulties inherent in this technique, see Depaepe, M. "How Should the History of Education be Written? Some Reflections about the Nature of the Discipline from the Perspective of the Reception of Our Work." *Studies in Philosophy and Education* 23, no. 5 (2004): 335. For a complementary approach see n. 40, below.

[24] Reinforced from 1981 by the founding of the specialist journal *History of Universities*.

[25] But see n. 20, above, for the late 1990s blip.

[26] Including over 800 that have been reviewed in the pages of *History of Education* since 1972.

[27] Most notably: *History of Education Quarterly* (USA: from 1961); *Paedagogica Historica* (Belgium: from 1961); *Journal of the Australian and New Zealand History of Education Society*, continued (from 1983) as *History of Education Review* (Australia/New Zealand: from 1972); *Histoire de l'Education* (France: from 1978); *Historical Studies in Education* (Canada: from 1984). See also Caspard, P., ed. *International Guide for Research in the History of Education*. Paris: Peter Lang, 1990, 2nd ed., 1995.

[28] Briggs, A. "The Study of the History of Education." *History of Education* 1, no. 1 (1972): 5.

brought to maturity by Peter Gosden,[29] and elements of the literature on economic history.[30]

Changing Gears

To counter the problem of professional isolation brought about by the demographics of the scholarly field from the mid-1980s—a diminished number of specialists concentrated heavily in the university departments of education, with few students to teach—historians of education sought in the 1990s to become better connected, thematically[31] and internationally.[32] This dynamic was influenced by, and received energy from, broader intellectual currents in the humanities and social sciences[33] which have had the effect of concentrating effort across national borders on a range of key concerns. The apparatus that has supported it over the past decade has been a revolution in scholarly connection via new information technologies, one result of which has been significantly increased co-ordination among the national learned societies.[34]

The UK History of Education Society has been as active in these developments as any of the equivalent learned societies worldwide, and most of the notable characteristics of the historiography of British education over the last decade can be traced through its publications (*History of Education* and the Society's *Bulletin*[35]), the wider activities of its prominent members, and commentary from overseas on its activities. Initial signs of a more organized approach to presenting theoretically informed scholarship were evident at the society's 1992 conference on 'Historical Perspectives on Feminism and Education', the published proceedings of which appeared under the title 'Feminism, Femininity and Feminization'.[36] By 1997, the editors of the Society's *Bulletin* could review trends through the middle of the decade expressive of a wide range of 'theoretical perspectives and critiques', along

---

[29] For Gosden on his own method, see "Twentieth Century Archives of Education as Sources for the Study of Education Policy and Administration." *Archives* 15, no. 66 (1981): 86.

[30] Such as Aldroft, D. *Education, Training and Economic Performance, 1994–1990.* Manchester: Manchester University Press (1990).

[31] Rousmaniere, K. "Fresh Thinking: Recent Work in the History of Education." *Paedagogica Historica* 37, no. 3 (2001): 649–52.

[32] Ibid.; Lowe, "Major Themes", Vol. I: xliii. For an earlier initiative see, Herbst J. "The International Standing Conference for the History of Education after the First Decade." *Paedagogica Historica* XXVI, no. I (1990): 85–89.

[33] Feminism and postmodernism in particular, see below nn. 84–89.

[34] By 2006 the International Standing Conference for the History of Education (founded in 1979) had affiliated to it 29 such national bodies.

[35] Renamed *History of Education Researcher* in 2003.

[36] 'Feminism referring to political expressions of the desire for a better deal for women; femininity, invoking the social, physical and cultural characteristics regarded as specific to women; and feminization, meaning the process of identification of a particular occupation with women', with coverage focusing mainly on nineteenth and twentieth century England, Europe and America, Summerfield, P. "Introduction." *History of Education* 22, no. 3 (1993): 213.

with a diversity of 'methods, methodologies and epistemologies'.[37] Towards the end of the decade there was further scope for innovation along these lines as the society's conferences embraced such themes as 'Teachers' Lives' (1996), 'Education and National Identity' (1998) and 'Breaking Boundaries: Gender, Politics and the Experience of Education' (1999), each designed to encourage international coverage and a broad methodological range.[38] Past the turn of the century this momentum was continued as the UK society's annual conference continued to promote diversity of subject matter, theoretical orientation and geographical location, while the expansion of *History of Education* (six issues *per annum* from 2000) allowed for more themed issues, often derived from other conferences or symposia.[39] In 2004, a 30-year tradition of single male editors came to an end when feminist scholars Joyce Goodman and Jane Martin took over the journal, inviting readers in their first editorial to think of the field as 'a space of struggle in which activity is structured and boundaries controlled, and a social system that functions according to its own specific logic or rules' before asserting, paradoxically, that 'of course' there cannot nor should there be 'closure' in academic debate.[40] In this context, it is notable that editorials since 2000 have been much more concerned than hitherto with theoretical considerations.[41]

Historiographical Preoccupations at the Turn of the Century, 1996–2006

In retrospect, it seems evident that the postwar nadir of purposefulness and confidence within the British history of education community occurred around 1990–1992,[42] for, although the overall volume of published work had continued to grow, much of it reflected the longstanding concerns of a generation passing from the scene, necessarily detached from emergent intellectual developments and presaging a short-term

---

[37] Goodman J., J. Martin, and W. Robinson. "Editorial: 'Retrospect and Prospect': Towards the Millennium with the *Bulletin of the History of Education Society.*" *History of Education Society Bulletin* no. 61 (1998): 1–7.

[38] Published proceedings appearing in: *Cambridge Journal of Education* 27, no. 3 (1997); and *History of Education* 28, no. 3 (1999) and 29, no. 5 (2000). Papers on education in England, Wales, Scotland, Aotearoa/New Zealand, India and South Africa were represented in the latter two collections.

[39] Examples of which were *History of Education* 29, no. 2 ("Progressive and Child-Centred Education"), 30, no. 2 ("Ways of Seeing Education and Schooling: Emerging Historiographies"), 35, no. 2 ("Early Years Education: Some Froebelian Contributions") and 35, nos 4–5 ("Making Education Soviet, 1917–53").

[40] Goodman, J., and J. Martin. "Editorial: History of Education-Defining a Field." *History of Education* 33, no. 1 (2004):1. This editorial comprises a very judicious review of the output of the journal over the previous 32 years, which, through its attention to theoretical and methodological strains (pp. 5–9), complements the appendices in Richardson "Historians and Educationists" (140–41) and in the present article.

[41] Starting with Brehony, K. "Introduction." *History of Education* 29, no. 2 (2000) (special issue on 'Progressive and Child-Centred Education').

[42] Richardson, "Historians and Educationists", 133.

contraction of the field.[43] However, since the mid-1990s the field—in Britain and internationally—has embarked on the biggest reappraisal of its academic methods and institutional aims since the early 1960s, and it is with aspects of this reappraisal that the remainder of this article is concerned.[44]

International Reappraisals

As already described, the most significant element of this intellectual reorientation over the last decade or so has been a substantial widening of the concepts, disciplinary frameworks, sources and methodologies deployed in the field.[45] Prominent and perhaps most programmatic among the examples available is the international collaboration of scholars from seven countries who, since first convening in Birmingham in 1995, have examined the images and artefacts of formal education. At its outset, the aim of this group was to recover 'the silent social history of the classroom'[46]—a sphere of enquiry lamented by Harold Silver in 1992 as profoundly absent in the literature[47]—and, later, the group applied these methods to schooling more broadly.[48] The editors of an initial set of papers explained that the group's concerns arose not merely from a sense that the routine activity of the classroom was a missing aspect of the historical record, but also from a desire to set 'a new direction in the history of education' given that, as they put it, the field 'appears to be stalled in methodological evolution'. In particular, they sought to generate a *modus operandi* characterized by essays that needed to be read 'relationally, and not as discrete entities' but as 'open narratives ... and parts of a larger conversation'.[49] This conversation was

---

[43] For an example of this continuity of outlook see, Coles J., "Editorial: The JEAH and the Millennium." *Journal of Educational Administration and History* 32, no. 1 (2000): 1–7. For the contraction, see Appendix I and n. 20, above.

[44] Institutional in the sense of how to secure the sustainability of the field within higher education.

[45] Although many of the most prominent themes of recent years have antecedents traceable in pioneering work of the previous two decades, see Goodman and Martin "Defining a field", 3–9.

[46] Grosvenor, I., M. Lawn, and K. Rousmaniere, "Introduction." In *Silences and Images: The Social History of the Classroom*, edited by I. Grosvenor, M. Lawn and K. Rousmaniere. New York: Peter Lang, 1999: vii, 1–3.

[47] Silver, H. "Knowing and not knowing in the history of education." *History of Education* 21, no. 1 (1992): 105.

[48] Grosvenor, I., and M. Lawn, eds. *History of Education* 30, no. 2 (2001) (special issue on 'Ways of Seeing in Education and Schooling: Emerging Historiographies'); Mietzner, U., K. Myers, and N. Peim, eds. *Visual History: Images of Education.* Oxford: Peter Lang, 2005; Lawn M., and I. Grosvenor, eds. *Materialities of Schooling: Design, Technology, Objects Routines.* Didcot: Symposium Books, 2005.

[49] Grosvenor *et al.*, *Silences and Images*, 2, 9.

continued through a series of four further conferences held in Europe during 1996–2000,[50] with the result that by 2005 the introductory editorials of resulting publications had taken a decidedly *avant-garde* turn, influenced strongly by theories of language and culture. For Martin Lawn and Ian Grosvenor—presiding over a genre they labelled 'material culture studies'—the objects and routines of schooling were now best considered as technologies which, once obsolete and available for historical scrutiny, form 'layers of object sedimentation'. This, in turn, allowed teaching to be seen as 'a series of networked operations' and 'the school site as a new text' where teachers can be governed by 'prescribed action, shaped possibilities and steering, especially by means of technologies of the self'.[51] For Nick Peim, historical method was best seen as archaeology, with the artefacts examined subsequently rendered as history, a procedure which is 'always something that has to be, in one way or another, told—or, at least, represented'. Sources of whatever form are signs; the historian then undertakes meaning-making in which 'atomistic signs and sign configurations are being construed into more or less coherent texts', a method he described as 'illustrative modes and occasions of engagement with signifying material'.[52] According to an editorial in 2001, the inherent variety of the endeavour illustrated the point that the academic network and its activities remained heterogeneous, since 'the net orthodoxy is to demand news ways of production and new modes of report'.[53] Four years later, it was stated that work of this kind made no claim 'to a new mode or model of history' but rather 'to positively supplement other kinds of historical evidence': historical judgements about 'what matters' had continued importance; circumspection rather than 'modish displacement of conventional histories' was a virtue; the idea of 'reality' remained a proper goal of historical studies.[54] Having established in this manner that the historical baby should remain in the bath, Peim nevertheless threatened to drown it in the water by asserting that 'history cannot be innocent of the sociology of knowledge', before drawing the postmodern conclusion that he and his co-workers shared 'an implicit consensus that history cannot be seen as the accumulation of a steadily growing stock of knowledge' since 'history is fundamentally hermeneutic in character' and saturated in myth. Thus, the 'visual turn' in the history of education had the 'promise to transform and re-energize' it, since the field was 'not simply expanded by the intrusion of hitherto excluded knowledge. Its borders are interfered with; its ontological status is problematized, reorganized and refined'.[55]

---

[50] Toronto (1996), Rotterdam (1998), Lahti (Finland) (1999) and Edinburgh (2000): Grosvenor and Lawn, *Silences and Images*, 1–2; Depaepe, M. *Order in Progress: Everyday Educational Practice in Primary Schools. Belgium, 1880–1970.* Leuven: Leuven University Press, 2000: 14, n. 28; Grosvenor and Lawn, '"Ways of Seeing"', 105; Meitzner *et al.*, *Visual History*, 9–10.

[51] Lawn and Grosvenor, *Materialities of Schooling*, 7–10.

[52] Peim, N. "Introduction." In Mietzner *et al.*, *Visual History*, 7, 25–26.

[53] Grosvenor, I., and M. Lawn. "Ways of Seeing in Education and Schooling: Emerging Historiographies." *History of Education* 30, no. 2 (2001): 107–08.

[54] Peim, "Introduction", 26, 34–35; Lawn and Grosvenor, *Materialities of Schooling*, 10.

[55] Peim, "Introduction", 25, 9, 30, 31.

A second example of innovation in the field, equally international in reach, and experimental and radical in its implications, comprises recent attempts to relate contemporary cultural theory developed in 'the West' to the issue of researching the history of education (or other phenomena) of indigenous, non-industrialized peoples. This enterprise is most developed among a loose network of scholars in Australia, New Zealand and Canada and, as such, exerts some influence over historiography in Britain, the former colonial power, in terms mainly of a critical stance toward historical representations of immigrant minorities.[56] At first sight, researching the histories of indigenous peoples, including their educational histories, would seem the ideal setting in which to test the ever closer relationship of history and anthropology over the last 20 years,[57] along with complementary and more conventional studies of the political milieu.[58] However, the Western empirical stance that such an enterprise implies is increasingly rejected by some historians of education in favour of a quite different approach to data generation. In the context of researching education among Aboriginals, Gillian Weiss has summarized three strands of this problem: 'the difficulty of attempting to analyse and interpret one culture, or set of cultures, through the medium of, and with the tools and methodologies of, another diametrically different culture'; different understandings within Western and indigenous cultures of the dynamic of time; and highly divergent understandings of the process of education.[59] Influenced strongly in their methodologies by theories of 'voice' first systematically explored in 1970s and 1980s ('second wave') feminism, historians of indigenous cultures set out, from the early 1990s, to establish rules of engagement. A decade later, these seem to have settled around the need for a cooperative approach across cultural boundaries to creating primary, non-documentary source material (despite 'a huge diversity of attitude and approach to the question of who should be involved in rewriting' on the part of indigenous peoples), both to reflect the difficulty of agreeing property rights in relation to the resulting data and also to promote the ideal of 'equality' between Western academic discourse and that of oral societies.[60]

Positioned at the conceptual and geographical boundaries of the field, the study of materialities of education and of native people's education is significant in its current reappraisal internationally, in terms of both academic methods and institutional aims.

---

[56] For example, Grosvenor, I. *Assimilating Identities: Recent Educational Policy in Post 1945 Britain*. London: Lawrence & Wishart, 1999. Lowe, "Major Themes", Vol. IV: ix–x.

[57] Cannadine, "Preface", ix.

[58] Weiss, G. "Inter-disciplinary but not Undisciplined: Writing the History of Aboriginal 'Education'." *Paedagogica Historica* 37, no. 1 (2001): 252 n. 2. See also, Axelrod, P. "Historical Writing and Canadian Education from the 1970s to the 1990s." *History of Education Quarterly* 36, no. 1 (1996): 28–30.

[59] Ibid., 251–52. For a North American view, see Marker, M. "'That History is more a Part of the Present than it Ever was in the Past': Towards an Ethnohistory of Native Education." *History of Education Review* 28, no. 1 (1999): 1–29. An emblematic New Zealand study is Simon, J., ed. *Nga Kura Maori: The Native Schools System, 1867–1969*. Auckland: Auckland University Press, 1998.

[60] Weiss, op cit., 253–55. For the unrepentant view of a minority, see ibid., 255, n. 10.

First, it comprises specific attempts to break with a dominant methodology depicted as stale and unproductive.[61] Weiss concludes that studies of native people's education have only been able to proceed fruitfully due to the foundations laid in the 1990s by oral and feminist histories in establishing personal memory as a legitimate source,[62] while Peim's account of the 'visual turn' in the educational historiography of schooling is the fullest exploration to date of the means by which it might epitomize 'new acceptable ways of working'—mould-breaking in its stance and use of sources yet circumspect enough in method and aim to draw into its wake the more conventional historian, while also riding the surf of contemporary cultural theory.[63] Second, these two areas of innovation are connecting the historiography of education to other inter-disciplinary currents in contemporary scholarship beyond 'straight' historical research. Indeed, both Peim and Weiss conclude that such work must necessarily be interdisciplinary, containing at the core of its methodology a need to go 'beyond the purely historical' and to 'step beyond the traditional boundaries' of the discipline.[64] Third, they are important for what they reveal about priorities, in terms of both the scope of 'education' to be studied and the purposes ascribed to such work. In terms of scope, strongly evident is renewed commitment to intensive study of systems of schools and schooling since 1850 as the key territory at a time when this emphasis is lessening in the wider literature (see Appendix IV). In histories of materialities in education, schooling is the enduring and core concern. Similarly, colonial and post-independence schooling has, so far, been the most prominent aspect of the emergent studies of native peoples' experience of education, even though, as Weiss points out, a much wider canvas is appropriate in work with groups such as Aboriginals whose experience of formal education is both 'minimal and marginal' and unrelated to their 'traditional forms of "education"'.[65] In terms of purposes, proponents of both genres maintain that such histories have purchase over contemporary educational debates. Study of the materialities of schooling in England has been deployed in a critique of current reforms,[66] while the collaboration of native peoples with Western historians is, first and foremost, political in nature. For Aboriginals, wresting control over the curriculum of community education is a key goal, while in North America native peoples seek a re-education, 'not just to inform, to redress the imbalance, but to offer a workable alternative to western culture and attitudes'.[67]

---

[61] Grosvenor *et al.*, *Silences and Images*, 2; Weiss, op. cit., 252.

[62] Weiss, "Aboriginal 'Education'", 258.

[63] In this context see also: Popkewitz, T., B. Franklin, and M. Pereyra, eds. *Cultural History and Education: Critical Essays on Knowledge and Schooling.* New York: RoutledgeFalmer, 2001; and Cohen S., *Challenging Orthodoxies: Toward a New Cultural History of Education.* New York: Peter Lang, 1999.

[64] Peim, "Introduction", 31; Weiss, "Aboriginal 'Education'", 260, 261.

[65] Weiss, "Aboriginal 'Education'", 252.

[66] Lawn and Grosvenor, *Materialities of Schooling*, 9. See also the essay in the same collection by Carey Jewitt and Ken Jones (201–14): "Managing Time and Space in the New English Classroom".

[67] Weiss, "Aboriginal 'Education'", 252 n. 3; 255; 255 n. 11.

In addition, these areas of innovation are significant in the context of varied changes in the field internationally over the last decade. By the mid-1990s they were contributing to strands of reappraisal within Europe and its former colonial countries, an undertaking that had got under way before, and which has been conducted largely in parallel with and separate from a similar process of reassessment in the USA.[68] The spark igniting widespread reassessment in America was a paper by Jurgen Herbst which claimed, in 1999, that over the previous 20 years there had been 'little genuine fresh input' in the field in the United States. With the exception of women's history, 'truly creative and innovative scholarship' had fled the scene and contemporary research internationally appeared to move on 'by sheer momentum' in neglect of its core concern—schooling and pedagogy—due to the long shadow cast by Barnard Bailyn and Lawrence Cremin, progenitors in the early 1960s of a modern historiography of American education that had reframed 'education' in history as all of the processes of cultural transmission in society.[69] Within six months of the appearance of Herbst's broadside, the Spencer Foundation had mounted a conference at Stanford University on New Directions in the History of Education. Comprising 40 participants, among them many of the most prominent United States scholars in the field of the previous 35 years, the discussion confirmed Herbst's contention that the 1960s and 1970s had, indeed, been a 'golden era'.[70] If, as at least one participant remarked, the whole event was highly insular in its concerns,[71] it was also instructive regarding the intellectual methods and institutional aims of the field that American scholars considered needed to be pursued. Reports of the discussions also suggested that delegates took for granted traditional methods of historical enquiry[72] and a continuing concentration on formal education in schools and universities. In this light, the key issue for the future appeared to be whether, in order to make the field sustainable, educational historians in America should commit to a wholesale engagement with contemporary policy. The answer arrived at was that, on balance, they should,[73] and for

---

[68] Although figures such as Geraldine Clifford, Barbara Finkelstein, Kate Rousmaniere and Wayne Urban have been involved in both.

[69] Herbst, J. "The History of Education: State of the Art at the Turn of the Century in Europe and North America." *Paedagogica Historica* 35, no. 3 (1999): 739, 741, 743.

[70] Donato R., and Lazerson M., "New Directions in American Educational History: Problems and Prospects." *Educational Researcher* 29, no. 8 (2000): 6.

[71] Mahony, K. "New Times, New Questions", ibid., 18. For concern about the insularity of American historiography of education, see also Rousmaniere K., "Fresh Thinking: Recent Work in the History of Education." *Paedagogica Historica* 37, no. 3 (2001): 649–52.

[72] For example in discussion on 'Writing the Educational Histories of People of Colour' the most controversial point reported was whether, in contemporary America, white scholars could continue to write about the history of minorities alongside historians of colour: Donato and Lazerson, "New Directions", 7–8. There was no suggestion that Native Americans were other than just another minority to be examined, in contrast to the sensibility in Australasia and Canada that more radical research methods are called for when exploring education in the histories of indigenous cultures (see above nn. 58 and 59).

[73] Donato and Lazerson, "New Directions", 13.

commentators such as Milton Gaither and Sol Cohen this underscored Herbst's point. Bailyn's insistence that, in history, 'education' be interpreted as the entire process of cultural transmission in society, far from being a liberation for the field, had proved unworkable in practice; instead, it had served only to intensify research—some of it decidedly unhistorical in its 'radical revisionism'—on the true heartland of schooling in the modern state.[74]

British Responses

British responses to Herbst's article were instructive and could be read as a cross-section of historiographical opinion across the Atlantic at the turn of the new century.[75] His lament found no place in Roy Lowe's celebratory, four-volume collection of key contributions to the Anglophone field over the period 1957–2000. Moreover, in contrast to Herbst's call for a renewed focus on 'teaching and learning in schools' in the setting of 'programs of professional education', Lowe specifically endorsed Bailyn's vision of the proper scope of the field as encompassing the entire process of acculturation. In turn, this led Lowe to characterize the achievements of the field in terms of the extent to which it had realized the dream of Brian Simon, and other founders of the UK History of Education Society, that the history of education be seen as 'a full and proper element in the study of history more generally'.[76] On closer inspection, however, Lowe's collection turned out to be heavily concerned with education systems developed under the modern state; indeed, he concluded that American controversies during 1970–1980 over the purposes and function of 'common schooling' had significantly 'overshadowed and anticipated all that has

---

[74] Gaither, M. *American Educational History revised: A Critique of Progress*. New York: Teachers College, Columbia University (2003): 5, 157–59, 161–64; Cohen, *Challenging Orthodoxies*, 277–94. Over prescriptions for the field they differed, however. For Gaither the future needed to lie with a closer engagement of history with policy, see Gaither, M. "Globalization and the History of Education." *Paedagogica Historica* 37, no. 3 (2001): 644–47. In contrast, Cohen envisioned a 'new cultural history of education' that sought to 'bring history of ideas or intellectual history back into the frame' alongside social history, ibid., viii.

[75] These are itemized and referenced in Goodman and Martin, "Defining a Field", 2 and McCulloch G., ed. *The RoutledgeFalmer Reader in History of Education*. Abingdon: RoutledgeFalmer, 2005: 3–4.

[76] Herbst, "State of the Art", 747; Lowe, "Major Themes", Vol. 1, xlvi, xliii and also Lowe, "Do we still need history of Education?", 502. For Brian Simon's dream, see Depaepe, M., "It's a Long Way to … an International Social History of Education: In Search of Brian Simon's Legacy in Today's Educational Historiography." *History of Education* 33, no. 5 (2004): 543.

come after in this field of study'.[77] Two years later, and with Herbst's 'significant challenge' specifically in view, Gary McCulloch commissioned a special edition of *History of Education* designed to 'inform and enhance the future direction of the field',[78] following this with his own edited collection of recent notable contributions focused mainly on Britain. In these two publications, many of the diverse theoretical concerns evident in the British literature since the mid-1990s were charted and discussed—voice, memory, gender, the limitations of the conventional archive— along with broader themes that have won increased attention and have been seen to benefit from methodological innovation in research: informal agencies of education, empire, youth transitions, education and national identity. However, like Lowe, the rationale of McCulloch's edited collection was to eschew Herbst's call for a more overt focus on schooling, instead invoking 'the prime avowed purpose' of the field over the previous 40 years, namely 'to explore relationships between education and the configurations of society as these have played themselves out over time'.[79]

These and other publications, which during 2000–2003 could be said to have comprised the British engagement with Herbst,[80] articulated a number of points regarding the main currents running in British historiography of education at the turn of the century and how these related to overseas influences and trends. First, and not least in significance, historians of education in Britain were, as a group, becoming much more eclectic and international in their historiographical outlook than a gener- ation previously.[81] Indeed, the barb that they were trapped in an 'Anglo-Saxon' ghetto[82] appears wide of the mark for, although the commitment to social history in a national context still predominated (and comprised the sustained empirical basis and identity of the field in an international context), there were now clear signs in the British journal literature of a resurgent interest in aspects that had characterized the field up to the 1950s and had remained a hallmark of concern in much of continental

---

[77] Lowe, "Major Themes", lii. In reviewing the collection, Gary McCulloch saw it as a broadly faithful mirror of the key traits of Anglophone writing in the field since 1960: an emphasis on nine- teenth- and twentieth-century schooling; the special significance accorded to 'detailed treatments of the origins and early development of modern systems of education'; a strong presence of male authors; a generally cautious approach to theoretical and methodological orientations; and a 'polit- ical and ideological hue' that 'generally favours left-wing and Marxist criticisms of modern school- ing': *History of Education* 31, no. 3 (2002): 303–07.

[78] McCulloch, G. "Introduction: Reflections on the Field." *History of Education* 31, no. 3 (2002): 204–05. The resulting essay were co–edited with Ruth Watts and published as the special issue "Theory, Methodology and the History of Education". *History of Education* 32, no. 2 (2003).

[79] McCulloch, *RoutledgeFalmer Reader*, 2.

[80] Many of the arguments they advanced are discussed in Aldrich. R. "The Three Duties of the Historian of Education." *History of Education* 32, no. 2 (2003): 133–43. See also n. 75, above.

[81] Lowe "Major Themes", xliii; Rousmaniere, "Fresh Thinking". Between 1977 and 1986 only three out of 189 articles in *History of Education* were primarily concerned with historiography; equiv- alent figures for 1996–2005 were 51 out of 312 articles.

[82] Depaepe, M. "What Kind of History of Education May We Expect for the Twenty-first Cen- tury? Some Comments on Four Recent Readers in the Field." *Paedagogica Historica* XXXIX, nos 1–2 (2003): 190–91, 196.

Europe subsequently: the study of educational ideas and influences, along with scrutiny of the philosophical and epistemological assumptions underlying working methods and thematic concerns.[83] Second, although the defining stamp of much published work still comprised histories of modern formal education, most notably aspects of state-sponsored schooling and university education, the dominance of this tradition had begun to weaken significantly in the mid-1990s. Forces at work included generational renewal within the historical profession more broadly and the gathering 'cultural turn' in history. The latter development has been, on the one hand, an intellectual movement, strongly influenced by theories of language, gender and identity. On the other, it is intimately linked with world affairs, and, most especially: the failure by the end of the twentieth century of almost all Marx's predictions concerning social and political development;[84] the implications for academic history of the working methods of feminism[85] and, later, postmodernism;[86] and the location of Western historians in what, by the 1980s, were starting to become self-consciously 'postcolonial' societies.[87] Within this broad context, and for several more specific reasons, it has remained the norm in Britain over the past decade for historians of education to uphold a public commitment to a wide definition of their field. In this way, Roy Lowe could remain true to the verity of the 1960s that only by this means could historians of education position themselves in the mainstream of social history (a battle fought and lost in England in the mid-1970s[88]) while, for a new generation, Gary McCulloch, Joyce Goodman and Jane Martin could value breadth of study for the interdisciplinary engagements that it promised across the humanities and social sciences, and beyond the boundaries of the nation-state.[89] Meanwhile, British architects of the materialities of education initiative had found common cause internationally with scholars from those countries where pedagogy had always been held to be at the core of the field (e.g. Belgium or Germany)[90] or where calls were now being advanced for the history of education to celebrate an institutional return to faculties

---

[83] See Appendix IV.

[84] Kolakowski, l. *Main Currents of Marxism: The Founders, The Golden Age, The Breakdown*. New York: W. W. Norton, 2005. See also, Brehony, K., "Education as a 'social function': sociology, and social theory in the histories of Brian Simon." *History of Education* 33, no. 5 (2004): 554.

[85] Offen, K., R. R. Pierson, and J. Rendall, eds. *Writing Women's History: International Perspectives*. London: Macmillan, 1991.

[86] Evans, R. J. *In Defence of History* London: Granta, 1997. See also Evans R. J. "Prologue. *What is History*-Now?", in Cannadine, *"What is History Now?"*, 6–8.

[87] Kennedy, D. "Imperial history and post-colonial theory." *Journal of Imperial and Commonwealth History* 24 (1996): 345–63; Hopkins, A. G. "Back to the Future: From National History to Imperial History." *Past & Present* 164 (1999): 198–43.

[88] Richardson, "Historians and Educationists", 117–32.

[89] McCulloch, *RoutledgeFalmer Reader*, 2, 9; Goodman and Martin, "Defining a Field", 1, 4, 10.

[90] Depaepe, *Order in Progress*, 14, n. 28; Depaepe, "What kind of history of Education?", 192; Depaepe, M. "History of Education Anno 1992: 'A Tale Told by an Idiot, Full of Sound and Fury, Signifying Nothing'?" *History of Education* 22, no. 1 (1993): 4.

of education after the 1970s and 1980s distraction of social history (e.g. the USA).[91] At the same time, senior historians of education in Britain—Roy Lowe from the perspective of traditional methods in historical scholarship and Richard Aldrich from a sense of the duties of the field both to history and to education—counselled that there was no substitute for 'painstaking', 'scientific' and 'expert' history[92] and that the lumpen condemnation of 'modernist' or 'empiricist' history by postmodernists and poststructuralists required consistent countering due to the historian's obligation to 'search after truth'.[93]

Sustaining the Endeavour

Despite the suppleness of these various positions, in the British context as elsewhere, the practical problem remained the weak institutional base for the study of the history of education.[94] On the one hand, mainstream historians continued to inhabit a clearly differentiated field with a strong undergraduate base[95] while, on the other, educational research was becoming ever more infused with the values and methods of social research. As Nick Peim observed, the history of education was a 'hybrid' field[96] and therein lay its vulnerability. The specialist journals were flourishing but, in contrast to mainstream history, the ebbing away of students and established curricula in all but a handful of institutions[97] ruled out one traditionally purposeful means of differentiation: debate among fellow scholars of the communal question

---

[91] Herbst, "State of the Art", 747; Levin R., "After the Fall: Can Historical Studies Return to the Faculties of Education?" *Historical Studies in Education* 12, nos 1–2 (2000): 155–62.

[92] Lowe, "Do we Still Need History of Education?", 496–501. For an alternative, postmodern view, critical of historians who place detail above interpretation, see Cohen, S. "An Innocent Eye: The 'Pictorial Turn,' Film Studies and History." *History of Education Quarterly* 43, no. 2 (2003): 258–59.

[93] Aldrich, "The Three Duties", 141–42.

[94] And not only in Britain: for North America, see Levin, "After the Fall"; for Australia, see Campbell, C., and G. Sherington. "The History of Education: The Possibility of Survival." *Change: Transformations in Education* 5, no. 1 (2002): 46–64; for Belgium, see Depaepe, M. "History of Education Anno 1992", 1.

[95] In 2006 history remained the sixth most popular A-level subject among school and college leavers after (in order of magnitude): English, general studies, mathematics, biology and psychology.

[96] Peim, N. "The State of the Art or the Ruins of Nostalgia? The Problematics of Subject Identity, its Objects, Theoretical Resources and Practices." *Paedagogica Historica* 37, no. 3 (2001): 654.

[97] During 2004–2006 four centres for the history of education in England were profiled in the *Educational Researcher*, each undertaking research and offering named courses for students: Cambridge (BA Education Studies: 'History of Education', see *Educational Researcher* no. 72 (2003): 94–97); London (Institute of Education) (MA in History of Education, see *Educational Researcher* no. 74 (2004): 111–14 and no. 75 (2005): 52–54); Winchester (BA Education Studies (various modules); 'MA in Social History: Education: 1800–1944', see *Educational Researcher* no. 76 (2005): 100–01); and Birmingham (BA in History, Heritage, Education; MA in History of Childhood and Youth in European Cultural History, see *Educational Researcher* no. 77 (2006): 46–47). In October 2006, due to under-recruitment, the University of Birmingham's Senate approved the closure of the School of Education's undergraduate course in History, Heritage, Education while protecting its programme in Applied Golf Course Management.

'What should we teach?'. Moreover, as Goodman and Martin had been pointing out for some years, the intellectual commitments of individual participants in the field were more overt and varied than in the past,[98] and while this embrace of 'identity politics'[99] by many historians of education was recognizably part of a wider development in the academic study of history,[100] it could hardly compensate for a lack of students to teach.

To what extent have these various characteristics of the field in Britain been perceived as evidence of strength and vitality among observers from within the international community of historians of education? In 1993 the view from Paris was that the foundations laid in the 1960s and 1970s—in particular the range and depth of the British 'descriptive and analytical' tradition, compared with the less flexible and innovative philosophical genre found on the continent—rendered the field stronger in England than anywhere in Europe.[101] In 2000, Aldrich and his colleague David Crook considered that this 'relatively strong position' persisted in terms of research and publications[102] despite the drastic erosion of the teaching base over the previous 15 years,[103] but in 2002 Marc Depaepe, the most internationally minded and probably the most widely read historiographer of education of the past 20 years,[104] dismissed this claim, and the 'hackwork' on which he considered it based, as 'the fruit of frustration and anger at the languishing position' of the field.[105] In contrast, the perspective from Miami the same year was that current research in England was as fresh and exciting as anywhere in Europe or North America.[106] When all of the opinions had been traded, the body of published work generated in the field in Britain stood as its monument: large scale and still growing; empirically rigorous; increasingly concerned with the past 150 years; widening in conceptual scope; and comprising a traditional division of labour in which work published in the mainstream history

---

[98] Goodman, Martin and Robinson, "Retrospect and Prospect", 2 and Goodman and Martin, "Defining a Field", 10.

[99] Peim, "The State of the Art or the Ruins of Nostalgia?", 655.

[100] See, for example, Jordonova, "*History in Practice*", 34–35, which illustrates the point with an example from education.

[101] Compère, M.-M. "Textbooks on the History of Education Currently in Use in Europe." In *Why Should We Teach History of Education?*, edited by K. Salomova and E. Johanningmeier. Moscow: Library of International Academy of Self-Improvement, 1993: 243. Compère also maintained that the low intellectual prestige of pedagogic research in England had freed historians of education based in the teacher training institutions from inertia; ibid.

[102] Aldrich R., and D. Crook. *History of Education for the Twenty-First Century*, London: Institute of Education (2000): x.

[103] See above nn. 12 and 97.

[104] By his own estimation, Depaepe had traced at least 600 articles on the historiography of education published before 1980, see "How Should the History of Education be Written?", 335, n. 3, while his own historiographical articles since the early 1990s have had extensive multilingual bibliographies.

[105] Depaepe, "What kind of history of Education?", 191, 189. Some of Depaepe's own annoyance had been stirred by the expansive title of the Aldrich and Crook collection, ibid.

[106] Rousmaniere, "Fresh Thinking", 649–50.

journals is more likely to centre on the premodern period, the history of universities, literacy and the history of the family, and the output of the specialist titles edited from the education faculties retains a dominant emphasis on the recent past, schooling, state policy, biography and educational ideas,[107] albeit with a recent and significant broadening of methods of enquiry and theoretical orientations.[108]

This assessment provokes a final question, that of the sustainability of the field, given its weak institutional basis. This, in turn, links British debates to a broader international discussion of the purpose and future orientation of the study of the history of education. In so far as there has been an English tradition, it has, in Anglo-American fashion, followed a descriptive and analytical course, present from the early seventeenth century[109] but dominant since the early 1960s, when bonds to the Germanic philosophical tradition established in the last quarter of the nineteenth century were severed.[110] In the absence of a founding historiographical text to set alongside Bailyn of Harvard's *Education in the Forming of American Society* (1960), the postwar English pioneer was Brian Simon: self-taught, working in parallel with, rather than among, those historians energizing emergent labour history and, in his interests, 'an "educational" historian in heart and soul', concerned to reach a readership of teachers.[111] Reflecting candidly in 2002, Roy Lowe concluded that the crucial organizational flaw underlying the outpouring of work that Simon's example had stimulated and inspired was (in contrast to the internationalism of Simon and that of Lowe himself [112]) the 'arrogance and complacency' of a university culture that led to the parochialism of a generation of academics trapped in 'a national culture, nation-alistic perceptions and a set of local prejudices which were never or rarely tested

---

[107] See Richardson, "Historians and Educationists", 28–29, 139–40 and Appendices III and IV, below.

[108] Goodman and Martin, "Defining a Field", 5–9. A small number of general historians have continued to produced highly influential work on education in Britain as it resonates within Jordonova's quartet of '"structural" phenomena' in society: the economic, political, social and intellectual (see above n. 9). Two recent examples are Rose, J. *The Intellectual Life of the British Working Classes.* New Haven, CT: Yale University Press, 2001; and Orme, N. *Medieval Schools: From Roman Britain to Renaissance England.* New Haven, CT: Yale University Press, 2006. However, this enterprise has been small scale and unable to establish education within mainstream history as a compelling theme for exploring and explaining past societies in the manner achieved by historians of equally pervasive social phenomena such as gender, religion or health.

[109] Evident, for example, in the writing about the history of the universities, see Cordeaux, E., and D. Merry. *A Bibliography of Printed Works Relating to the University of Oxford.* Oxford, Clarendon Press, 1968.

[110] This linkage established an emphasis, embraced across the Anglophone world, on the ideas of educators in history. The pioneering British work was Quick, R. *Essays on Educational Reformers.* London: Longmans, Green, 1868.

[111] "Professor Brian Simon in Conversation with Ruth Watts." *Educational Researcher* no. 71 (2003): 5–6; Richardson, "Historians and Educationists", 15–18; Depaepe, "In Search of Brian Simon's Legacy", 541.

[112] Ibid., 537–41; Crook, D. "Society, Economy, Politics and Education from Wilson to Thatcher." *Oxford Review of Education* 24, no. 4 (1998): 535.

against experience'.[113] For the majority of historians of education—those based in the departments of education—the implications of this academic isolation become increasingly hard to ignore as the 1980s unfolded,[114] with perhaps the most spirited response coming from the Institute of Education at the University of London, where Richard Aldrich set out in 1988 on a course of research projects designed explicitly to reconnect with a professional audience around the organizing theme of 'historical perspectives on current educational issues'.[115] Whereas in the early 1990s such a development was patterned recognizably within a postwar bifurcation of an 'academic' history of education contrasted with an 'applied' educational history,[116] the general momentum toward interdisciplinarity and the epistemological debate of the past 15 years has signalled a realignment,[117] creating a new historiographical climate, strongly influenced by postmodern critique, in which 'presentism' is no longer regarded as the enemy of good history but accepted as integral to the condition of writing history.[118]

In Britain, with its still-generous funding of 'lone scholarship' in the humanities and social sciences, neither the lack of a student base nor the rarity of programmes of funded research has yet to imperil the viability of continued scholarship in the field,[119] most of which is coordinated through the university departments of education.[120] As such, there has been little overt challenge to Bailyn's dictum that the field should be focused broadly and on the processes of education throughout society even if, as we have seen, it has until recently been honoured mainly in the breach and is currently regarded by some in the United states as a cul-de-sac.[121] So long as

---

[113] Lowe, "Do We Still Need History of Education?", 495, 497.

[114] Richardson, "Historians and Educationists", 132–38.

[115] Aldrich, R. "Historical Perspectives on Current Educational Issues." *Bulletin of the History of Education Society* 41 (1988): 9–10 and Aldrich, R. *The End of History and the Beginning of Education.* London: Institute of Education, 1997: 5. This orientation-with its attendant problems-was discussed by American delegates at the Spencer Foundation Conference in 2000 (Donato and Lazerson, "New Directions": 9–10) and has been strongly resisted in numerous essays by Marc Depaepe. At the London Institute the orientation has been continued by Aldrich's successor since 2003, Gary McCulloch: see, *Documentary Research in Education, History and the Social Sciences.* London: RoutledgeFalmer, 2004: 6, 10.

[116] Richardson, "Historians and Educationists", 138, n. 205. For a riposte, see Aldrich R. "A Contested and Changing Terrain: History of Education in the Twenty-First Century" in Aldrich and Crook, *History of Education for the Twenty-First Century*, 70–79.

[117] Interpreted by Aldrich in 1997 as a cultural shift more favourable to education as a discipline than to history, "End of History", 24–27.

[118] For example, Black. J. *Using History* London: Hodder Arnold, 2005: 1 and Jordonova, *History in Practice*, 206.

[119] See above, nn. 14 and 97.

[120] See Appendix II.

[121] Where a major reassessment of Bailyn's influence is under way prompted by, among others, Jurgen Herbst, Sol Cohen and Milton Gaither (see above nn. 69 and 74), which is echoed in Australia by Craig Campbell and Geoffrey Sherington (see "The Possibility of Survival", 60). As previously noted (above nn. 90 and 110), the turn to social history that Bailyn prompted has had less influence in continental Europe.

current funding conditions apply, the field looks set to continue on its present trajectory of increasingly varied types of investigation into aspects of formal and informal education, with a primary focus on educators, schooling and the universities.[122] Indeed, the current spate of scholarly output, coupled with its conceptual and geographical diversity, suggests that the UK History of Education Society, through its journals and conferences, is currently as important a catalyst for the field in Britain as it was in the re-founding period of 1967–1972. Meanwhile, if we ask, as did the seminar series on 'Social Change in the History of Education' held in England during 2004–2006, what have been the achievements of the field over the last 40 years,[123] the inescapable conclusion is that, as a result of a sustained, rigorous and enlarging endeavour, our understanding of the historic processes of education and social change is much fuller and more sophisticated than a generation ago.[124] As with other spheres of history recently reviewed by David Cannadine, we can further conclude that the consequence of this endeavour, coupled with the questions that concern contemporary society, is resulting in a contemporary history of education that would, half a century ago, have been not only 'completely unthinkable' but 'literally unimaginable'.[125]

---

[122] A storm cloud on the current horizon (February 2007) is how humanities scholarship will fare in social science 'units' such as Education under metrics-based research funding, due to be introduced in 2014.

[123] Economic and Social Research Council award no. RES-451-26-0169. The organizers were Gary McCulloch (University of London: award holder), Joyce Goodman (University of Winchester) and William Richardson (University of Exeter).

[124] Moreover, it can be claimed in response to those who criticize British research in education at large for being besettingly faddish and shallow (see Richardson, "Educational Studies", 41, 47), that no aspect of that field has maintained a greater consistency of methodological rigour over the last half-century (albeit that recent postmodernist critique maintains that such consistency does not necessarily amount to an increased stock of knowledge, see above n. 55).

[125] Cannadine, "Preface", x.

Appendix I. Number of articles on the history of education published in leading historical journals established or edited in the universities of the British Isles, 1956–2005* (n = number of journals)

1956–60	1961–65	1966–70	1971–75	1976–80	1981–85	1986–90	1991–95	1996–00	2001–05	Total (whole period)
61	67	159	230	332	358	403	471	439	578	3,098
(n = 24)	(n = 26)	(n = 33)	(n = 37)	(n = 41)	(n = 44)	(n = 50)	(n = 55)	(n = 56)	(n = 56)	

*Coverage from 1956:

Transactions of the Royal Historical Society
Church Quarterly Review (ceased publication after 1968)
Journal of Hellenic Studies
English Historical Review
Classical Review
Scottish Historical Review
Classical Quarterly
Journal of Roman Studies

History
Cambridge Historical Journal (continued as *Historical Journal* from 1958)
Bulletin of the Institute of Historical Research (continued as *Historical Research* from 1987)
Economic History Review
Greece and Rome
University of Birmingham Historical Journal (ceased publication 1969; continued as *Midland History* from 1971)
Journal of Ecclesiastical History
History Today

Appendix I. (*Continued*).

Irish Historical Studies

British Journal of Educational Studies (coverage to the end of 1971)

Amateur Historian (continued as *Local Historian* from 1968)

Past and Present

Journals founded from 1957:

Medical History (founded 1957)

Business History (founded 1958)

Bulletin of the Society for the Study of Labour History (founded 1960; continued as *Labour History* from 1990)

Welsh History Review (founded 1960)

History of Science (founded 1962)

Studies in Church History (founded 1964)

Journal of Contemporary History (founded 1966)

Northern History (founded 1966)

History of Education Society Bulletin (founded 1968; continued as *History of Education Researcher* from 2003)

Journal of Educational Administration and History (founded 1968)

Local Population Studies (founded 1968)

Society for the Social History of Medicine Bulletin (founded 1970; continued as *Social History of Medicine* from 1988)

Oral History (founded 1970)

European Studies Review (founded 1971; continued as *European History Quarterly* from 1984)

History of Education (founded 1972)

Journal of Imperial and Commonwealth History (founded 1972)

Urban History Yearbook (founded 1974; continued as *Urban History* from 1992)

History Workshop Journal (founded 1976)

Social History (founded 1976)

Southern History (founded 1979)

Journal of Legal History (founded 1980)

History of Universities (founded 1981)

Parliamentary History (founded 1982)

British Journal of Sports History (founded 1984; continued as *International Journal of the History of Sport* from 1987)

Rural History (founded 1986)

Contemporary Record (founded 1987; continued as *Contemporary British History* from 1996)

Social History of Medicine (founded 1988)

History of Human Sciences (founded 1988)

Gender and History (founded 1989)

20th Century British History (founded 1991)

Contemporary European History (founded 1992)

Early Medieval Europe (founded 1992)

International Yearbook of Oral History (founded 1992; ceased publication after 1996)

Women's History Review (founded 1992)

Historical Studies in Industrial Relations (founded 1996)

Appendix II. Proportion of articles enumerated in Appendix 1 published in five specialist journals of the period established or edited in Education departments of universities in the British Isles, 1956–2005* (n = number of articles)

	1956–60	1961–65	1966–70	1971–75	1976–80	1981–85	1986–90	1991–95	1996–00	2001–05	Whole period
%	66	60	60	63	67	61	57	50	54	54	57
	(n = 40)	(n = 40)	(n = 96)	(n = 144)	(n = 223)	(n = 218)	(n = 232)	(n = 235)	(n = 236)	(n = 310)	(n = 1,774)

*British Journal of Educational Studies (coverage: 1952–71); Journal of Educational Administration and History (1968–); History of Education Society Bulletin (1968–); History of Education (1972–); British Journal of Sports History (1984–86: continued as International Journal of the History of Sport, 1987–).

Appendix III. Chronological distribution of the articles enumerated in Appendix I (1956–2005) (%)* (n = number of articles)

	1956–60	1961–65	1966–70	1971–75	1976–80	1981–85	1986–90	1991–95	1996–00	2001–05	Whole period	% over whole period comprising articles from journals in Appendix II
	%	%	%	%	%	%	%	%	%	%	%	
The ancient world	0	6	2	2	1	3	2	2	5	3	3	10
The medieval world	8	7	3	5	4	11	10	10	5	4	7	17
1500–1750	35	18	15	17	19	15	14	14	8	11	13	30
1750–1864	37	54	46	39	44	32	29	29	23	25	30	62
1865–1913	14	11	25	26	28	22	23	23	27	24	25	70
1914–1960	6	4	9	10	13	16	20	20	26	29	19	61
1961 to the present	0	0	0	1	1	1	2	2	6	4	3	66
	100	100	100	100	100	100	100	100	100	100	100	
	(n = 51)	(n = 54)	(n = 131)	(n = 201)	(n = 282)	(n = 331)	(n = 383)	(n = 446)	(n = 412)	(n = 510)	(n = 2,801)	

* Excludes bibliographical, historiographical and overview articles.

Appendix IV. Thematic distribution of the articles enumerated in Appendix I (1956–2005) (%) (n = number of articles)

	1956–60	1961–65	1966–70	1971–75	1976–80	1981–85	1986–90	1991–95	1996–00	2001–05	Whole period	% over whole period comprising articles from journals in Appendix II
	%	%	%	%	%	%	%	%	%	%	%	
Bibliography; historiography; overviews	21	25	21	15	10	9	7	7	6	11	10	83
Ideas; influences; biography; organizations and movements	13	19	13	11	10	9	8	3	11	15	10	78
The churches; religion	3	5	6	3	4	6	5	5	4	6	5	52
Policy and administration	14	13	18	21	17	16	17	15	11	7	14	77
Pre-school education; education at home	0	3	1	1	0	1	1	1	1	1	1	64
Schools	8	7	9	10	10	11	10	11	6	7	9	78
Universities	16	9	13	14	11	18	21	20	14	18	17	21
Adult, worker and industrial education	7	6	6	4	9	8	8	5	6	5	6	46
Teachers and teacher training	7	3	5	3	5	4	3	6	6	4	5	72
Education and gender	0	0	0	1	3	2	5	4	4	4	3	65
Libraries; literacy and books	0	2	4	4	5	5	1	4	6	4	4	34
Disadvantaged and marginal groups; education & welfare	0	0	1	1	1	1	1	2	4	4	2	68
Curriculum	7	6	2	7	10	7	7	6	11	6	7	56
Qualifications and training schemes	2	2	0	0	2	1	1	1	1	1	1	63
Childhood; family; youth	2	0	1	5	3	2	5	10	9	7	6	4
	100	100	100	100	100	100	100	100	100	100	100	
	(n = 61)	(n = 67)	(n = 159)	(n = 230)	(n = 332)	(n = 358)	(n = 403)	(n = 471)	(n = 439)	(n = 578)	(n = 3,098)	(n = 1,774)

The History of Education as the History of Reading*

Jonathan Rose

My fundamental premise is simply this: that the history of reading is essential to recovering the history of education. All education involves some form of reading: that is, deciphering and extracting information from a text. It might be a printed text (like a primer), an oral text (say, a professorial lecture), a broadcast text (a television news programme), or even a musical text (you can learn a lot by listening to a concert). But all texts educate. This axiom, of course, leads to a very expansive definition of education, which would include formal, informal and self-education. It certainly presumes that education is a lifelong process that takes place both inside and outside classrooms. Such a broad remit would make the historiography of education essential to, and practically coextensive with, the historiography of culture. I, for one, have no problem with such an all-inclusive approach. However, it would probably compel historians of education to devote less attention to institutional structures and more to the intellectual experiences of actual students—because, as we all know, bureaucratic directives do not necessarily determine what goes on in the classroom, and pupils may read textbooks in ways that teachers, superintendents and cabinet ministers never imagined or intended.

Historians of education may therefore find it useful to know what historians of reading have done, the theoretical models they have used, and some of the tentative

---

*An earlier version of this paper was published in *Historically Speaking* (January 2004), under the title 'Arriving at a History of Reading'. It is published here with some revisions and with the kind permission of the editors.

conclusions they have reached—conclusions which are often quite different from anything predicted by literary theorists. But on one point historians of reading agree with postmodern critics: all things are texts, which can be read, and are open to interpretation. The thrashings administered by Edwardian schoolmasters, for example, were read by some pupils as pointless sadism, which taught them nothing but an abiding hatred of injustice, whereas another student might read them as 'tough but fair' discipline which 'made me the man I am today'.[1] Either way, it was an educational experience, which can only be understood by employing the methods of the historiography of reading.

Twenty years ago the historiography of reading scarcely existed. Many historians at that time doubted that we could ever recover anything so private, so evanescent as the inner experiences of ordinary readers in the past. Where were such experiences recorded? What sources could we possibly use?

Yet since then the historiography of reading has advanced more quickly than anyone expected. It constitutes one-third of the mission of that new scholarly organization, the Society for the History of Authorship, Reading and Publishing (SHARP), founded in 1991. Scholars have sketched in some of the blank spaces on this vast empty map. With considerable ingenuity, they have located and used a wide range of raw materials that offer some insight into the mental world of ordinary readers:

Police records should be mentioned first and foremost. Say what you like about inquisitors and secret policemen: no one has been more helpful to historians of reading. They asked precisely the questions we want to ask: *What did you read, and how did you read it? Where did you obtain this book? Did you discuss it with anyone? How did you interpret this particular passage?* The proceedings of the Inquisition were famously used to investigate the reading of a sixteenth-century Italian miller in Carlo Ginzburg's *The Cheese and the Worms* (1980)—and Ginzburg is by no means the only historian to rely on that kind of documentation.[2]

Probate and booksellers' records of course cannot reveal how or even whether a particular book was read, but they can generate useful statistics of book ownership and distribution. Wills in particular provide one of the few records we have of readers in medieval Europe. In *Reading Becomes a Necessity of Life: Material and Cultural Life in Rural New England, 1780–1835* (1989), William J. Gilmore used these sources to reconstruct in astonishing detail the literary culture of a Vermont backwater in the early American republic.

Sociological surveys of reading go back much farther than you might imagine. *The Statistical Account of Scotland* was compiled in the 1790s, and it is a mother lode of information on reading habits and local libraries. The USSR made a large academic investment in the sociology of reading, and as long as one allows for ideological biases, one can use these studies to recover the Soviet common reader, as Stephen

---

[1] Rose, Jonathan. *The Intellectual Life of the British Working Classes.* New Haven, CT and London: Yale University Press, 2001: 168–172.

[2] For example, see also Nalle, Sara T. "Literacy and Culture in Early Modern Castile." *Past & Present* 125 (November 1989): 65–96.

Lovell did in *The Russian Reading Revolution: Print Culture in the Soviet and Post-Soviet Eras* (2000).

Reading groups and literary societies seem to have been ubiquitous in modern Western societies, among all races, all social classes and both sexes. And, fortunately, they often kept minutes. Elizabeth McHenry drew on these records to rediscover a literary tradition that we scarcely knew existed, for her prize-winning book *Forgotten Readers: Recovering the Lost History of African American Literary Societies* (2002).

Memoirs and diaries of ordinary people have been collected and used by social historians to illuminate family life, work experiences, gender roles and popular mentalities. It is significant that, when the 'inarticulate masses' write their own history, they have quite a lot to say about their reading. These documents made possible David Vincent's *Bread, Knowledge, and Freedom* (1981), Thomas Augst's *The Clerk's Tale: Young Men and Moral Life in Nineteenth-Century America* (2003), as well as my own book, *The Intellectual Life of the British Working Classes* (2001). Of course, some literary cultures produced more autobiographies than others. Britain seems particularly well favoured in this respect: for my book, I was able to draw on about 900 working-class memoirs for the nineteenth century alone, whereas Martyn Lyons could only locate 22 such autobiographies for his *Readers and Society in Nineteenth-Century France* (2001). But bear in mind that no one suspected that so many British proletarian memoirs existed until David Vincent, John Burnett and David Mayall began to track them down in a systematic way. Eventually they found and catalogued about 2000 of them, creating an indispensable resource for historians of popular education as well as historians of reading.[3] More recently Sven Steffens (Université Libre de Bruxelles) has recovered several hundred francophone workers' memoirs. There is an important scholarly lesson here: the next time a fellow historian tells you 'The sources simply don't exist,' ask: 'How hard have you looked?'

Commonplace books, or notebooks of literary extracts, convey not only which books the compiler read, but which passages he considered important and how he assembled them into a coherent world-view. The genre can be traced back to Aristotle and has proved particularly useful in investigating Renaissance reading, though it continued to flourish well into the twentieth century.[4]

Records of educational institutions of course reveal a great deal about literacy acquisition and early reading habits. Often our prime sources of information on disenfranchised readers are the papers of the pedagogical agencies that served them, such as the Workers' Educational Association in Britain. The archives of the Freedmen's Bureau were a key source for Heather Andrea Williams's recent book *Self-Taught: African American Education in Slavery and Freedom* (2005).

---

[3] Burnett, John, David Vincent, and David Mayall, eds. *The Autobiography of the Working Class: An Annotated, Critical Bibliography*, 3 vols. New York: New York University Press, 1984–89.

[4] See, for example, Moss, Ann. *Printed Commplace-books and the Structuring of Renaissance Thought*. Oxford: Clarendon Press, 1996, and Miller, Susan. *Assuming the Positions: Cultural Pedagogy and the Politics of Commonplace Writing*. Pittsburgh, PA: University of Pittsburgh Press, 1998.

Library registers can provide a hard quantitative record of books read (or rather, books borrowed, which may not be quite the same thing). However, lists of loans by themselves tell us very little. They become revealing only when they are situated in a thick description of the community that the library in question serves. That is precisely the method used by the most innovative library historians today, notably Christine Pawley in *Reading on the Middle Border: The Culture of Print in Late-Nineteenth-Century Osage, Iowa* (2001). It may be that the next big breakthrough in library history will be a quantitative study of borrowing patterns among African-American common readers—made possible by the fact that, until the 1960s, many American public libraries were racially segregated.

Letters to the editor may seem an unreliable source, given that they are selected, edited and (occasionally) written by editors. Besides, most contemporary magazines and newspapers devote only a miserable half-page to readers' responses. But in the nineteenth century especially, periodicals were largely reader-written. William Lloyd Garrison's *Liberator*, Alexander Herzen's Russian dissident paper *Kolokol*, and the *People's Journal* (Scotland's largest working-class weekly) in many ways resembled a twenty-first century electronic bulletin board, filled with contributions and exchanges from subscribers. They offer a salutary reminder that print literature too is interactive, shaped by constant reader feedback. And the particularly lucky researcher may stumble upon an archive of unpublished readers' letters, uncontaminated by editorial intervention, and David Nord did when writing *Communities of Journalism: A History of American Newspapers and Their Readers* (2001).

Fan mail can offer an especially intimate portrait of a particular author's reading public, provided we remember that these samples over-represent enthusiasts and under-represent disgusted or lukewarm readers. Of course many writers either burned readers' letters (e.g. Charles Dickens) or simply neglected to save them. But where they have survived, even letters to now-forgotten writers can reveal a great deal about readers, as Clarence Karr shows in *Authors and Audiences* (2000), his study of five Canadian middlebrow novelists.

Canvassers' reports, especially those filed by colporteurs for evangelical publishers, often contained remarkably sophisticated and detailed market research. Amy M. Thomas[5] and David Nord[6] used them effectively to reconstruct the audience responses and socioeconomic status of antebellum American readers.

Oral history is of course useful only for investigating the fairly recent past, but it allows historians to do literally what we can otherwise only do figuratively: interrogate the audience. In *Australian Readers Remember: An Oral History of Reading 1890–1930*

---

[5] Thomas, Amy M. "Reading the Silences: Documenting the History of American Tract Society Readers in the Antebellum South." In *Reading Acts: U.S. Readers' Interactions with Literature, 1800–1950*, edited by Barbara Ryan and Amy M. Thomas. Knoxville: University of Tennessee Press, 2002: 107–36.

[6] Nord, David Paul. *Faith in Reading: Religious Publishing and the Birth of Mass Media in America.* Oxford: Oxford University Press, 2004: ch. 7.

(1992), Martyn Lyons and Lucy Taska fully exploited the opportunity to pursue questions that written sources do not always answer.

Iconography may appear to be a suspect source: can we accept painted images of readers reading as photographically realistic? In fact, Laurel Amtower has offered some ingenious inferences about medieval readers, based on their depictions in illuminated manuscript.[7] Peter Stallybrass has noted how frequently, in medieval art, books are portrayed with multiple bookmarks: sometimes the reader has his fingers on several pages at once. That suggests to him the reason why the codex superseded the scroll in the early Christian centuries: where scrolls permitted only linear reading, codices allowed the reader to flip back and forth. For the first time, one could easily compare different parts of the same text—compare, in particular, the Old and New Testaments.

Marginalia (I used to think) was as a general rule too scattered, too abbreviated, too cryptic to ever tell us much about the readers who scribbled it in the white spaces of printed pages. Happily, Heather Jackson has proved me wrong. Her *Marginalia: Readers Writing in Books* (2001) offers a rare combination of solid historiography framed in delightful belletristic prose. She shows us how to accumulate a large database of marginalia, and how to use it to frame useful historical generalizations about readers.

The Reading Experience Database (RED), a joint project sponsored by the British Library and the Open University, has since 1996 collected information about readers in history. RED (http://www.open.ac.uk/Arts/RED/) has mobilized a corps of volunteers who report back whenever they come across an example of a reading experience, filling out a form which asks for basic sociological data about the reader and the book read. The database will only cover reading experiences in Britain between 1450 and 1914. But historians working in other periods and cultures may find this machinery of scholarship worth imitating.

Drawing on all these sources, historians of reading have advanced to the point where they can test theories of reading. Did a 'public sphere' arise in bourgeois Europe as Jürgen Habermas postulated? James Van Horn Melton has produced a book-length synthesis of all the research that bears on that question: *The Rise of the Public in Enlightenment Europe* (2001). In 1974 Rolf Engelsing argued that a 'reading revolution' (*Leserevolution*) swept through the North Atlantic world around 1800. This involved a threefold shift: from reading aloud to private reading, from predominantly religious reading to predominantly secular reading, and from 'intensive reading' (close and repeated reading of a few canonical texts, such as the Bible or *Pilgrim's Progress*) to 'extensive reading' (rapid reading of a large body of ephemeral texts, mainly newspapers, magazines and novels).

The jury is still out on Engelsing's hypothesis. Though the shift to private reading did take place, it now looks much more drawn out than Engelsing suggested. In *Privacy and Print* (1999) Cecile Jagodzinski contends that in England reading became more

---

[7] Amtower, Laurel. *Engaging Words: The Culture of Reading in the Later Middle Ages*. New York and Basingstoke: Palgrave, 2000: ch. 2.

private during (and as a result of) the religious conflicts of the seventeenth century, while I found that reading aloud was still common in half of all working-class households as late as 1900. But it could be argued that the 'reading revolution' comes as close to a fairly messy reality as any historical model. It works reasonably well for nineteenth-century Britain, where paper production multiplied sixty times over between 1800 and 1901, while newspaper circulation grew exponentially. In 1814–1846 religion accounted for 20.3 per cent of all books published, falling to 8.6 per cent by 1901. And when he investigated rural Vermonters in the age of Jefferson and Madison, William Gilmore found what looks like a reading revolution in progress: families devoted to intensive reading of religious literature tended to live on poor and remote farms, and possessed an average of only 1.6 books, while families who read secular literature extensively were more prosperous and owned an average of 136.6 volumes.[8] It may be that we should treat the 'reading revolution' as we have learned to treat the 'industrial revolution': as a rough generalization concerning a ragged and uneven process, a concept which has some usefulness as long as we bear in mind that reading habits evolved differently in different societies.

Women's reading choices were somewhat different from men's, but not as different as many feminist critics once assumed. One could generalize that female authors tended to be more popular among female readers than among male readers. A sampling of books published by subscription in eighteenth-century Ireland found that 14.2 per cent of the subscribers were women, but the proportion rose to 30.0 per cent for female-authored books.[9] In 1888 about 1800 British adolescents were asked to name their favourite writers: nearly 30 per cent of the girls' votes (and almost none of the boys') were cast for women authors.[10]

In antebellum America, Mary Kelley observed, 'Female readers identified with learned women, and they modeled themselves on such women'. Beyond that, however, 'the selection of reading matter was not sharply gendered. Men [and women] appear to have read the same history, biography, travel literature, and fiction'.[11] In *The Woman Reader 1837–1901* (1993) Kate Flint found that middle-class Victorian women were reading heavily in philosophy, politics and the hard sciences— so heavily that she ended up doubting whether it made sense to analyse readers by

---

[8] Gilmore, William J. *Reading Becomes a Necessity of Life: Material and Cultural Life in Rural New England, 1780–1835.* Knoxville: University of Tennessee Press, 1989: 277–82.

[9] Kennedy, Máire. "Women and Reading in Eighteenth-Century Ireland." In *The Experience of Reading: Irish Historical Perspectives*, edited by Bernadette Cunningham and Máire Kennedy. Dublin: Rare Books Group of the Library Association of Ireland and Economic and Social History Society of Ireland, 1999: 88–94.

[10] Rose, Jonathan. "How Historians Study Reader Response: or, What Did Jo Think of *Bleak House*?" In *Literature in the Marketplace: Nineteenth-Century British Publishing & Reading Practices*, edited by John O. Jordan and Robert L. Patten. Cambridge: Cambridge University Press, 1995: 196. The survey, carried out by Charles Welsh, was reported in Salmon, Edward. *Juvenile Literature as It Is.* London: Henry J. Drane, 1888: ch. 1.

[11] Kelley, Mary. "Reading Women/Women Reading: The Making of Learned Women in Antebellum America", in *Reading Acts*, 56.

gender. Conversely, in turn-of-the-century Osage, Iowa, 'women's novelists' like Dinah Mulock Craik, Harriet Beecher Stowe and Susan Warner were also very popular among men.[12] Even Mrs Henry Wood, that sentimental Victorian sob sister, was in 1910 the novelist most frequently borrowed from British prison libraries. Clarence Karr found that gender did not much affect responses to Canadian authors Ralph Connor and L. M. Montgomery: men as well as women were moved to tears, women as well as men were inspired to rational critical analysis.[13]

Nineteenth-century moralists projected a host of anxieties on the woman reader, whose brain was assumed to be incapable of digesting a strong literary diet. Over-consumption of romance novels (they warned) could overheat the female imagination, producing sexual arousal, discontent, confusion of fiction and reality, even hysteria. One woman who exhibited all these symptoms was Emma Bovary: in this respect Gustave Flaubert, for all his reputation as a subversive, shared the bourgeois prejudices of his age, as Martyn Lyons tellingly notes. Those attitudes and the influence of Catholicism discouraged *femmes savantes* in Flaubert's France, but such women did exist, even in the ranks of the proletariat. Lyons points to Suzanne Voilquin, a St Simonian agitator who gave up romance novels for Voltaire, Rousseau and Volney.[14]

Flaubert's bias has been an astonishingly common one among intellectuals of both the Right and the Left. We have been told again and again, from all points on the ideological compass, that the common reader cannot be trusted to read intelligently. The masses will be misled by Enlightenment philosophy or romantic fiction or penny dreadfuls or advertising or mass culture or middlebrow culture. One can trace this fear back at least as far as the Reformation and the anxieties aroused by unrestricted reading of vernacular bibles—anxieties by no means limited to Catholics. Similar apprehensions about mass literacy were voiced by the English Romantics (see Alan Richardson, *Literature, Education, and Romanticism: Reading as a Social Practice, 1780–1832* [1994]), the Victorians (see Patrick Brantlinger, *The Reading Lesson: The Threat of Mass Literacy in Nineteenth-Century British Fiction* [1998]), and the Modernists (see John Carey, *The Intellectuals and the Masses: Pride and Prejudice among the Literary Intelligentsia, 1880–1939* [1992]). In *Howards End*, E. M. Forster portrays Leonard Bast, the self-educated clerk, as a pathetic victim of bourgeois cultural hegemony, who reads Ruskin simply because he has been told that Ruskin is 'the greatest master of English Prose'. (In fact, the founders of the Labour Party discovered their vision of social justice in Ruskin, more than in any other author.) Feminist critics since Mary Wollstonecraft have warned that women will be nobbled by romance novels, but these warnings only make sense if you assume (as many nineteenth-century males assumed) that women are particularly susceptible and soft-headed, and

---

[12] Pawley, Christine. *Reading on the Middle Border: The Culture of Print in Late-Nineteenth-Century Osage, Iowa*. Amherst: University of Massachusetts Press, 2001: 108–11.

[13] Karr, Clarence. *Authors and Audiences: Popular Canadian Fiction in the Early Twentieth Century*. Montreal and Kingston: McGill: Queen's University Press, 2000: ch. 10.

[14] Lyons, Martyn. *Readers and Society in Nineteenth-Century France: Workers, Women, Peasants*. Basingstoke: Palgrave, 2001: chs 4–5.

cannot be trusted to roam the bookshelves without special guidance. That assumption was only finally scotched when Janice Radway (for her 1984 book *Reading the Romance*) interviewed romance fans and found them far more intelligent and discerning than Emma Bovary.

The new historiography of reading is marked by a general dissatisfaction with the Frankfurt School, *marxisant* criticism, poststructuralism, semiotics and much feminist criticism, all of which tended to treat the ordinary reader as the passive victim of mass culture or capitalism or discourses of patriarchy. 'In the final analysis there is one facet of the reading experience which remains individual and private', concludes Clarence Karr in his exploration of fan mail. 'With many readers this journey into the inner self concluded with greater knowledge of themselves and an increased ability to cope in the world. With others it was a life-changing experience.'[15]

In his study of manuscript letters sent to the *Chicago Tribune* and *Chicago Herald* between 1912 and 1917, David Nord shows how radically individualistic reader response can be. One might object that those newspaper readers were to some extent socially determined, inasmuch as they all had to respond to the same text—but some of them slipped even that constraint. The correspondents included publicity seekers ('We are two young athletic women and we expect to walk from Chicago to New York in the very near future') and crackpots ('I am that messiah that the Jews are looking for') who wrote with no apparent reference to anything published in the papers. Others began by mentioning a specific article, but then veered off onto totally unconnected personal obsessions. Reactions to coverage of the First World War were more coherent but equally unpredictable: the *Chicago Tribune* was variously damned as pro-German or pro-Allied, depending on the reader. And some responses to discourses embedded in the newspaper were of a type not generally anticipated by poststructuralists: 'If the officers of my union would find me Guilty of useing any part of your scabby paper in my toilet, I would be subject to a $100 fine at the next meeting'.[16]

Martyn Lyons and I found the same pattern of independence among (respectively) French and British working-class autodidacts of the nineteenth century. Their reading was not generally dictated by middle-class patrons or bourgeois cultural hegemony: rather, they exchanged books and ideas among their friends, family and workmates. 'Working-class networks protected the autodidact's autonomy as a reader', Lyons observes. 'They ensured that he or she did not always respond predictably to the literary culture diffused by middle-class mediators.'[17]

Heather Jackson located 80-odd marked-up copies of Boswell's *Life of Johnson*, and examined the marginal scribbles for evidence of reader response over two centuries. She found one consistent pattern: There is no pattern. It is impossible to generalize about readers' comments or what they chose to comment on. But of course, as Jackson realizes, that variousness is itself enormously significant:

---

[15] Karr, *Authors and Audiences*, 165.

[16] Nord, David Paul. *Communities of Journalism: A History of American Newspapers and Their Readers*. Urbana and Chicago: University of Illinois Press, 2001: ch. 11.

[17] Lyons. *Readers and Society in Nineteenth-Century France*, 55.

Boswell's alert, annotating readers respond to topics that touch them personally. Their selection of passages for marking and comment tend, in consequence, to be individual and idiosyncratic. If it seems perverse to say that idiosyncrasy constitutes a pattern, it must at least be acknowledged that ... Boswell's readers were looking for help with their own lives and were most struck by those places in which there was something at stake for them personally.... Their collective portrait can only be a group portrait of individuals.[18]

The eighteenth- and nineteenth-century guidebooks that told Englishwomen what they should and should not read were, as Kate Flint and Jacqueline Pearson have shown, largely disregarded by actual readers, who might even flout the novelist's intentions by identifying with the villainess rather than the heroine.[19] Cecile Jagodzinski argues that the proliferation of books in post-Caxton England, combined with the need to conceal heretical religious views, encouraged the growth of private reading, which in turn 'bred a new sense of personal autonomy, a new consciousness of the self'. By the seventeenth century male readers could think more independently about politics, and male and female readers alike could think more independently about religion. Thus 'the concept of privacy as a personal right, as the very core of individuality, is connected in a complex fashion with the history of reading'.[20]

Postcolonial critics might object that this independence is a Western construct, a liberty that the colonized did not enjoy. They were more or less compelled to consume the literature prescribed by the colonizer: the readings required by an imperialist educational system, or the books 'dumped' on colonial markets by metropolitan publishers. Those assumptions have been sharply and effectively challenged by historians of reading. In *Literary Culture in Colonial Ghana*, Stephanie Newell finds the same kind of self-improving readers that Thomas Augst, Martyn Lyons and I found in the United States, France and Britain: 'Charles Dickens and John Ruskin were the favourites of colonial educators and *also* of ambitious, but socially powerless, African young men'. Far from being indoctrinated, these readers adapted English literature to their culture and appropriated it to develop a voice of their own. *Wuthering Heights* and *The Pickwick Papers* were not 'thrown like a punch at Ghanaian society, knocking existing interpretive practices out of action', rather they were 'dropped like a pebble into a pool of existing literacies and narrative conventions, sending ripples through the multiplicity of reading practices which operated already in local cultures'.[21] Priya Joshi independently arrived at much the same conclusion in *In Another Country: Colonialism, Culture, and the English Novel in India* (2002). Though the novel as a genre was a British import, not indigenous to India, it was enthusiastically embraced by Indian readers. This was

[18] Jackson, H. J. *Marginalia: Readers Writing in Books*. New Haven, CT and London: Yale University Press, 2001: 165–78.

[19] Pearson, Jacqueline. *Women's Reading in Britain 1750–1835: A Dangerous Recreation*. Cambridge: Cambridge University Press, 1999: 16–21.

[20] Jagodzinski, Cecile M. *Privacy and Print: Reading and Writing in Seventeenth-Century England*. Charlottesville and London: University Press of Virginia, 1999: 1–2.

[21] Newell, Stephanie. *Literary Culture in Colonial Ghana: 'How to Play the Game of Life'*. Bloomington: Indiana University Press, 2002: 2–3.

a demand-driven phenomenon, as Joshi discovered in London publishers' archives and Calcutta library catalogues. Nor were colonial readers slavishly mimicking the colonizer: Indians devoured G. W. M. Reynolds while West Africans adored Marie Corelli, two novelists who were judged hopelessly trashy by London critics.

Medievalists, as Laurel Amtower notes, may be surprised to find Christine de Pisan criticizing and rejecting a misogynist tract by Mathéolus, given 'that the medieval world has been largely characterized in terms of a suppression of subjective or individual response'. But perhaps the reader—even the late fourteenth-century female reader—was never so rigidly imprisoned in dominant discourses as Michel Foucault imagined. In fact, Amtower concludes, Christine 'demonstrates a viewpoint that was widely taking hold among readers of the later Middle Ages: that the individual has both the ability and the duty to engage texts analytically and to question or doubt those opinions that may turn out to be dangerous or false'.[22]

Historians of reading, then, generally agree that readers play an important role in constructing the meaning of texts, which may sound suspiciously postmodern. But though postmodernists talk as if they were the first to discover the 'active reader', in fact they were the last. The 'obstinate audience' is well-known to the 'uses and gratifications' school of media researchers, who have been active since the 1960s. It was evident in Paul Lazarfeld's mass communication studies of the 1940s. It was familiar to Francis Bacon ('how easily with a little dexterity and discourse of wit meanings which it was never meant to have may be put upon it') and Montaigne ('I have read in Livy a hundred things that another man has not read in him').[23] As John Locke noted, the Reformation encouraged readers to 'bring the sacred Scriptures to their opinions, to bend it to them, to make it, as they can'. The King James Bible stated explicitly that, 'to exercise and whet our wits', God sometimes expressed Himself in purposefully ambiguous terms: 'They that are wise, had rather have their iudgements at libertie in differences of readings, then to be captivated to one, when it may be the other.'[24] As Stephen Dobranski notes, Renaissance authors commonly encouraged the active readers, sometimes in prefatory exhortations, sometimes by deliberately leaving gaps or cryptic passages in the text (a common practice in a climate of state and ecclesiastical censorship). John Milton's proclamation that books 'contain a potencie of life' implied that the text has only potential meaning, which can be realized by the reader.[25] Evidence of that active reading may be found in annotations: H. S. Bennett estimated that a quarter of the 'thousands' of Renaissance books he inspected contained some marginal corrections, even if they were rarely found beyond page 50.[26]

---

[22] Amtower, *Engaging Words*, 1–2.

[23] Noted in Sharpe, Kevin. *Reading Revolutions: The Politics of Reading in Early Modern England.* New Haven, CT and London: Yale University Press, 2000: 41–42.

[24] Quoted in Dobranski, Stephen B. *Readers and Authorship in Early Modern England.* Cambridge: Cambridge University Press, 2005: 29–31.

[25] Ibid., ch. 1.

[26] Bennett, H. S. *English Books & Readers 1603–1640.* Cambridge: Cambridge University Press, 1970: 208.

One can trace this idea back as far as Thomas à Kempis, who observed that 'The voice of books informs not all alike'. We always knew, in a general way, that texts may be indeterminate, but only recently have we begun to study systematically the responses of actual historical readers. As David Nord argues, 'What is needed is not more philosophy, not more theory about audience activity or passivity, but rather more empirical research, research that links different levels of analysis, research that links actual readers not only to texts but to social contexts in which the readers lived and the texts were read'.[27] Without that research, Robert Darnton warned, literary critics tend 'to assume that seventeenth-century Englishmen read Milton and Bunyan as if they were twentieth-century college professors'.[28] Of course we inevitably encounter epistemological questions when we try to make sense of texts: the post-modernists were not wrong to point that out. But what better way of addressing those questions than a historiography of reading, which asks how readers in the past made sense of texts?

Broadly understood, then, *reading, education* and *interpretation* are synonymous. Laurel Amtower makes the point that, in Old English, *raedan* could refer to any kind of 'interpretation and glossing of signs in a world in which all was text'. It might involve reading a *boc* (an Anglo-Saxon term that included all sorts of documents, not just books per se). But one could also read things that were not (strictly speaking) documents, as when Aelfric said 'Ic raede swefn' [I read dreams].[29] That wider meaning survives in colloquial English today, as in 'How do you read this situation?'. I attempted to write *The Intellectual Life of the British Working Classes* as a history of reading/education/interpretation in that expansive sense: it considers how individuals read books, magazines, newspapers, advertising bills, films, radio programmes, musical performances, school lessons and adult education classes. The rationale behind this method is simply this: We can only understand the mentality of a given audience by reconstructing (as far as possible) its cultural diet, and then asking how that audience interpreted those cultural experiences.

None of this compels us to drive off a postmodern cliff proclaiming that there are no facts, only interpretations. That was always a false dichotomy. There are facts, but they all require interpretation. There may be a right and a wrong way of reading a CAT scan, spy satellite data or John Donne's poetry, but all demand highly sophisticated hermeneutic skills. And of course, wars have been fought over different readings of scriptures, treaties and intelligence reports. As sociologist Erving Goffman put it, we are always 'reading' the sensory data that shower in on us, always asking ourselves 'What is it that's going on here?'. If all forms of education pose this question, then historians of education must inevitably address 'reading'.

---

[27] Nord, *Communities of Journalism*, 266–70.

[28] Darnton, Robert. "First Steps Toward a History of Reading." In *The Kiss of Lamourette: Reflections in Cultural History*. New York: W. W. Norton, 1990: 181.

[29] Amtower, *Engaging Words*, 7–9.

From the 'Eye of History' to 'a Second Gaze': The Visual Archive and the Marginalized in the History of Education

Ian Grosvenor

Ways of Seeing [1]

> We don't really debate education and its fundamental purpose in this country.
> Nor do we relate educational policy to the social arena. How we educate young people relates
> to our social vision, how we see the world and ourselves.... (Nicholas Tate, 1996[1])

> Birmingham children are white and they're black
> Immigrants come, we can't send them back

---

[1] *The Guardian*, 8 October 1996. Nicholas Tate is a historian, who after a career in teaching and teacher training joined the English National Curriculum Council in 1989 at the time of the establishment of the English national curriculum. From 1994 to 1997 he was chief executive of the School Curriculum and Assessment Authority and from 1997 to 2000 chief executive of the Qualifications and Curriculum Authority. In both of these positions he was the chief curriculum adviser to the Secretary of State for Education. From 2000 to 2003 he was headmaster of Winchester College, one of England's oldest independent boarding schools. He is currently director general of the International School of Geneva.

Really we'd like to but now they're here
Millions who multiply year after year
It's our job to teach them to live just like us
Nicely and soberly without any fuss
God knows how we'll do it, we'd all like to cry
Have you the desire to give help and to try
And teach in our schools—we'll see you get paid
May we please employ you to give us your aid. (Draft advertisement, Birmingham Education files, 1960s[2])

Trials and Tribulations

In the 1970s an article was published in the British journal *Race Today* called 'Trials and Tribulations of a Self-Help Group'. The article detailed the difficulties encountered by Birmingham's Afro-Caribbean Self Help Organisation in running a Saturday school. Gus John, in an earlier report on Handsworth, *Race in the Inner City* (1972), had described the organization as: 'the most hopeful growing-point for an active and relevant community self-help effort'. Not the least of the difficulties faced by the Saturday school, which took place at Wilkes Green Infants' and Junior School, was a concern about its teaching of 'culturally relevant' history. Black parents supported the school's teaching; one parent who was interviewed said: 'they've got to know what their forefathers did. They should know about their history'. However, this was not a view shared by members of the Education Committee. Alderman Dawes said: 'I've interviewed these people running the school and I am rather worried about certain aspects of the teaching of history at the school. In fact it came out loud and clear that their intention was to teach the supremacy of the black.' When pressed by the reporter to define what he meant by 'black supremacy' he said he found it 'difficult to be specific' and 'it was only a feeling from what they said to me when I interviewed them'. Local Handsworth head teachers endorsed Dawes comments: 'there's a strong political element in the teaching at the supplementary school. I think they preach the revolution' and 'I know that in one school—Handsworth Wood Girls' Secondary Modern—they're trying to infiltrate little cells...'.[3]

Some thirty years later in April 2001 the *Race Relations (Amendment) Act 2000* came into force and established a new 'legislative and administrative framework for a

---

[2] Birmingham Central Library, Archives Department, Immigrant Education Files

[3] Bergman, J., and B. Coard. "Trials and Tribulations of a Self-Help Group." *Race Today* 4(4) (1972): 112–14. The article ends on an interesting note-an account of the similarities of the Polish experience in Birmingham. The Polish Supplementary School met every Saturday at St Michaels Roman Catholic Secondary School, Floodgate Street and in 1972 had 325 pupils and held classes on the Polish language, history, geography and culture. The Headmistress of the school was interviewed and it is useful to quote her in full: 'Originally the authorities and teachers complained about the school and tried to occupy the Polish children on Saturdays with sports and other activities as a means of stopping them coming to our school when it was founded in 1950. But now they've changed their attitude because they see the positive job we're doing. After all, if you have a plant, no matter from where it comes, it has a special soil that requires special treatment' (p. 114).

successful multicultural Britain'. The legislation outlawed discrimination in all public services and placed a statutory duty on public authorities to promote race equality in carrying out their functions. For the Labour Government the promotion of 'race equality' was a 'positive way of tackling the institutional problems' highlighted by the Macpherson Inquiry into events surrounding the murder in London on 22 April 1993 of the black teenager Stephen Lawrence.[4] To offer guidance around issues of implementation the Home Office produced a consultation paper, *Race Relations (Amendment) 2000: New Laws for a Successful Multi-Racial Britain* (2001). The first chapter of the paper opens with a series of arguments about 'race equality'. It was, in the Government's view, 'essential in order to build strong, inclusive communities'. 'Race equality' was 'a basic human right' and there was a 'moral case' for striving 'for equality and fairness'. There was also an 'economic case' as 'everyone's potential can be utilized. In a diverse society such as ours, whose history has seen *successive waves of migration* both in and out of the country, that is all the more important' [emphasis in the original]. The arguments are then followed by a series of brief statements about '40,000 years of migration to Britain', 'the significant contribution made by black and Asian people fighting for Great Britain in the two great wars' and the involvement of labour from the Caribbean, India and Pakistan in the postwar 'reconstruction effort'. Two photographs from the Ministry of Defence archives accompany these statements showing black and Asian men on active war service. More details and images of Britain's multicultural history are presented in a three-page appendix. Finally, the importance of this history is also stressed in the foreword to the paper by the then Home Secretary, Jack Straw, 'our great nation is built on diversity, change and immigration'.[5]

Two sets of events some 30 years apart: the first, 1972, is about the fear of history; the fear of a challenge to the status quo, to received notions about the past. The second, 2001, is about celebrating history; recognizing that there is more than one story of the nation; it is about bringing different stories to the surface as part of a strategy for creating a fair and just society. In presenting this alternative story of the nation the Home Office gave power to its argument concerning diversity and social change by including images from national archives that showed black and Asian men participating in an iconic moment in the story of modern Britain.

It is a truism that history is essentially about stories. 'Stories', as the novelist Ben Okri wrote in *Birds of Heaven* (1996), 'are the secret reservoir of values: change the stories individuals and nations live by and tell themselves and you change the individuals and the nations'. Okri continues:

> Nations and peoples are largely the stories they feed themselves. If they tell themselves stories that are lies, they will suffer the future consequences of those lies. If they tell themselves stories that face their own truths, they will free their histories for future flowerings.[6]

---

[4] For the full report see http://www.archive.official-documents.co.uk/document/cm42/4262/4262.htm

[5] Home Office, *Race Relations (Amendment) Act 2000. New Laws for a Successful Multi-Racial Britain.* London: Home Office, 2001: 1, 7, 36–38.

[6] Okri, B. *Birds of Heaven.* London: Phoenix, 1996, 21.

This paper is about both the stories we tell and the images we place with those stories; it is also about historical practice and the power of the image to generate new research approaches.

The 'Eye of History': Historians and the Visual Archive[7]

When one looks at the literature around using visual sources in research, particularly photographs, there is a general historical myopia. Raphael Samuel tellingly observed in the early 1990s:

> It is a curious fact that historians, who are normally so pernickety about the evidential status of their documents, are content to take photographs on trust, and to treat them as objective correlatives of fact … [T]here are not even the rudiments of an agreed scholarly procedure which would allow photographs to be treated with the high seriousness accorded to much less problematical sources. As one curator puts it caustically, most of them are treated as 'eye-wipes'.[8]

More recently, Peter Burke in *Eyewitnessing* (2001) has warned historians about the potential dangers in using images. He cites, for example, Samuel's complaint about being seduced by the 'inventions' of Victorian photography: 'Much of what we [British social historians of the 1960s] reproduced so lovingly and annotated … so meticulously was fake'. He questions the veracity of social documentary photographs of Jacob Riis, Margaret Bourke-White, Dorothea Lange and Robert Capa and cites an epigram of the American photographer Lewis Hines: 'While photographs may not lie, liars may photograph'. Throughout the text Burke constantly returns to the 'problem of authenticity' and 'the reality effect'. In short, *Eyewitnessing* is a treatise on the untrustworthiness of images.[9] However, when we narrow our focus and turn to the literature relating to the history of education and the visual it is interesting to find a growing engagement with visual culture and the uses of images as historical evidence, an engagement which appears to straddle the space between a lack of agreed scholarly procedure and concerns about representation, realism and objectivity.[10] I do not intend to detail here the content of this corpus of writing other than to list what I take to be key texts, but I would like to conjecture about why the visual is proving increasingly attractive to historians of education. I am reminded of Catherine

---

[7] The phrase the 'eye of history' originates with the American photographer Matthew Brady; see Ryan, J. *Picturing Empire: Photography and the Visualization of the British Empire*. London: Reaktion Books, 1997: 16.

[8] Samuel, R. "The 'eye of history'." *New Statesman & Society,* 18 December 1992/I January 1993: 41.

[9] Burke, P. *Eyewitnessing: The Uses of Images as Historical Evidence*. London: Reaktion Books, 2001: 21–23.

[10] See the following collections Grosvenor, I., M. Lawn, and K. Rousmaniere, eds. *Silences and Images: The Social History of the Classroom*. New York: Peter Lang, 1999; "The Challenge of the Visual in the History of Education." *Paedagogica Historica* 36, no. 1 (2000); "Ways of Seeing." *History of Education* 30, no. 2 (2001); Myers, K., U. Mietzner, and N. Peim, *Visual History*. London: Peter Lang, 2005.

Burke's observation that images—line drawings, still photography, film, video and digital technologies—have accompanied the development of state education from its beginnings and that 'the camera within the school has its own historical narrative reflecting change and continuities in ways of seeing education and children over time'.[11] It may be that the research agendas which are attracting historians of education—identity, sexuality, mentalities, material cultures, the body—are areas where the visual archive is particularly rich. It may also be that the experience of using the visual instead of the literary 'touches on the limitations of language', and has freed the research imagination beyond the traps of language and raised a new research agenda.[12] That said, it must be noted that not all historians of education have been seduced by the visual.[13]

Before leaving this brief exploration of the visual in historical research and moving the focus to the marginalized in British society I want to signal an emerging problem for anyone interested in the 'pictorial turn'.[14] Just as every picture tells at least one story, so every image produced today becomes evidence of the past tomorrow. For a long time the photographic image, in the sense of its mechanical reproduction, materialized seeing in such a way that the image produced its own 'aura of believability'[15]. Today, new technology is challenging this level of believability and the boundaries between what is fact and what is fiction, between what is real and what is artificial, are becoming more porous. This challenge to believability will have to be addressed by those future historians who adopt the pictorial turn. As one commentator observed, we are at an 'important historical juncture' just before the widespread adoption of electronic technology and 'we must try to take some responsibility for the future of the immensely popular and still believable medium of photography'.[16]

So what research agenda does the visual offer when we consider the educational history of black and minority ethnic children in British schools? In order to answer this question, we first need to appreciate and be aware of that history, or rather histories.

---

[11] Burke, C. "Visualising the body of the school child: critical reflections on spaces of representation." Unpublished paper, 2.

[12] Walker, R. "Finding a Silent Voice for the Researcher: Using Photographs in Evaluation and Research." In *Qualitative Voices in Educational Research*, edited by M. Schratz. London: Falmer Press, 1993: 52.

[13] See, for example, Catteeuw, K., K. Dams, M. Depaepe, and F. Simon. "Filming the Black Box: Primary Schools on Film in Belgium, 1880–1960: A First Assessment of Unused Sources." In Mietzner *et al.*, *Visual History*, 203–32. See also a reply to their arguments: Margolis, E., and Sheila Fram. "Caught Napping: Centuries of School Surveillance, Discipline, and Punishment." *History of Education* 36, no. 2 (2007): 191–212.

[14] This phrase was coined by Mitchell, W. J. T. *Picture Theory: Essays on Verbal and Visual Representation.* Chicago: University of Chicago Press, 1995.

[15] Strauss, D. Levi. *Between the Eyes: Essays on Photography and Politics.* New York: Aperture, 2003: 71.

[16] Ritchin, F. *In Our Own Image: The Coming Revolution in Photography.* New York: Aperture 1990, reissued 1999: Preface.

Histories of Black and Minority Ethnic Schooling

From the outset, it is important to note that the historical study of the educational experiences of black and minority ethnic children in British schools is and continues to remain a minority interest amongst historians.[17] At a recent History of Education Society (UK) conference which took as its theme *Education for All*, consequent on 2005 being the twentieth anniversary of the publication of the Swann Report,[18] only seven scheduled papers addressed the conference theme from the angle of 'race' and education in the UK.[19] At present there is a dominant policy-driven narrative which tells the story of black and minority ethnic schooling and divides this history into a series of phases beginning in the late 1940s and finishing in the late 1990s. In the first phase, 1945 to late 1950s, we find large numbers of black and ethnic minority children beginning to enter the education system in Britain. These children appeared in state schools as a result of black migration prompted by the demands of Britain's chronic postwar labour shortage. The colonies, or ex-colonies, offered a reserve supply of cheap labour. The needs of British industry, especially because of high emigration from Britain, led to a heavy reliance on this reserve of labour. Migrants from the West Indies, India and Pakistan came to urban centres in Britain as labour, to work and settle. The state response to the presence of these children in the system was essentially one of ignorance and neglect. Riots in London, Nottingham and nearby Dudley in 1958 saw 'white' racist attacks on migrant communities which were misrepresented in the media as popular demands for action regarding a growing 'colour problem'. The policy response was to restrict further immigration. The policy goal was 'assimilationism', which involved the teaching of the English language and dispersing or 'bussing' immigrant children to minimize their numbers in any single class/school. The key concern of this period was to protect the stability of the system and placate the fears of white parents and communities. This phase ran from the late 1950s to the mid- to late 1960s. It was followed by a period characterized by ideas concerning integration, 1966 to the late 1970s, in which there was recognition that there were inequalities of opportunity. Education, while withdrawing support for the idea of white cultural superiority, assumed a need to build 'compensatory' programmes to make good supposed cultural deficits suffered by minority pupils. The late 1970s to the late 1980s was a period in which cultural pluralism and multiculturalism flourished. There was a general recognition of cultural difference and this was accompanied by work on the promotion of positive, albeit superficial, images: the three Ss—'saris, samosas and steelbands'. Racism and its effects were talked about in some Local Education Authorities (LEAs)

---

[17] One can speculate as to why this is case and it may relate in the UK to the politically charged nature of the debate around issues of 'race'. Nevertheless, the amount of contemporary studies of 'race' and education which are now historical texts is significant.

[18] Swann Report. *Education for All: Committee of Inquiry into the Education of Children from Ethnic Minority Groups.* London: HMSO, 1985 was the result of a government initiated inquiry into the education of children from ethnic minority groups.

[19] See "Education for All: papers from the 2005 Conference of the History of Education Society (UK)." *History of Education*, 35, no. 6 (2006).

and interventionist policies and practices developed, notably in the Inner London Education Authority. The mid-1980s through to 1997 was characterized by the influence of Thatcherism and new racism. There was a strong assertion of national identity, where the interests of the majority had to come first, not because of 'superiority' but because this was 'our' country. The education reforms that the Conservatives introduced—the National Curriculum, the Market—paid no heed to cultural diversity and disregarded the likely consequences for minority pupils, parents and communities. Colour-blindness was the sanctioned approach.[20]

A Second Gaze into the Visual Archive

This narrative has essentially emerged out of the work of sociologists and policy analysts rather than historians and while one can point to problems with this narrative—for example, it draws too much attention to the elements of change in policy rather than signifying the elements of continuity[21]—it does, however, offer an organizing framework around which we might consider visual approaches. While the position in archive and record offices parallels to some degree what the American sociologist and ethnographer, Eric Margolis,[22] found during his research into archived documentary images of public schools between the 1880s and the 1940s in the USA, that the official record contains within it silences and absences, what he terms a 'historical amnesia', and that such collections reproduce overwhelmingly images of hierarchy and dominance, there is no actual shortage of visual evidence relating to black and minority ethnic children during this 50-year period. Images can be found on the covers and inside contemporary texts, which tell the story of the 'immigrant school[s]', they can be found in newspapers reporting on individual LEAs and schools, and in reports produced by bodies associated with race relations, such as Community Relations Councils and the Commission for Racial Equality (CRE).[23] No systematic historical work has addressed the content of these publications and their associated images, and certainly no attempt has been made to map

---

[20] See, for example, Mullard, C. "Multiracial Education in Britain: from Assimilation to Cultural Pluralism." In *Race, Migration and Schooling*, edited by J. Tierney. Eastbourne: Holt, Rinehart & Winston, 1982: 120–33; Gillborn, D. "50 years of failure: 'race' and education policy in Britain." In *The British Education Revolution: the Status and Politics of Educating Afro-Caribbean children*, edited by R. Majors. London: Falmer Press, 1999; Gillborn, D., and D. Youdell. *Rationing Education: Policy, Practice, Reform and Equity*. Buckingham: Open University Press, 2000.

[21] See, for example, Grosvenor, I. *Assimilating Identities: Racism and Education in post 1945 Britain.* London: Lawrence & Wishart, 1997.

[22] Margolis, E. "Class Pictures. Representations of Race, Gender and Ability in a Century of School Photography." *Visual Sociology* 14 (1999): 7–38.

[23] See Green, M., and I. Grosvenor. "Making Subjects: History-Writing, Education and Race Categories." *Paedagogica Historica* XXXIII, no. 3, (1997): 883–908. In the Local Studies Department of Birmingham Central Library there are several volumes of clipping files relating to black and minority ethnic settlement. The first volume is called 'The Coloured Problem' and the last 'Birmingham Ethnic Minorities'.

representation against policy developments.[24] When, for example, was there a shift in the job advertisements circulated in the professional press which simply acknowledged the presence of black pupils in schools and indicated that in teaching there was a career for black and minority ethnic teachers beyond, to use Mukherjee's phrase, 'race-cast roles'?[25] It may be useful at this point though to remember Simon Gikandi's observation that in visual as well as literary art, 'any sustained [white] contemplation of blackness is also an act of self-reflexivity: it is through the black figure that [white] Englishness acquires the metaphorical structure that enables it to gaze at itself in crisis'.[26]

As I suggested earlier I have some reservations about this narrative of black and minority ethnic schooling and the chronology of history which it reinforces. Recently, I have been trying to reconstruct the educational life of a black girl attending Nelson Street School, Birmingham, in 1913.[27] One could object that her story is an exception to the rule, that the presence of non-white children in both Birmingham and British schools in general was unusual before the 1950s, in other words before the opening decade of the narrative of schooling we have just explored. A decade ago I would have accepted this observation and the chronology it suggests; however, history moves on. The 2005 exhibition *Black Victorians: Black People in British Art 1800–1900,* organized by Manchester Art Gallery and Birmingham Museums and Art Gallery (BMAG), had a significant impact on black visitors to BMAG.[28] Such a response should come as no surprise for as Jan Marsh, the curator, writes in the accompanying exhibition book: 'The fact that the black presence in British art through the nineteenth century has been ignored and that art historians, virtually all white, have seldom looked for it, is no accident but the result of class and cultural power'. The exhibition was 'a modest endeavour' to bring to view a forgotten or hidden element in cultural history and as such connected with a universal desire to know our individual and collective pasts.[29] Such efforts are neither new nor confined to the world of art, as for several decades research into the black presence, into a neglected element in Britain's cultural history, has been going on in local

---

[24] The author and Richard Rose recently looked at the front covers of the journal produced by the forerunner of the National Association for Special Educational Needs (NASEN) and it was interesting to observe a clear shift in the representation of children from images in the 1960s and 1970s, where there were no visual clues relating to any form of disability or special needs, to the 1980s where 'difference' increasingly was celebrated

[25] Mukherjee, T. "The journey back." In *Multi-Racist Britain*, edited by P. Cohen and H. S. Bains. London: Macmillan, 1988: 213.

[26] Gikandi, S. *Maps of Englishness: Writing Identity in the Culture of Colonialism.* New York: Columbia University Press, n.d. [c. 1996]: 69.

[27] Grosvenor, I. "'Seen but not heard': city childhoods from the past into the present." *Paedagogica Historica* 43, no. 3 (2007), 405–429.

[28] Manchester Art Gallery, 1 October 2005–6 January 2006, BMAG, 28 January 2006–2 April 2006.

[29] Marsh, J. "The Black Presence in British Art 1800–1900: Introduction and Overview." In *Black Victorians. Black People in British Art 1800–1900*, edited by J. Marsh. Aldershot: Ashgate, 2005: 17.

community centres, adult education classrooms and libraries, and has been circulating through temporary exhibitions, small publishing enterprises and word of
mouth.[30] It is the local nature of these other explorations that is significant—these
explorations are mining rich seams of information, finding stories that for too long
have been either sedimented in the archive or stored amongst papers and albums
held in family attics and suitcases, stories which incrementally reshape our picture of
the past. In this process the photographic record, as Caroline Bressey has argued, is
an important source for researchers—it is, she argues, an 'immediate way of combat-
ing British history', it is 'proof' of a black presence and the people we learn about

---

[30] See, for example, Leech, K. *Brick Lane 1978*. Birmingham: AFFOR, 1980; Prescod-Roberts,
M., and N. Steele. *Black Women: Bringing it All Back Home*. Bristol: Falling Wall Press, 1980; Law,
I., and J. Henfrey. *A History of Race and Racism in Liverpool*. Liverpool: n.p., 1981; Alexander, Z.,
and A. Dewjee. *Roots in Britain*. Brent: Brent Library, 1981; Grosvenor, I., and R. L. Chapman.
West Africa, West Indies, West Midlands. Oldbury: Sandwell LEA, 1982; Dabydeen, D. *The Black
Presence in English Literature*. Wolverhampton: Wolverhampton CRC, 1984.; Sherwood, M. *The
British Honduran Forestry Unit in Scotland, 1941–1943*. London: One Caribbean, 1982; *Papers
Presented to the Conference on the History of Black People in London*, University of London, 27–29
November 1984; Thakoordin, J., and T. Gilbert. *Eradicate Racism a Murderous Crime*. London:
Liberation, 1985; *I Remember*. Wolverhampton: Wolverhampton Borough Council, 1986; Faizi,
Ghazala. *The Black Presence in London*. London: GLC, 1986; Lotz, R., and I. Pegg, *Under the
Imperial Carpet: Essays in Black History*. Crawley: Rabbit Press, 1986; *Caribbean Connections:
Southampton and the West Indies*. Southampton n.d.; Collicott, S. *Local–National–World Links: A
Case Study of Haringey History*. Haringey: Haringey Borough Council, 1986; *Moving Stories*. Leeds:
Leeds City Council, 1987; *Destination Bradford*. Bradford: Bradford Heritage Recording Unit, 1987;
Whose Freedom. London: Savannah Press, 1988; *Forty Winters On: Memories of Britain's post war
Caribbean Immigrants*. Lambeth, 1988; Small, S. *The Politics of British Black History, with Special
Reference to Liverpool*. Northampton: Wellingborough District Racial Equality Council, 1991;
Staying Power: The Black Presence in Liverpool. Liverpool: National Museums and Galleries on
Merseyside, 1991; *Newham: The Forging of a Black Community*. London: CARF, 1991; *Llafur 5*
(1991); *The Black Presence in Nottingham*. Nottingham: Nottingham County Council, 1993;
Sherwood, M. *Pastor Daniels Ekarte and the African Churches Mission*. London: Savannah Press,
1994; Layton, J. *Black People in Warwickshire*. Leamington Spa: Warwickshire County Council
1994; "The Black Presence in the North West,." *North West Labour History* 20 (1995–96); *Forty
Years On*. Lambeth, 1998; *Roti, kapra or makaan*. Nottingham: APNA Arts, 1998; Stacey, M. *The
Black Presence*. Liverpool: National Museums and Galleries on Merseyside, 1999; Edmead, P. *The
Divisive Decade*. Birmingham: Birmingham Libraries1999; Garfield, J. *Black Angels from the Empire*.
Stratford: Eastside Community Heritage, 2000; Choudhury, Y. *From Bangladesh to Birmingham*.
Birmingham: Birmingham Libraries, 2001; Bell, G. *The Other Eastenders: Kamal Chunchie and West
Ham's Early Black Community*. Stratford: Eastside Community Heritage, 2002; Dosanjh, J. S. *The
Development of Gurdwaras in Nottingham*. Nottingham: Nottingham City Council, 2002; Grosvenor,
I., R. Mclean, and S. Roberts, eds. *Making Connections: Birmingham Black International History*.
Birmingham: Black Pasts, Birmingham Futures Group, 2002; Grosvenor, I. *Hidden Histories.
Cultural Diversity in the West Midlands*. London: HLF, 2005; *Multiple Heritage Voices, Birmingham
1950–2006*. Birmingham: Race Equality West Midlands and HLF, 2007. These are only a selection
and do not include autobiographical writings such as Prem, D. R. *The Parliamentary Leper*. Aligarh:
Metric Publications, 1965; Marke, E. *Old Man Trouble*. London: Weidenfeld 1975; Thompson, C.
Born on the Wrong Side. London: Black Amber, 2006. See, also, the *Black and Asian Studies Newsletter*
(BASA) and the regular listing of projects in back numbers of the journal *Oral History*.

through it are part of 'a new historical geography, the forgotten geographies of people ignored, erased and forgotten' in the island story. The images in the collections from prisons, asylums and children's homes which she retrieved from the past are not just elements in 'black histories or even black British histories; they are British histories in the fullest sense.[31] The girl in the Nelson Street School photograph was not the only non-white child in Birmingham schools in the early years of the twentieth century. Neither was Birmingham the only city to have such youngsters on the school roll. The more we look into the archive, the more our stories change. As ever, what is needed is more time and more research in the photographic archive. However, this is not always as simple as it sounds. Photographs have an uncertain status being at the same time very often both exhibition objects (held by museums) and documentary sources (held by archives). In addition, the location of collections is not well known and access is often hindered because collections, as a consequence of staffing shortages and chronic underfunding in the UK archives and museums sectors, are often not catalogued.[32]

Returning to the girl in the Nelson Street photograph, she was a school pupil at the end of a 40-year period which saw a flood of illustrated nursery tales, recitation materials, children's books, juvenile literature and historical novels that flattered the British and stereotyped the world's non-white populations. It was a period where 'patriotism, militarism, adulation of the monarchy, and … imperial expansion came to be the central concerns of school history texts'.[33] I have argued elsewhere[34] that historians of education should embrace the grammar and the 'choreography', the routines and the rituals, and the symbolic events of everyday schooling to ask questions about the learning of folk-sayings and proverbs, drill and other exercises that regulated behaviour, memories of collective worship and celebrations involving the Union Jack, such as Empire Day, the imagery in the hymns that children sang every day—'England's green and pleasant land', 'Land of hope and glory', 'We plough the fields and scatter' (see Figure 1). Also, that we should look beyond formal school processes to the material culture of schooling and consider the impact of the friezes displayed on classroom walls, the history timelines, the 'lantern-slides' in the geography classroom, the wall-charts and maps depicting the Empire, the display of reproduction paintings, the symbols printed on exercise books, the world globe, the units

---

[31] Bressey, C. "Victorian Photography and the Mapping of the Black Presence." In Marsh, *Black Victorians*, 68, 78.

[32] The Heritage Lottery Funded project *Connecting Histories* (2005–2007) has addressed this problem through a unique partnership project between Birmingham City Archives, the School of Education, University of Birmingham and the Sociology Department, University of Warwick, which is cataloguing culturally diverse collections, including photographs, developing online catalogues and learning packages, and engaging in outreach work to generate new communities of archive users.

[33] Mackenzie, J. M. *Propaganda and Empire: The Manipulation of British Public Opinion 1880–1960.* Manchester: Manchester University Press, 1984: 176.

[34] Grosvenor, I. "'There no place like home': education and the making of national identity." *History of Education* 28, no. 3 (1999), 235–50.

of measurements on rulers, images on shields, cups, medals and certificates, class, team and prize-day photographs on pupils' sense of who they are and their place in the world. In other words, there is another line of research where the visual can be central to enriching our picture of the past and the emergence and perpetuation of ideas about what it was to be British; ideas which in turn shaped and reinforced policies about immigration and nationality. Further, such research is essential to test the argument advanced by Bernard Porter, and to a lesser degree by David Cannadine, that the imperial adventure did not really impinge on the English imagination at home and, in Porter's case, a clear reluctance to accept a dynamic link between the circulation of ideas about 'race' difference and manifestations of racism in British society.[35] It is interesting that both Cannadine and Porter seem to have been unaware of the work of James Ryan, whose book *Picturing Empire* (1997) documents how the development of photography coincided with the dramatic expansion of the British Empire and how in this period of expansion photography served a variety of purposes—as a tool of surveillance; a process of appropriation; a reinforcer of stereotypes; a symbol of personal memories; and as a form of education and entertainment. Ryan also forcibly argues that photographic practices articulated the ideology of imperialism and through exhibitions, newspapers, books, lantern-slide shows and picture postcards photography played a significant role in the popularization of the imperial spirit within and beyond Britain.

Figure 1. Empire Day, early twentieth century, unknown school. Private collection.

---

[35] Cannadine, D. *Ornamentalism: How the British Saw Their Empire.* London: Penguin, 2001, especially 181–99; Porter, B. *The Absent-Minded Imperialists.* Oxford: Oxford University Press, 2004.

To stay with the theme of Britishness, but to tackle it from a different angle, Gary McCulloch recently gave a paper at Birmingham on the theme of 'Security and settlements and history of education' where in the context of the changes in Britain following the London bombings he drew attention to a reassertion by the state of the need to define Englishness and to reclaim the idea of patriotism.[36] Both of these state agendas he demonstrated had links to schooling and the curriculum. As historians of education we can be alert to the emergence of different policy imperatives and their related practices, but we should also recognize how we can intervene in this debate. I have in mind one of Edward Said's final essays where he promoted the idea of 'communities of interpretation' as a rejoinder to the 'terrible reductive conflicts' that herd people under falsely unifying rubrics like 'the West' or 'Islam' and invent collective identities for large numbers of individuals who are actually very diverse.[37] For Said, these 'communities of interpretation' would investigate, analyse, apprehend, criticize and judge in a mission of understanding. These are all elements that are central to our practice as historians and we should seek out material in the archive which challenges such crude reductionism. Again, the visual offers such opportunities. Let me give an example. *From Negative Stereotype to Positive Image* was the title of an exhibition in 1993 which juxtaposed images from three Birmingham photographers—Sir Benjamin Stone[38], Ernest Dyche[39] and Vanley

---

[36] McCulloch, G. "Security, settlements and the history of education." Unpublished Domus seminar paper, University of Birmingham, 20 February 2006.

[37] Said, E. "Preface" (2003). In *Orientalism*. London: Penguin Books, 1978, reprinted 2003: xxii.

[38] Stone had systematically collected images recording people and places since the 1860s, but actively pursued photography as an interest in the 1880s. Seven years after his death in 1914, the trustees of his estate presented a collection of 22,000 photographs, 600 stereographs, 2500 lantern slides, 14,000 glass negatives, and 50 albums of collected prints to Birmingham Central Library. The size of this collection reflects Stone's era and the Victorian desire to capture and catalogue 'all' knowledge. In this desire to record knowledge pictorially Stone photographed and collected images during his travels in the West Indies and in Southern Africa. The images from these travels are of unnamed sitters, selected and posed by Stone. These images visualized the Empire. Stone also traded in images and amongst the collection of photographic albums are 'Types and Races of Mankind', which include captions by Stone; 'The Negress of the West Indies'; 'Trinidad Coolie'; 'Trinidad Hindoo from Madras'. Stone's concern here was with documenting 'race' typologies and we know very little about any of the people captured by the camera lens.

[39] Ernest and Malcolm Dyche had a photographic studio in Balsall Heath, Birmingham and in the 1950s and 1960s new black settlers in Birmingham sought portraits to send home to family and friends. The desire to convey messages about their success in Britain, as Peter James observed, 'led to the evolution of new hybrid images, constructed in partnership between photographer and subject, the final picture incorporating elements from different photographic and cultural traditions', James, P. *Coming to Light: Birmingham's Photographic Collections*. Birmingham: Birmingham Libraries and Birmingham Museums and Art Gallery, 1998: 42.

Burke[40]—taken between the 1890s and the 1990s to illustrate very different photographic practices—from the imperial gaze of ethnographic 'typing' (including photographs of schools in the Caribbean) to black photo-documentary. The effect was to draw attention to the processes of 'othering'—the capturing on film of unnamed colonial subjects as part of an imperial project to order and catalogue knowledge about the world, the migration and exchange of such images in the empire, their arrival in metropolitan collections, which in turn gave authority to what the image represented (see Figure 2), and the questioning of such representations by juxtaposing images taken of and by the black community in 1990s Birmingham (see Figure 3).[41] The 2006 exhibition *Making History: Art and Documentary in Britain from 1929 to Now* at Tate Liverpool also addressed the ways in which black artists in the 1970s and 1980s used and frequently subverted documentary modes and conventions in order to explore the construction of a multicultural image of Britain. Of course, as David A. Bailey and Stuart Hall have pointed out, 'politically progressive' images produced later or as a response to earlier representations do not necessarily stabilize earlier and more problematic images.[42] However, as Gen Doy writes: 'if we do not take account of the histories of the subjects in the archive as articulated by the subjects themselves, then the archive remains the determining discourse...'.[43] The Liverpool exhibition also included the work of black filmmakers—Horace Ove's *Pressure* (1975), Isaac Julien's *Territories* (1984), John Akomfrah's *Handsworth Songs* (1986)—and while space does not allow any discussion of this other visual form, its importance as historical evidence and its tremendous potential for generating new insights into the making of social relations must not be ignored.[44]

---

[40] Vanley Burke has spent four decades photographing the lives, peoples and scenes of the Black-British diaspora and the cultural theorist Stuart Hall has argued that this corpus of work represents both 'the first time that an intimate, insider's "portrait"-as opposed to a sociological study-of a settled British "colony" and its way of life had found its way into print in the form of a memorable set of images' and, through his photographic technique, an exploration 'of "blackness", of varieties of blackness, and ways of being "black" in Britain'. Hall, S. "Vanley Burke and the 'Desire for Blackness'." In *Vanley Burke: A Retrospective*, edited by M. Sealy. London: Lawrence & Wishart, 1993: 12–14.

[41] See James, P. "Rethinking Representation: Photographic Archives and Exhibitions in Birmingham Central Library." In *Cultural Diversity and Citizenship: Report of the Joint UNESCO/University of Birmingham Seminar*, edited by S. Wright. Birmingham: Department of Cultural Studies and Sociology, University of Birmingham, March 1998; Courtman, S. "A journey through the Imperial Gaze: Birmingham's Photographic Collections and its Caribbean Nexus." In *Visual Culture and Decolonisation in Britain*, edited by A. Ramamurthy and Simon Faulkner. London: Ashgate, 2006. See also, Hall, S. "Reconstruction Work." In "The Critical Decade, Black British Photography in the 80s." *Ten-8*, Spring 1992: 106–13. The nineteenth-century documenting of 'racial' types was not confined to British photographers like Stone; see, for example, the photographic album by Dammann, Carl W. *Anthropologisch-Ethnologisches Album in Photographien* (1873–1876) Berlin: BGAUE/Wiegand & Hempel.

[42] Bailey, D. A., and S. Hall. "The Vertigo of Displacement." *Ten-8*, Spring (1992): 15.

[43] Doy, G. *Black Visual Culture, Modernity and Postmodernity*. London: I. B. Tauris, 2000: 136.

[44] The exhibition ran from 3 February to 23 April 2006; see the accompanying exhibition book *Making History: Art and Documentary in Britain from 1929 to Now*. Liverpool: Tate Publishing, 2006.

Figure 2.   'Types of Races of Mankind', a photographic album complied by Sir Benjamin Stone, MP, 1870–1893. Birmingham Central Library, Stone Collection Album 50.

Figure 3. WELD (Westminster Endeavour for Learning and Development) playscheme, Birmingham, 1978. Photographs were taken by young people attending WELD photography workshops. Birmingham City Archives, MS 2478/A/7/1.

To return to the photographic image and a final observation: photographic meaning, as Allan Sekula has written, is essentially conditional: 'The photograph is "an incomplete" utterance of a message that depends on some external matrix of conditions and presuppositions for its readability'.[45] While I accept this conditionality I was recently struck by another observation about looking. The French poet Edmond Jabès wrote:

> That is why his [*sic*] gaze cannot stop at the level of simple appearances. To his eyes these are never more than a stage. It is as if he had a second gaze widening the visual field excessively and giving credit to the idea that behind every reality there lies an even more tangible reality.

Jabès was reflecting on the aftermath of Auschwitz, but I think this idea about a second gaze also has resonance for other marginalized groups. What Jabès seems to suggest is that photographs can also speak for themselves—the photograph functioning as an

---

[45] Sekula, A. "On the invention of photographic meaning." In *Thinking Photography*, edited by V. Burgin. London: Macmillan, 1982: 85.

emanation of the referent in the image.[46] Historians engaged in exploring and documenting diversity and change in modern Britain need to take note that for those who identify with the images of the forgotten, with the silent, there can be a level of recognition and connectivity that goes both before and behind the image—a second gaze that moves beyond appearances, and to which we need to be sensitive. By so doing we may be better placed to understand why in a period of significant social change meaning systems of subordination have survived and, in turn, how they continue to shape social relations.

Ways of Seeing [2]

> I don't like this school because children hit me and call me names. They call me "second hand", "toilet paper", "bloody Asian".... Sometimes I tell my teacher. She tells them off ... then they go to the Head and he is also angry with them ... now they don't fight in the school, they fight when we are coming home.[47]

> ... the most political decision you make is where you direct people's eyes. In other words: what you show people, day in and day out, is political ... [and] the most politically indoctrinating thing you can do to a human being is to show him [*sic*], every day, that there can be no change. But by showing that something is open to change, you keep the idea of change alive. (Wim Wenders[48])

---

[46] The quote is from Jabès, E. *From the Desert to the Book: Dialogues with Marcel Cohen*. Translated by Pierre Joris. Barrytown, NY: Station Hill Press, 1990 and is used by the poet, storyteller and commentator David Levi Strauss in a powerful reflective essay about a photographic installation, *Hotel Polen*, a work of fragments and silences that addressed issues around amnesia, memory and the Holocaust. The exhibition was by the Polish-born artist Ania Bien and is now permanently installed in the Israel Museum in Jerusalem. See, Strauss, D. Levi. "A Second Gaze." In Strauss, *Between the Eyes*, 115–23.

[47] "'They call me blacky'-a story of everyday racism." *Times Educational Supplement* 19 September 1986.

[48] Wenders, W., in conversation with Jansen, P. W. "The truth of images." In Wenders, W. *The Act of Seeing: Essays and Conversations*. London: Faber & Faber, 1997: 52.

Notes on Contributors

Felicity Armstrong is a Reader in Inclusive Education at the Institute of Education, University of London. Her research interests focus on cross-cultural, cross-disciplinary and historical research in education and difference. Her publications include *Spaced Out: Policy, Difference and the Challenge of Inclusive Education* (Kluwer, 2003), Barton, L., and F. Armstrong, eds. *Policy, Experience and Change: Cross-cultural Reflections on Inclusive Education* (Springer, 2007), Armstrong, F. and L. Barton, eds. *Disability, Human Rights and Education* (Open University Press, 2007) and Armstrong, F. "The historical development of special education: humanitarian rationality or 'wild profusion of entangled events'?" *History of Education* 31, no. 5 (2002). Felicity Armstrong is on the editorial board of the *International Journal of Inclusive Education*, *Disability and Society*, and a member of the Comité Scientifique of the French journal *Reliance*. Address: School of Educational Foundations and Policy Studies, Institute of Education, University of London, 20 Bedford Way, London WC1H OAL, UK. Email: F.Armstrong@ioe.ac.uk

Philip Gardner is Senior Lecturer in Education at the Faculty of Education, University of Cambridge. He is a Fellow of St Edmund's College, where he is also College Archivist. He is currently working on a new book on historical methodology, to be published by RoutledgeFalmer, entitled *Hermeneutics, History and Memory*. Address: Faculty of Education, University of Cambridge, 184 Hills Road, Cambridge CB2 8PQ, UK. Email: pwg1000@cam.ac.uk

Ian Grosvenor is Professor of Urban Educational History and Head of the School of Education, University of Birmingham, UK. He is the author of numerous articles and books on racism, education and identity, the visual in educational research, the material culture of education and the history of urban education. Books include *Assimilating Identities: Racism and Education in Post 1945 Britain* (1997), *Silences and Images: The Social History of the Classroom* (1999) with Martin Lawn and Kate Rousmaniere, *The School I'd Like* (2003) with Catherine Burke and *Materialities of Schooling* (2005) with Martin Lawn. He is co-founder of the History of Education Network within the European Education Research Association and also co-founder of the Domus Centre for Interdisciplinary Research into the Cultural Histories of Education and Childhood at Birmingham. Address: The School of Education, University of Birmingham, Edgbaston, Birmingham B15 2TT, UK. Email: i.d.grosvenor@bham.ac.uk

Joyce Goodman is Professor of History of Education at the University of Winchester, UK, co-editor of *History of Education*, vice-president of the History of Education Society GB and secretary of the International Standing Conference for the History of Education. Her publications include *Women and Education, 1800–1980* (Palgrave, 2004) (with Jane Martin), *Gender Colonialism and Education* (Woburn, 2002) (with Jane Martin) and *Women, Educational Policy-Making and Administration in England, Authoritative Women since 1800* (Routledge, 2000) (with Sylvia Harrop). Her research interests focus on girls' secondary education; women teachers, educational administrators and policy-makers; gender, colonialism, internationalization and education; and aesthetic education. Address: Faculty of Education, The University of Winchester, Winchester, SO22 4NR, UK. Email: Joyce.Goodman@winchester.ac.uk

Gareth Elwyn Jones is an Emeritus Professor of Education in the University of Wales. He is a former head of the Department of Education, and Dean of the Faculty of Education in the University of Wales, Aberystwyth. His most recent book, jointly authored with Gordon Wynne Roderick, is *A History of Education in Wales* (University of Wales Press, 2003). Email: gejsouthgate@btinternet.com

Jane McDermid is Senior Lecturer in History at Southampton University, with research interests in Russian and British women's history. Her most recent relevant publication is *The Schooling of Working-class Girls in Nineteenth Century Scotland: Gender, Education and Identity* (Routledge, 2005). She was an adviser and contributor to the *Biographical Dictionary of Scottish Women* (Edinburgh University Press, 2006), and is on the Steering Committee of the UK's Women's History Network. Address: History, School of Humanities, University of Southampton, Southampton, SO17 1BJ, UK. Email: J.McDermid@soton.ac.uk

Jane Martin is Reader in History of Education at the Institute of Education, University of London. Her research interests are focused on the educational experiences of girls and women, women's engagement in educational policy-making through participation in local and national politics, socialist politics around education, teachers and teaching, social identities and action, biographical theory and biographical method, historical theory and methodology, gender, education and empire. She is the author of *Women and the Politics of Schooling in Victorian and Edwardian England* (Leicester University Press, 1999), which won the History of Education Society Book Prize for 2002, and *Women and Education 1800–1980* (Palgrave, 2004) with Joyce Goodman. She is currently preparing a book-length manuscript for Manchester University Press under the title: *Making Socialists: Mary Bridges Adams and the Fight for Knowledge and Power*. She is Co-editor of the journal *History of Education*. Address: School of Educational Foundations and Policy Studies, Institute of Education, University of London, 20 Bedford Way, London WC1H OAL, UK. Email: j.martin@ioe.ac.uk

Gary McCulloch is Brian Simon Professor of the History of Education and Assistant Director (Research and Consultancy) at the Institute of Education,

University of London. He is currently the President of the History of Education Society (UK) and is a past Editor of *History of Education*. His recent publications include *Documentary Research in Education, History and the Social Sciences* (2004), *Cyril Norwood and the Ideal of Secondary Education* (2007), *The Death of the Comprehensive High School? Historical, Contemporary and Comparative Perspectives* (edited with Barry Franklin, 2007) and *History, Politics and Policy Making in Education: A Festschrift presented to Richard Aldrich* (edited with David Crook, 2007). He is series editor (with Barry Franklin) of the book series 'Secondary education in a changing world' (Palgrave Macmillan). Address: School of Educational Foundations and Policy Studies, Institute of Education, University of London, 20 Bedford Way, London WC1H OAL, UK. Email: G.McCulloch@ioe.ac.uk

Rosemary O'Day is Professor of History at the Open University, Milton Keynes. She took first class honours in history from the University of York. She gained her Ph.D. from the University of London under the supervision of Patrick Collinson and James Cargill Thompson. She began her career as a Research Associate working with Kenneth Charlton (and was then a lecturer) at the University of Birmingham. Following this, she moved to the History Department at the Open University. Her research has concentrated on several related areas: education; the social history of religion; professions; family; and gender. Her books include: *The English Clergy, 1560–1640* (Leicester, 1979); *Education and Society, 1500–1800: The Social Foundations of Education in Early Modern Britain* (1983); *The Family and Family Relationships* (1995); *The Professions in Early Modern England, 1450–1800: Servants of the Commonweal* (2000); *Women's Agency in the Early Modern British Isles and the North American Colonies: Patriarchy, Patronage and Partnership* (2007). Address: Department of History, Faculty of Arts, The Open University, Walton Hall, Milton Keynes MK7 6AA, UK. Email: M.R.Oday@open.ac.uk

Deirdre Raftery is Deputy Head of the School of Education, University College Dublin, and Senior Lecturer in History of Education. Recent books include: *Women and Learning in English Writing, 1600–1900* (Four Courts Press, 1997); *Emily Davies: Selected Letters, 1861–1875* (University of Virginia Press, 2002; co-edited with A. B. Murphy); and *Female Education in Ireland, 1700–1900* (Irish Academic Press/Frank Cass, 2007, co-authored with Susan M. Parkes). She is currently working on a book entitled *Irish Education, a Visual History*. Address: School of Education and Lifelong Learning, University College Dublin, Ireland. Email: deirdre.raftery@ucd.ie

William Richardson is Head of the School of Education and Lifelong Learning at the University of Exeter, and Reviews Editor of *History of Education*. He is currently researching histories of further education in postwar England. Address: School of Education and Lifelong Learning, St Luke's Campus, Heavitree Road, Exeter EX1 2LU, UK. Email: w.b.richardson@exeter.ac.uk

Jonathan Rose is a Professor of History at Drew University. He was the founding president of the Society for the History of Authorship, Reading and Publishing, and he now co-edits (with Ezra Greenspan) the society's journal, *Book History*. His most recent publication is *A Companion to the History of the Book* (Blackwell, 2007), co-edited with Simon Eliot. His other books include *The Intellectual Life of the British Working Classes* (Yale University Press, 2001) and *The Holocaust and the Book: Destruction and Preservation* (University of Massachusetts Press, 2001). Address: Department of History, Drew University, 36 Madison Avenue, Madison NJ, 0794, USA. Email: jerose@drew.edu

Michael Sanderson graduated from Cambridge University MA, Ph.D. as a Scholar of Queens' College. His Ph.D., supervised by J. P. C. Roach, was on education in the Industrial Revolution in Lancashire, an early foray into the borderlands of economic and social history. He was an assistant lecturer at Strathclyde University and then lecturer and subsequently professor at the University of East Anglia, Norwich, 1964–2004. His publications include *The Universities and British Industry 1850–1970* (1972), *The Universities in the Nineteenth Century* (1975), *Educational Opportunity and Social Change* (1987), *The Missing Stratum, Technical School Education in England* (1994), *Education and Economic Decline in Britain 1870 to the 1990s* (1999), *The History of the University of East Anglia 1918–2000* (2002). An interest in theatrical history led to his book *From Irving to Olivier, a Social History of the Acting Profession in England* (1984). He served on the Council of the Economic History Society 1994–2000 and was Commissioning Editor of the Society's Studies in Economic and Social History. Address: School of History, University of East Anglia, Norwich NR4 7TJ, UK.

Harold Silver is a Visiting Professor of Higher Education at the University of Plymouth and Visiting Research Professor at the Open University. He graduated from Cambridge, taught English and modern languages at further education colleges in Hull and Huddersfield, was Reader and Professor of education and social history at Chelsea College, University of London and then Principal of Bulmershe College of Higher Education. He has contributed extensively to the historical literature on policy and education, notably higher education. His score of books include *A Higher Education: the CNAA and British Higher Education 1964–89*, *An Educational War on Poverty: American and British Policy Making 1960–1980* (with Pamela Silver), and *Higher Education and Policy Making in Twentieth-Century England*. Forthcoming in 2007 is *Tradition and Higher Education*. He has a Cambridge Ph.D. and honorary doctorates from the Universities of Plymouth and Winchester, UK. Address: 2 William Orchard Close, Oxford OX3 9DR, UK. Email: harold@silver489.fsnet.co.uk

Tom Woodin is a researcher in history of education at the Institute of Education, University of London. He has written on working-class writers' movements and community publishing in *History of Education*, *Sociology* and the *International Journal*

of Lifelong Education. He is also currently researching the co-operative movement and education. Address: School of Educational Foundations and Policy Studies, Institute of Education, University of London, 20 Bedford Way, London WC1H OAL, UK. Email: t.woodin@ioe.ac.uk

Index